BEOWULf

AND OTHER OLD ENGLISH POEMS

BEOWULf

AND OTHER OLD ENGLISH POEMS

Edited and translated by

CRAIG WILLIAMSON

With a foreword by TOM SHIPPEY

PENN

UNIVERSITY OF PENNSYLVANIA PRESS

PHILADELPHIA

Published by
University of Pennsylvania Press
Philadelphia, Pennsylvania 19104-4112
www.upenn.edu/pennpress

10 9 8 7 6 5 4 3 2 1

Library of Congress Cataloging-in-Publication Data
ISBN: 978-0-8122-2275-3

This book is dedicated to

J. R. R. Tolkien,

who first drew me into the medieval world

through the gates of Middle-earth;

to the teachers and scholars who taught me the language—especially

Jim Rosier, Ted Irving, John Pope, Bruce Mitchell;

to my children—

Telory, Caden, Marc, and Milena—

who listened to the poems and loved to tell riddles;

to my Mother and Father

who helped me find my way;

to my wife and fellow traveler Raima Evan,

who has been my steadfast companion in words and worlds;

and to the unknown poets

who wrote or chanted these poems.

The poets pass over; the poems pass on.

CONTENTS

FOREWORD

Tom Shippey

SONG AND POETRY

About fourteen hundred years ago, mourners buried a man in what archaeologists have now labeled "Grave 32" in the Anglo-Saxon cemetery at Snape, in Suffolk. He was laid out carefully and respectfully, in pagan fashion, with a spear by his right side and a round shield covering the left side of his torso. Underneath the shield, though, the mourners placed what may have been the dead man's most precious possession: his harp. (Technically speaking, it is a lyre, but Anglo-Saxons would have called it a *hearpe*.) Made of maplewood, with a sound-board of thin oak, and with attachments including a wrist-strap which would allow it to be played two-handed, it is an unusually fine instrument even compared with the similar harps recovered elsewhere, one of them from the lavishly furnished royal burial at Sutton Hoo a few miles away. The report of the archaeologist Graeme Lawson notes that it was left "cradled in the crook of the [dead man's] left arm, almost as though in preparation for performance," and adds that such graves provide us with "direct archaeological links" to the world in which Old English poetry was composed and preserved (215, 223). The "warrior-poet" of Grave 32 was surely a *scop*, one of those who (see "The Fortunes of Men" ll. 74–77 below) "sits with his harp at his lord's feet, / Takes his treasure, a reward of rings, / Plucks with his harp-nail, sweeps over strings, / Shapes song: hall-thanes long for his melody."

What we now know as poetry, then, began as song, though the tunes and the music have been lost beyond recall. Performers nowadays, such as

Ben Bagby, try to reimagine it, though one may wonder whether any one person can now recreate a whole art form developed long ago by many minds and marked by delighted virtuosity. The Anglo-Saxons' word for "harp-nail," or plectrum, was *sceacol*, and the poet of "The Fortunes of Men" calls it, in very literal translation, "the shackle, which leaps, the sweet-sounding nail." It is "the harp's sweet songs, the poet's music" that provoke Grendel to envious fury in *Beowulf*, and there are "sound and music mixed" when Hrothgar's poet plays the "joy-wood" and sings the story of Finnsburg to the Danish court and its guests (see ll. 1064, 1062–1162). At a much lower social level, Bede's story of Cædmon (see pp. 191–93) indicates that it was normal at an Anglo-Saxon drinking-party for a harp to be passed round so that everyone could sing. Cædmon is unusual in that he cannot sing (or play?) and has to hide his embarrassment in the cowshed, from which the angel rescues him by the gift of inspiration. Of course, Bede's story may not be true, but it cannot have seemed implausible either to the first readership of Bede's own version written in Latin, or to the readership of the translation into Old English made more than a century and a half later. For the pagan and pre-literate Anglo-Saxons of the early Anglo-Saxon period, poetry delivered as song was at once the main channel of their own traditions, their highest intellectual art form, and their most valued entertainment. When the Messenger who announces Beowulf's death says that their lord has "laid down laughter," he is thinking of *gamen and gleodream*, "game and glee-dream," or as we would say, "merriment and joy in music."

The very high cultural value placed on their native skill by Anglo-Saxons must account for the preservation of Old English poetry in relatively large quantities, rather more than 30,000 lines of it all told, enough to fill the six thick volumes of *The Anglo-Saxon Poetic Records* (to which the best overall guide is Fulk and Cain's *A History of Old English Literature*). This body of literature is a striking anomaly on the early medieval European scene. Anglo-Saxons were still writing poems in the traditional style, with fairly strict adherence to the old rules of meter and use of traditional "kennings" (see pp. 8–9) almost up to 14 October 1066, when the last Anglo-Saxon king Harold died on the battlefield of Hastings: the latest datable poem we have is the one preserved in *The Anglo-Saxon Chronicle* on the death of his predecessor King Edward nine months before. How long they had been doing this is a much harder question. Bede's *Historia Ecclesiastica Gentis Anglorum*, or *History of the English Church and People*, was finished by 731, and his story of Cædmon is set many years earlier, so that "Cædmon's

Hymn" is often taken to be the earliest Old English poem. But it has been pointed out by Kevin Kiernan (1990) that Bede gives only a Latin version of the "Hymn," the Old English poetic versions (in both Northumbrian and West Saxon) being added much later, so that they could have been composed on the basis of the Latin at that later date—though it is an odd coincidence, as Fulk and Cain remark (142, 255), that the Latin falls so neatly into Old English poetic form.

Other contenders are carved rather than written (Old English used the same verb, *writan*, for both), and use the old "runic" alphabet rather than the Latin alphabet brought in by Christian missionaries. The poem "The Dream of the Rood" survives in long and probably expanded form in the "Vercelli Book"—an Anglo-Saxon manuscript found against all probability in the cathedral library of Vercelli in Northern Italy, perhaps left there by a pilgrim—but some twenty lines of a version of the same poem are carved in stone, in fragmentary form, in runic letters and in a very different far-Northern dialect, on the stone obelisk now known as "the Ruthwell Cross" in Dumfriesshire in southern Scotland. Everything about the Ruthwell Cross is enigmatic, but it could be three hundred years older than the Vercelli Book. There are five lines of Old English poetry, also in runic script, on "the Franks Casket," a whalebone box discovered in France, and an early date is suggested by the fact that the engraver not only carved his runes clockwise round the box edges, but did them in mirror-writing along the bottom, as if the left-to-right convention was unknown to him (Fulk and Cain, 45–47).

Our written records of Old English poetry, then, last more than three hundred years, from 1065 back to at least the early 700s. But there can be no doubt that the verse-form was old even in Cædmon's time. We possess a considerable amount of Old Norse poetry, in a language related to Old English but recorded centuries later, much of it in far more complex meters and with the "riddlic" quality also found in Old English (see pp. 161–77, 186, 208 below) developed almost into incomprehensibility. Some Old Norse poems, however, are written in the meter they called *fornyrthislag*, "old-word-meter," and this is effectively identical with Old English, in meter and often in turns of phrase. Poems have also survived in Old Saxon and Old High German, again with similar meter and phrasing, all of which indicates that the various Germanic peoples at one time, before any records survive, and when their languages were much more similar to each other than they later became, had a shared tradition of poetry. J. R. R. Tolkien's son Christopher has even pointed out that some names surviving in Old Norse must have originated as Gothic, the stories attached to them going back to the wars of the Goths and Huns in far Eastern Europe before the fall of the Western Roman Empire, and also remembered by Old English poets (xxiii–xxvii). But the reason poetry is preserved much earlier and in much greater quantity in Old English than in its cousin-languages must be—apart from a certain dogged conservatism in the English psyche—England's early conversion to Christianity, with the associated import of writing skills. To put this in its proper place, one needs to give a general account of Anglo-Saxon history over some six hundred eventful years.

IMMIGRANTS, MISSIONARIES, AND INVADERS

Immigrants

Between 400 and 600 a massive and fateful change for the whole history of the world, which we still do not fully understand, took place in Britain. In the year 400 most of Britain, as far west as the Irish Sea, and as far north as Hadrian's Wall, and to some extent beyond it, was securely under Roman rule as the various provinces of Britannia. Its upper classes spoke good grammatical Latin, reinforced by the import of tutors for their children. Probably many soldiers, and many urban dwellers, spoke the Vulgar Latin common across the Western Empire. Most of the population, however, spoke a Celtic language that was the ancestor of modern Welsh, which had hung on in Britain after other western provinces had started speaking the variants of Vulgar Latin which would become French, Spanish, Portuguese, and so on (see Jackson, chaps. 1–6).

Two hundred years later most of eastern and central Britain was English-speaking, and almost everywhere in it had been literally renamed. A few large towns and rivers retained their Latin names, more or less, so that Roman *Londinium* became Old English *Lundene*, while the *Tamesis* was the *Temese*, or Thames. The names of quite large settlements, however, had been forgotten, so that *Ratae Coritanorum*, or maybe *Corieltavorum*, was now *Ligoraceaster*, modern Leicester. Others survived barely recognizably, the major legionary base of *Eboracum* becoming *Eofor-wic*, "Boar-town," and eventually York, while *Venta Bulgarum* was *Win-ceaster*, Winchester. Lower down the scale, towns, villages, streams, and fields had all acquired Anglo-Saxon names that must have been totally unknown two hundred years earlier. There are signs that English speakers had heard Welsh words and not understood them. There are several river Avons in modern England, but *afon* is just the Welsh word for "river." Someone must have been told the word, and taken it to be a name, which argues for a low degree of bilingualism.

What is the explanation? The simplest, and the one accepted for many years, is that after the Roman army withdrew from Britain in 407 there was a massive invasion from what is now south Denmark and north Germany, leading to extensive population change at best and genocide at worst. Most modern scholars now reject this as overly dramatic, and in any case logistically impossible, while some argue that all that happened was the arrival of a new ruling class who succeeded in imposing their language on a relatively undisturbed base population. The German archaeologist Heinrich Härke, however, has observed that opinions in this area tend to be colored by scholars' national experiences. German scholars, familiar with mass population movements from their own living memory, find a major immigration easy to imagine (1998, 21). British scholars, equally familiar with small numbers of invaders setting themselves up as ruling elites, as in British India and much of Africa, see this as the most natural explanation. Mark Thomas, in collaboration with others including Härke, offers a nuanced compromise, with fairly large numbers of Germanic speakers seeping in over an extended period, establishing themselves as a landowning minority, and then outbreeding the native British population as a result of the greater advantages which come with superior wealth and status. An important point supporting their argument is the revised opinion about the early seventh-century boat preserved in the barrow at Sutton Hoo. The naval architects Edwin and Joyce Gifford, who built and successfully sailed a half-size replica of it, are sure that, although the boat was buried without mast or sail, probably to make room for the burial chamber with its lavish grave-goods, it and the later and smaller Anglo-Saxon boat found at Graveney were not rowboats but sailing-ships, and furthermore "fully resolved designs, difficult to improve upon even with today's knowledge" (23). A craft like the one found at Sutton Hoo could easily have operated a "shuttle service" across the North Sea, bringing perhaps thirty passengers at a time and returning for more (unlike a rowboat) with a crew of only five or six.

Whatever the number of incomers, however, there has never been any doubt that much of the British population survived, for the late seventh-century laws of King Ine of Wessex assign a status and a compensation-tariff (or *wergild*) to *Wealas*, non-Anglo-Saxons, but one significantly lower than for their own people (Whitelock 1955, 367–68). This legal disability has disappeared by the time of King Alfred's laws two centuries later, suggesting that by then the populations had merged. One fact seems to be that mitochondrial DNA, which is maternally inherited, gives different results from Y-chromosome DNA, found only in males (Härke 2002, 150): a predominantly male immigration, mixing disproportionately with the female native population, would explain this and fit with the complex mathematical calculations of Thomas et al. It is likely in any case that every small area arrived at a different balance, under different circumstances, and very likely also that whatever happened was soon "airbrushed" into a politically convenient form. The *Anglo-Saxon Chronicle*, for instance, gives a triumphalist narrative (compiled centuries later) of the seizure of Wessex from the Welsh, but there are doubts about the whole story, and the name of the founder of the Wessex royal dynasty, Cerdic, may be a repronounced Welsh one, Caradoc (see Myres, 144–73).

The most authoritative account of the arrival of the Anglo-Saxons is, however, the one given by Bede in his *History of the English Church and People* and it has been accepted ever since; but since Bede's work was not completed until 731, almost three hundred years after the date he gives for that arrival (449), there may still be some doubt about it. According to Bede, the fifth-century invaders came from "the three most formidable races of Germany, the Saxons, Angles and Jutes" (Bede, trans. Sherley-Price, 56). Some airbrushing can be detected already, for the Angles and Jutes hardly show up in Roman accounts of Germany, though there is no doubt about their presence in Britain. The Saxons are prominent in the names of four Anglo-Saxon kingdoms, Wessex, Sussex, Middlesex, and Essex, but it is a strange thing that even Alfred, King of Wessex, whose mother was a Hampshire Jute (Lapidge and Keynes, 68), nevertheless always called his own language *englisc*, never *seaxisc*, and claimed to be the rightful ruler of all *Angelcynn*, the whole English race, which clearly included his own Wessex. Whatever the reason, the Angles seem to have established themselves as the definitive group among the invaders, even among peoples calling themselves Saxon. There are linguistic indications that the Old English language itself is a mixed form derived from different Germanic dialects (Nielsen, 221–23, 290–93). We should note that the modern term "Anglo-Saxon" is a learned one, rarely used by "Anglo-Saxons" themselves, which is one reason why philologists prefer the term "Old English" for their language.

One interesting point is that the leader of the first invaders is named by Bede, and the *Anglo-Saxon Chronicle*, and the Welsh writer of the *Historia Brittonum*, as Hengest, with his brother Horsa, and they are said to be Jutes. In the background of *Beowulf* there is another Hengest fighting *against* the Jutes (see ll. 1082–1158), but fighting your relatives was normal enough in Germanic heroic legend. They are the only two Hengests recorded in Old English, the dates are not impossible, and they may be the same man, especially as they appear to be guilty of similar deeds of oath-breaking or treachery.

Whatever the story, between about 450 and about 600, most of what is now England settled down into a number of conflicting kingdoms, each ruled by an English (or Saxon) dynasty that claimed descent from Woden, except for that of Essex, which claimed descent from the god Seaxneat. The main ones were the two Northumbrian kingdoms of Deira and Bernicia, Mercia or "the Mark" in the Midlands, and East Anglia and Wessex farther south, with Essex, Middlesex, Kent, and Sussex increasingly subordinate to one of the larger kingdoms. All of them sparred among themselves, while the Northumbrian, Mercian, and West Saxon kings also continued to try to extend their rule over the still independent British, Pictish, or Scottish states to the west and north. Matters would, however, be changed by the arrival in Kent in the year 597 of Christian missionaries sent to England by Pope Gregory the Great, and led by St. Augustine of Canterbury.

Missionaries

One might wonder why a mission was necessary. By 400 Roman Britain was officially Christian, Christianity having become the official religion of the Empire twenty years earlier, after seventy further years of increasing imperial favor. Even after the Roman withdrawal from Britain the native British states remained Christian, as did Ireland, never part of the Empire but converted during the fifth century initially by the agency of St. Patrick, a Briton with a Roman name (*Patricius*). One sign of less-than-friendly relations between the native British and the incoming Anglo-Saxons is that either the Britons made no effort to convert the immigrants, or the immigrants took no notice. Unlike other Germanic peoples moving into the former Empire—Franks, Goths, Vandals—the Angles and Jutes at least had had no border with the Empire, and no direct contact with it or with its religion; they remained entirely pagan. The names of their gods—Tiw,

Woden, Thunor (later affected by the Norse equivalent Thor), and Frig, "the Lady"—survive in place-names like Tysoe and Wednesbury, as well as in the days of the week, but there is little trace of them in the surviving poetry: one poem (*Maxims I*) says dismissively, "Woden made idols, the Almighty [made] the firmament."

The Anglo-Saxon conversion took place surprisingly quickly and successfully, as a result of a kind of pincer movement. In the south was the mission sent from Rome, hosted initially by the king of Kent, whose Frankish wife was a Christian. This mission had mixed fortunes. Kings of Kent and Essex accepted the faith, but their successors reverted to paganism. Rædwald, king of East Anglia, tried to be a Christian without abandoning paganism. If he was the man for whom the Sutton Hoo grave-mound was raised, his hesitation is reflected in the grave-goods, which include a pair of baptismal spoons, labeled "Saulos" and "Paulos" to signal conversion, but also all the apparatus of a pagan warrior-king: weapons, whetstone-scepter, gold and jewelry, and most impressive of all, the boat in which to sail to the other world like Scyld Sceafing in *Beowulf* (Evans; C. Green, see also ll. 28–53). Some Roman missionaries accordingly grew disheartened and left, or tried to leave, only to be sent back by the pope or by a threatening vision of St. Peter. The major success of this mission was the conversion of King Edwin of Northumbria, for a while an exile at Rædwald's court, but Edwin was killed in battle against a coalition led by Penda, the pagan Anglo-Saxon king of Mercia, and Cadwalla, the British Christian king of Gwynedd in Wales.

Fortunately for the future of Christianity in Britain, northerners were meanwhile coming into contact with Irish missions in Scotland, notably on the isle of Iona. Edwin's eventual successor Oswald is said to have been baptized during his exile in Scotland, and after defeating and killing Cadwalla at the battle of Heavenfield, a few hundred yards from Hadrian's Wall, he called in many preachers from the north. Their personal asceticism, coupled with what may have been a more tolerant idea of mission, made a lasting impact that survived even the death of Oswald, killed like Edwin by the pagan Penda. Potential competition between the Romanists and the Irish church was settled by the famous decision of King Oswy at Whitby in the year 664, that the Northumbrian church should follow Rome, on the grounds that St. Peter, holder of the keys of heaven, had more authority than St. Columba. Nevertheless, ascetic hermit-saints like St. Cuthbert (d. 687) and St. Guthlac (d. 714) continued to attract popular devotion of a kind not given to St. Wilfrid (d. 710), who won the debate at Whitby but who comes across as an organizer-saint, efficient, authoritarian, at times ruthless. Cuthbert's body still lies in Durham Cathedral, with his coffin and his pectoral cross; the Gospel-book that went with him into the grave is currently on loan to the British Library. "Lives" of all three of the saints last mentioned were written soon after their deaths (Webb and Farmer; Colgrave).

Most professors will be familiar with the phenomenon of the student who has had little early exposure to intellectual life, but who on first encountering it realizes that this is what he or she had been waiting for all along. Anglo-Saxons seem to have taken to literacy, and the new religion that brought it, with the same enthusiasm. Bede's story of King Edwin and his counselors (see p. 190) suggests that the main draw of Christianity was its message of hope and certainty, of a world other than the brief lit circle surrounded by darkness that was the pagan image of life. Another element may have been relief from fear: the Northern pagan religion, English or Norse, relied on propitiation of its gods by sacrifice, and there is evidence for human sacrifice in early England, some of it gruesome, like one woman's grave in Yorkshire. The mourners there laid their relative out carefully and closed her coffin, but then threw an older woman in the grave, threw a rock on top of her to hold her down, and buried her alive. She was still trying to push herself up on her elbows as she died (Fleming, 139–40, 347–48). Many besides King Edwin's priest-counselor must have been glad to be released from this kind of ritual behavior: one might note that the *Beowulf*-poet seems to have heard of sacrificial rites, though he presents them as a desperate emergency measure by the Danes and expresses strong disapproval (ll. 175–88).

As for books, before the conversion century was over, rich Anglo-Saxon churchmen like Benedict Biscop (d. 690) were arriving in Rome like twentieth-century Texas oilmen in Paris, anxious to build up their collections. The libraries of York and Jarrow, while modest by Italian standards, soon became a source of pride (Lapidge), and Anglo-Saxon scholarship began to be respected far afield. Its phenomenally rapid growth is illustrated by the career of Bede. When he was a young teen in 686, his first monastery at Wearmouth was all but wiped out by plague, so that the boy had to learn to sing antiphonally with his abbot Ceolfrid, there being no choir-monk left to join the service (Bede, trans. Sherley-Price, 15–16). But by the time he died in 735 Bede was probably the most learned man in Europe, author of many works of Bible commentary and chronology besides his famous *History,* all in impeccable Latin. Fifty years later the York deacon Alcuin, or Alhwine, was "headhunted" by Charlemagne to produce, among other tasks, an authoritative text of the Bible (Garrison et al.). One of the most praiseworthy features of this first era of Anglo-Saxon Christianity was their immediate determination to spread the Gospel to what they recognized as their kin in the still pagan lands across the North Sea. St. Willibrord (d. 739) became the Apostle of the Frisians. St. Boniface, whose birth name was Wynfrith, is known as the Apostle of Germany: he was martyred in 754 at Dokkum in the Netherlands (Talbot). Anglo-Saxon and Irish missionaries were probably the more successful for not always being associated with the Frankish church, seen with some justice as an arm of Frankish imperialism.

The Anglo-Saxon church nevertheless had its own special qualities, one of which was perhaps a certain lack of interest in humility. It did produce "fundamentalists" like Bede, who says nothing about his own birth, but the Anglo-Saxon monasteries that were soon founded—sometimes double foundations for men and women, sometimes ruled by royal-family abbesses like Cædmon's Hild at Whitby—were aristocratic places, rich and status-conscious (see Wormald). This fact may well explain the survival of Old English poetry, and the kind of poetry that survived. Until at least the ninth century, and probably later, the church had an effective monopoly on writing, but aristocratic churchmen did not lose interest in their own traditions, including heroic legends of the past. Some thought they took too much interest in the stories of what must have been pagan heroes. Alcuin wrote angrily to one "Speratus" (an unidentified Mercian bishop, see Bullough) that he had heard a harper was being allowed to sing stories of Ingeld at mealtimes (a character who appears in *Beowulf,* see ll. 2025–69), instead of a lector reading the word of God; but this only tells us what was actually happening (Garmonsway and Simpson, 242). An evident compromise was to put Christian story into the kind of poetic form Anglo-Saxons were used to, and that is what we often have. Bede tells us that Cædmon, himself illiterate, had the Bible read to him so he could turn it into poetry, and we have long poems paraphrasing Genesis, Exodus, and Daniel, and the apocryphal Book of Judith, though they are not now thought to be by Cædmon. A man called Cynewulf, probably a Mercian monk, added a runic "signature" to four poems, including the female saints' lives of *Elene* and *Juliana.* The long poem *Andreas,* which translates another apocryphal story of St. Andrew's conversion of the cannibal Meremodonians, would have made inspiring listening for trainee missionaries, and we have two poems on the life of St. Guthlac, who (like St. Juliana) knew how to deal with demons. A considerable "wisdom literature" also survives in poetry, of which more is said below.

Another aristocratic interest, however, was history, and it may be no coincidence that the three most famous literary works produced by Anglo-Saxons are all in their different ways historical: Bede's *History of the English Church and People* in Latin, completed in 731; *The Anglo-Saxon Chronicle*, in Old English prose with poetic insertions, first compiled in the 890s but kept up at Peterborough monastery till 1154; and the poem *Beowulf,* whose date is not known, but which gives a surprisingly detailed account of events in south Scandinavia in the early sixth century, a little of which can be confirmed. Portions of two other heroic poems survived up to modern times: the so-called *Finnsburg Fragment,* which duplicates part of a story told in *Beowulf,* and *Waldere,* an epic about events in the fifth century, which was evidently discarded by some hardline librarian who however used a few scrap pages to reinforce the cover of a book now in the Royal Library in Copenhagen. Some abbots at least must have given permission for the considerable expenditure of time and vellum needed to write and copy these poems, and we are now grateful for their open-mindedness.

Invaders

The "golden age" of English saints and scholars was abruptly terminated by a new wave of attacks on Britain by fierce pagans from across the sea, this time much better documented than whatever happened in the fifth and sixth centuries. The newcomers were the Vikings, mostly from Denmark, though the first attack recorded—a small affair at Portland in Dorset in 789—was carried out by Norwegians. Four years later came what one could call the "Pearl Harbor" of the Dark Ages, the destruction of St. Cuthbert's island monastery at Lindisfarne. No-one saw it coming. Alcuin wrote in dismay to King Ethelred of Northumbria, "Lo, it is nearly 350 years that we and our fathers have inhabited this most lovely land, and never before has such terror appeared in Britain as we have now suffered from a pagan race, nor was it thought that such an inroad from the sea could be made" (Whitelock 1955, 776). It was the start of an era of all-but-continuous warfare that lasted from 793 until the late eleventh century. The last Anglo-Saxon king, Harold Godwinsson, defeated a major Norwegian attack on

England at Stamford Bridge in Yorkshire in 1066 three weeks before Hastings, killing his namesake Harald Harthræthi ("Hard-Ruler"), the giant Varangian, but Danish fleets continued to try their luck for some years following.

Important turning points in the Viking wars were these. The Anglo-Saxon kingdoms coped fairly well for two or three generations, until in 865 a force arrived that they called the *micel here*, "the big army," led in tradition and probably in fact by the sons of Ragnar Lothbrok ("Hairy-Breeches"). In quick succession this army overran East Anglia, Northumbria, and Mercia, killing the kings or forcing them into exile. The decisive battle that took place at Repton in Mercia may be marked by the discovery of the Repton charnel-house, which contains the bones of more than 250 people, mostly men of unusual size and strength, grouped round a Roman stone sarcophagus that may have held the Viking leader. One of the men buried close by was certainly a Viking, for he had a "Thor's hammer" amulet round his neck, as well as a sword by his side. He had suffered several ghastly wounds, one of them a blow to the groin that must have emasculated him (Richards, 388).

One should admit that the Anglo-Viking wars were a fair fight, for Anglo-Saxon culture had remained warlike, a result of the continuous fighting among the native kingdoms, as one can see from many archaeological finds and from the names they chose for their sons. The latter are characteristically two-part compounds, and include Ecg-bryht ("Edge-bright"), Beaduheard ("Battle-hard"), Ead-gar ("Wealth-spear"), Here-beald ("Army-bold"), and so on. Beowulf's uncle Hyge-lac's name means "Mind-play," and some have taken this to mean that he was a frivolous person, but the *lac* intended is much more likely to have been the *ecga gelac* of the poems, "edge-play, sword-play," as with St. Guth-lac, "war-play." Warlike finds include the Coppergate helmet, found in 1982 down a well in York (why throw such a valuable item away?); the Viking-era longsword found in 1976 in a stream near Richmond in Yorkshire by a boy looking for minnows (but who dropped it, and why was it never picked up?); and the very recently unearthed Staffordshire hoard (2009), its hundreds of gold, silver, and jeweled items so broken up and so military in character that some think they must be *wæl-reaf* or "spoils of slaughter" (see *Beowulf*, l. 1206 below), accumulated by one of King Penda's Mercian successors, whose capital Tamworth was close by (Fleming, 207–8: but why was it buried and never recovered?).

Even a poem as late as "The Battle of Maldon" can still celebrate an Anglo-Saxon "last stand" in traditional heroic style, with only a hint of regret at the leader Alderman Byrhtnoth's Custer-style rashness. Nevertheless, in spite of stiffening resistance, the Vikings were increasingly professional, and to begin with they had soft targets in the shape of large, rich abbeys and cathedrals staffed by men of peace. Success in Britain and Ireland, and elsewhere in Europe, swelled their numbers.

Once the Mercian king had fled, the Ragnarssons turned their attention to Wessex, the last surviving English kingdom. By 878 its king was Alfred, last survivor of five brothers, and the Vikings almost caught him by a surprise attack just after Christmas. Alfred fled into the marshes of Somerset, where, in legend though not in fact, he "burned the cakes" while hiding out in a peasant hut. If he had given up then, the world might now be speaking Danish. But he managed to rally resistance from his hideout, defeated the Vikings and forced them to deal (and their king to accept Christianity), and started a long period of military, civil, and religious reorganization. In the "Preface" he wrote, or probably dictated, for his translation of Gregory the Great's book on *Pastoral Care*, he mused over events of the past, going back to the Northumbrian "golden age," and concluded, surprisingly, that what had been missing was literacy: literacy in English, not Latin. The "Life" of him written by his Welsh bishop Asser notes that he ordered all his officials and county aldermen to learn to read, or find a proxy who could (Lapidge and Keynes, 110). Several works in Old English survive, written or commissioned by him, including the *Anglo-Saxon Chronicle*, a translation of Bede, and a translation of Boethius's *Consolation of Philosophy*. Alfred's armies (and embryo navy) fought renewed Viking attacks to a standstill in the last years of his life (d. 899). He is the only English king regularly awarded the title "the Great."

His son, daughter, grandson, and later descendants continued the process, completing Alfred's policy of annexing the counties of Mercia not under immediate Danish occupation—and so consolidating *Angelcynn*—and then bringing the "Danelaw" in northern and eastern England back under some kind of control. All this was, however, achieved at great cost. By Alfred's time the libraries of York and Jarrow had been destroyed and dispersed. Abbeys had been sacked, churches abandoned; priests and bishops fled and did not always return. In the far north the strongholds of Durham and Bamburgh held out, the former eventually under the control of a hereditary corporation descended from the men who had for many years carried the body of St. Cuthbert from refuge to refuge till they found a lasting home, the latter under an English "high-reeve."

One further result of the Viking wars was that England received a new element to its ethnic mix through large numbers of Danish settlers in the north and east, and Norwegians in the northwest, who made a considerable imprint even on the English language: many common Old English words were replaced by Norse ones, and there are some signs of this process in late poems like "The Battle of Maldon." Another development was the "Benedictine Reform" of the late tenth century, in which "hardliners" led by St. Dunstan and St. Æthelwold, with royal support but against a good deal of local resistance, seized control of the church and attempted to restore stricter standards, making a particular target of married nonmonastic clergy. It is the reformers who have left us most of the surviving writings in Old English, but it is doubtful they would have approved of many of the poems written in earlier times. Works like the Vercelli Book, and the Exeter Book—two of the four biggest collections surviving—were lost or disregarded. No-one knows where the manuscript of *Beowulf* and *Judith* came from, but it is unlikely to have been a first-rate reformed institution.

The efforts of the Wessex kings were then frittered away round the year 1000 by the inept rule of King Ethelred Unræd (often translated as "the Unready," though "No-idea" would be more accurate), and a fairly united England passed into the control of the Danish king Knut (often written Canute). Stubborn English conservatism meant that his descendants were eventually replaced by one more member of the old Wessex royal dynasty, Edward "the Confessor," but when he died without an heir the throne passed to his brother-in-law Harold Godwinsson, and then, after Hastings, to the Norman William "the Conqueror." Many of the Anglo-Saxon ruling class died on the battlefield and many more were dispossessed, William brought in Norman bishops to replace Anglo-Saxon ones, and Anglo-Saxon civilization, at least in its upper reaches, came to an end.

THE INDIVIDUALITY OF ANGLO-SAXON

Much scholarly work has been done in recent years on Anglo-Saxon intellectual background, as one can see from the ongoing multi-author online projects *Fontes Anglosaxonici* and *Sources of Anglo-Saxon Literary Culture* (*SASLC*). Such inquiries have, however, told us relatively little about the poetry, with the exceptions in this volume of the "Advent Lyrics" (based on Latin liturgy, see Burlin), the "Panther" and "Whale" poems, derived (much altered) from a Latin bestiary (Fulk and Cain, 141–42), and the poem "Vainglory." This latter interestingly echoes a non-Benedictine "Rule," that of St. Chrodegang of Metz (d. 766), which itself recalls a sixth-century sermon by Caesarius of Arles. But as Fulk and Cain remark (135), this learned material is skillfully and originally embroidered "to produce a grand scene of drunken boasting in the meadhall." The online projects have meanwhile concerned themselves mostly with Anglo-Latin writers, or with the works of the Benedictine reformers, notably Ælfric, author of many Old English homilies and saints' lives in prose, and Wulfstan, homilist and legislator. Such writers fit, or can be made to fit, into a European context. But there is little that resembles Old English poetry anywhere else in the world, except for Old Saxon and Old High German poems that may well owe their existence to Anglo-Saxon models.

One way of responding to such poetry involves a certain humility. Is it possible that Anglo-Saxons, ill-informed and pre-scientific though they were, had skills we have lost: skills not of reading and writing, but of speaking (and singing) and listening? If one considers the "riddlic" quality of much of the poetry, mentioned several times below, the rules for a proper riddle are, first, that everything said in it must be true (or else it's not a fair riddle), but at the same time misleading (or it's not a good, testing riddle). But there are other ways of not-quite telling the truth. Lines 21–22 of "Wulf and Eadwacer" as translated here (and also very much as in the original) simply do not make sense, not literal sense. They say that it is "easy" to tear apart what has never been joined, or in Williamson's masterful rendering, "to rip an unsewn stitch." Logically speaking, this is not easy, it is *impossible!* If it has never been "sewn," there can be no "stitch" there to rip! Nevertheless we may well guess what the speaker means. What she says is desperately regretful for something that never existed, that has been prevented from existing—but is terribly and paradoxically powerful in her mind, in her imagination. To feel the force of what she says, you have to be aware of both the surface literal nonmeaning and the underlying emotional meaning: the point is in the agonizing contrast, just as the point of a riddle is the contrast between misleading surface and hidden solution.

The female speaker's statement in "Wulf and Edwacer" is also put with generalizing force, like a modern proverb (e.g., "It's no use crying over spilt milk," which we all know does not refer to milk). Beowulf likewise uses a proverb to clinch his farewell speech to Hrothgar (see ll. 1837–38 below). But what does he mean by it? And why does Hrothgar reply, politely and flatteringly, but raising the unwelcome issue of a dire fate for Beowulf's uncle Hygelac (which by that stage of the poem we know is going to happen)? One advantage of proverbs is that, in a way, the speaker does not say them. They are what everyone says, and everyone accepts: if the listener knows how to apply them, well and good; if not, the speaker takes no responsibility. At this point, one may well think, Beowulf and Hrothgar would each do well to listen to the veiled warning the other has given, but each perceives only the other's danger. The astute Anglo-Saxon listener could perceive both at once, and also the characters' matching nonperceptions. In the same way, one may well wonder what the queen Wealhtheow is saying in her long speech to her husband (ll. 1174–87). It took fifty years of scholarship before anyone began to understand it, and many scholars would not believe it once they did—one of them insisted that the ironically unexpected situation revealed was just too difficult for Anglo-Saxon warriors to take in, men "not chosen mainly for intellectual qualities," as he rather superciliously remarked (Sisam, 9). But how did he know? Maybe men who could not take a hint did not last long in an Anglo-Saxon warband. Talking tactfully round a subject could be a survival skill, as could recognizing the intention when someone else was doing it.

Proverbs may veil truth (see Deskis). Generalizing statements can also insist on it. Byrhtwold, the old retainer in "The Battle of Maldon," says as he prepares to die (ll. 319–20), "Ever may a man mourn / Who thinks to flee . . ." What he says is not true: one can easily imagine someone running away from a lost battle, and congratulating himself later on every time he thought of it. But once again we know what Byrhtwold means. He means no one *ought* to feel like that, has any right to feel like that. What he says is not true, it is super-true, a cultural imperative. Sayings like that give some of their force to poems like "Maxims II" (p. 179), which move easily up and down a truth-scale without giving clues as to where we are on it. A similar poem (the second section of *Maxims I*) begins, word for word, "Frost shall freeze." That is so true it is undeniable, or even not worth saying: of course frost freezes, that is what the words mean. Is "A king shall rule a kingdom" a saying of the same kind? Or is that a Byrhtwold-type saying, one that *must* be true? "Winter" may well be "coldest," but is "Truth . . . the trickiest"? It is if it is an Anglo-Saxon poet talking. One should note that charms are as super-true as maxims, but in a different way (see pp.

183–86). They are true because they work, they do what they say (if you say the right words): "Get out, little spear" ("Charm for a Sudden Stitch," ll. 6, 12, 15, 17).

The "leaping shackle" of Old English poetic virtuosity shows at its most extreme, however, in poems like "The Wanderer," "The Seafarer," and "Deor." For many years what drew attention was their personal quality, which they share with the "women's songs," "The Wife's Lament" and "Wulf and Eadwacer," and which is indeed strong and moving. Slowly it was recognized that unlike Victorian "dramatic monologues" (to which they had been unconsciously assimilated by Victorian readers), they were impersonal too. "The Wanderer" uses the words "I, me, my" nine times in its first thirty lines, three times near the middle (ll. 10–29, 63–65), but then never again. The poem is studded with imaginary speakers, who may or may not be the "wanderer" himself: the "wise man," the "wise warrior," "The wise man who ponders," the "man wise in mind." One thing the poem is certainly saying is that true wisdom comes only from experience, from the heart not the head: no-one without such experience has a right to declare truth. "The Seafarer" follows a similar pattern, but with a markedly more Christian conclusion. "Deor" goes the other way, from the far-distant to the immediately personal, starting with a sequence of "fates worse than death" drawn from old legend—Weland's torture, Beaduhild's rape-pregnancy, monstrous love, long exile, impotent despair—generalizing first that that is the way things often go (as said at much greater length in the poem "The Fortunes of Men"), but then applying it personally, to the harper "Deor" himself. All the "fates worse than death" found some cure or consolation, and for those fully aware of old legends there may even have been a consolation hidden from Deor: the fate of Heorrenda of the Heodenings, the harper who displaced him in the poem, was not a lucky one.

The poets claim the role of "soothsayers," those who state ultimate truth about reality, but they move easily between riddle-truth, proverb-truth, maxim-truth, charm-truth, felt-truth, and learned-truth, as well perhaps as states which modern people do not readily recognise. One connecting feature is that the poems show a continuing interest in things which simultaneously are and aren't—like the unsewn stitch, "the song of us two together" in "Wulf and Eadwacer," the "unwoven web" of the lamenting wife's wedding, the dream-memories of the "wanderer," or the ruins on which he broods, hard stone which certainly exists, but by existing proves that something greater no longer exists. All these poems resist paraphrase and throw off analysis, but it is no wonder that they have intrigued generations of modern readers with no interest in purely intellectual culture. They are best taken as poetry, as they are presented here.

A LONG AFTERMATH

Old English poetry did not quite die with its patrons on the battlefield at Hastings. Three hundred years later poets were again writing alliterative poetry, with too many themes and phrases carried over from Old English for there to be no connection. The Alliterative Revival, as it is called, was a survival, returning from a long period when it may have been composed, but (as in the beginning) was not written down. It sprang up most strongly in the West Midland counties where "ure leden, that is ald inglis," as one writer called it ("our language, that is Old English"), was left most undisturbed. Shakespeare, a Warwickshire man, comes up with many Old English poetic phrases, most strongly in *Macbeth*, his only play to feature an Anglo-Saxon king, Edward the Confessor, and a Danelaw hero in Old Siward (Sige-weard, "Victory-guardian"). Many modern poets have drawn inspiration from its recovered relics, including Geoffrey Hill, with his *Mercian Hymns*, W. H. Auden, Seamus Heaney (see Jones), and J. R. R. Tolkien, whose "Rider" poems scattered through *The Lord of the Rings* show what can still be done through strict alliterative meter even in modern English. Craig Williamson's poems presented here both introduce us to a long-lost tradition and encourage us to believe that it need not be lost. In them the dead "warrior-poet" of Grave 32 can be heard again, like his lovingly and painstakingly reconstructed harp.

NOTE ON EDITIONS

T hroughout this book I have referred to Beowulfian critical discussions and textual matters in *Klaeber 4*, which is the common abbreviation for the most recent full-scale scholarly edition of the poem, *Klaeber's Beowulf and the Fight at Finnsburg*, 4th edition, edited by R. D. Fulk, Robert E. Bjork, and John D. Niles, with a Foreword by Helen Damico. This work is a monument of Old English textual scholarship and critical commentary. It is based on the earlier editions of *Beowulf and the Fight at Finnsburg*, edited by Fr. Klaeber, whose history is traced in Damico's Foreword to *Klaeber 4* (vii–ix). The first edition of this groundbreaking work appeared in 1922. The second and third editions appeared in 1928 and 1936; the third edition was reissued in 1950 with supplements. The third edition was the one I used when first studying the poem in graduate school at the University of Pennsylvania under two fine mentors of Old English, James L. (Jim) Rosier and Edward B. (Ted) Irving, Jr. This *Beowulf* text was the standard text for many generations of scholars and students and has now been revised and brought up to date to include scholarly discussions of the last sixty years. Each of the Klaeber editions has been a model of Old English scholarship in its time, and this fourth edition, prepared with such scholarly devotion and deep wisdom by Fulk, Bjork, and Niles, is no exception. It is, in the words of Tom Shippey (who happily has written the Foreword to my own work here), "A Triumph for a Triumvirate" (see Shippey 2009, 360ff. for a thorough and appreciative review of *Klaeber 4*).

For translating *Beowulf*, I used both Klaeber, *Beowulf and The Fight at Finnsburg*, 3rd ed., and later *Klaeber 4*; also *Beowulf: An Edition*, ed. Bruce

Mitchell and Fred C. Robinson.. For the riddles, I used my own edition, *The Old English Riddles of the Exeter Book* and took the translations with minor revisions from my edition of *A Feast of Creatures: Anglo-Saxon Riddle-Songs*. For the Exeter Book poems, I used Muir's *The Exeter Anthology of Old English Poetry*, 2nd ed. rev., and also consulted several versions of the short poems in grammars and readers such as *A Guide to Old English*, rev. 7th ed., ed. Mitchell and Robinson; Peter Baker, *Introduction to Old English*, 2nd ed.; *Eight Old English Poems*, 3rd ed., ed. Pope, rev. Fulk; and *Old English Language and Literature*, ed. Marckwardt and Rosier. For the charms, I used *Anglo-Saxon Magic*, ed. Dr. G. Storms. For all the poems, I consulted *The Anglo-Saxon Poetic Records*, ed. Krapp and Dobbie, as well as other later editions of the texts such as those in the Methuen Old English Library series, along with scholarship about the poems.

GUIDE TO PRONOUNCING
OLD ENGLISH

W hat follows is a simplified guide to the pronunciation of Old English to aid the reader in pronouncing the occasional words and passages quoted in the original in the commentaries on the poems. For a fuller explanation, see the pronunciation guides in any of the Old English grammars such as those by Mitchell and Robinson or Baker listed in the Bibliography. There is not always absolute agreement about the finer details of pronunciation, especially with respect to the vowels and diphthongs. I have followed a common editorial practice of indicating long vowels with a macron and also indicating the difference between the hard and soft c forms and g forms by the presence or absence of a superscript dot. Such markings, which are used as an aid to students learning the language, are not in the poetry manuscripts themselves.

OE letters	Pronounced as in
Vowels	
a	cot
ā	calm
æ	cat
ǣ	band
e	pet
ē	fate
i	sit
ī	beat
o	bought

Vowels (continued)

ō	boat
u	full
ū	food
y	French tu
ȳ	French ruse

Diphthongs

ea = æ + a
ēa = ǣ + a
eo = e + o
ēo = ē + o
ie = i + e
īe = ī + e

Consonants

Most OE consonants have the same pronunciation as in Modern English. Exceptions are noted below. All consonants must be pronounced; there are no silent consonants. So, for example, the *w* must be pronounced in *wrītan*, "write," and the *c* in *cniht*, "young man." All double consonants must be pronounced, so *biddan* has the *dd* sound of "bad debt."

c	as in <u>c</u>at	
ċ	as in <u>ch</u>urch	
g	as in <u>g</u>ap	
ġ	as in <u>y</u>ield	
h	as in <u>h</u>ot	at the beginning of a word
	as in Germ a<u>ch</u>	elsewhere in a word
f	as in <u>f</u>ox	when not between voiced sounds
	as in <u>v</u>ixen	when between voiced sounds
s	as in <u>s</u>it	when not between voiced sounds
	as in <u>z</u>ip	when between voiced sounds
ð, þ	as in <u>th</u>in	when not between voiced sounds
	as in <u>th</u>is	when between voiced sounds
cg	as in e<u>dg</u>e	
sc	as in <u>sh</u>ip	
ng	as in fi<u>ng</u>er	

Between back vowels, as in OE *āgan* (own), or finally after a back vowel, as in OE *plōg* (plow), the g sound is like German *ach*, only voiced. For the distinction between back and front vowels, see Algeo and Pyles.

All vowels are voiced. Some consonant sounds (b, d, g, j, l, m, n, r) are normally voiced; others (p, t, k, ch) are unvoiced. For more on the voiced/unvoiced distinction, see Algeo and Pyles.

ON TRANSLATING
OLD ENGLISH POETRY

INTRODUCTION

W hen poets are asked to describe the act of writing or translating poetry, they often turn to metaphor to unravel or explain a process that remains in part mysterious. If writing poetry is like dancing solo with the world, translating poetry is like dancing with a partner you get to know over time. My partner usually comes from a different homeland with a different personal or cultural way of perceiving and performing in the world. Our rhythms, our dances, our expectations are different. We do, however, share a sense of rhythm, and we both utilize bone, muscle, sinew. We do different dances on similar legs. We have brains that process music, rhythm, movement. This is true for any translation dance—it's a shared movement between worlds.

My dance with the Old English poet is special in that his or her language is part of my linguistic inheritance. The poet says *bān* where I say "bone" and *hūs* where I say "house," but the meanings remain largely the same (even if the Anglo-Saxon house is quite different from my own). On the other hand, when the poet says *dōm*, drawing on a complex linguistic and cultural storehouse, he or she means something like "judgment, reputation, honor, glory," which is a far cry from the meaning of "doom" that I have inherited, meaning "fate, destruction, death," which first arises in the fourteenth century. So we speak a different but related language. Some of our words mean the same thing; the great majority do not. My partner's language is vastly more inflected than my own, though we share similar inflections that have survived the centuries. We come from different worlds but we are both human, and what we share makes the act of translation possible, even if finally what we recognize is a strange but human otherness together. We are both poets who love the written word. We dream up worlds with these words which reflect the worlds we inhabit. We cherish human connection (though we connect in different ways) and lament the loss of loved ones (though our lamenting rituals are different). We dance together what we might call a dance of difference. My Old English poetic partner may be a court composer or a Christian monk. His or her natural mode of dancing out rhythms is alliterative strong stress where mine is metrical feet and rhyme. In order to make this dance work, we must share ideas and languages—or at least I must do this since I'm the living partner doing the translator's choreography, but sometimes it seems, in the middle of a line, when we are sitting poetically together with warriors at the meadhall table, that my partner is communicating movements, inviting meanings, teasing me and my world with differences in language and culture or tongue-in-cheek ambiguity. We communicate together across the long space of time and shape the dance.

When the dance is done, I can analyze the movement and the steps, as I've done below, but something of this dance remains a mystery. This is as it should be. We can use critical language to understand the language of poetry, but this has its limitations. There is always an unconscious element to the process that remains hidden like some mysterious force in some unknown place. Sometimes after a hard night's work on my own lines or lines in *Beowulf*, the right words, both beautiful and true, just pop into mind without prompting. This is what makes writing and translating poetry both a transcendent experience and a true delight.

OLD ENGLISH POETIC METER

Old English poetry is built on an alliterative, strong-stress pattern. Each line normally contains four strongly stressed syllables, for example:

1	2	3	4
Iċ swiftne	ġeseah	on swaþe	fēran
I a swift (thing)	saw	on the road	travel

The words that are stressed depend on their nature and function in the sentence (verbs, for example, are more important than adverbs) and in their placement (the first word in a poem or section is often important). The initial consonants of accented syllables normally alliterate only with them-selves (b alliterates with b, m with m, sp with sp, etc.); any vowel can alliterate with any other vowel (a alliterates with a, e, i, etc.). The third stress in the line always alliterates with the first or second stress or both. The fourth stress in a line never alliterates (or almost never alliterates), but it can sometimes alliterate with a stressed syllable in the preceding or follow-ing line. Thus the possible alliterative patterns in a particular line are stresses 1 and 3; 2 and 3; and 1, 2, and 3.

Each line is also divided into two half-lines, each with a syntactic integ-rity, and is separated by a relatively strong caesura or pause, and the half-lines fall into a number of possible patterns of stressed and unstressed sylla-bles. Each half-line normally has two stressed syllables and a somewhat flexible number of unstressed syllables. Sometimes there also occurs a sec-ondary stress, midway in weight between a stressed and an unstressed sylla-ble. The basic half-line patterns, with illustrations in modern English, are as follows:

$'$ x $'$ x	Type A	grim and greedy
x $'$ x $'$	Type B	his mighty band
x $'$ $'$ x	Type C	the ship waited
$'$ $'$ $`$ x	Type D^1	high horn-gabled
$'$ $'$ x $`$	Type D^2	bold, battle-famed
$'$ $`$ x $'$	Type E	wind-waters roll

In this scheme, the sign $'$ represents a stressed syllable or lift; x represents an unstressed syllable or drop; and $`$ represents a secondary stress or half-lift. Some but not all of the drops can be expanded into more unstressed syllables, and there are several subtype variations for each of the major types. Occasionally there are longer lines, called hypermetric lines, which have three stressed syllables in each half-line instead of two; they seem to follow the pattern types above but add an extra foot (translators vary on whether to try to imitate these). There is only rarely rhyme in Old English poetry. This is a somewhat simplified summary of Old English meter; readers inter-ested in a more detailed explanation should consult the Old English gram-mars or handbooks on style listed in the Bibliography.

What was common to the literate Anglo-Saxon, the controlled strong-stress line, often proves strange to modern readers of poetry who are used to the iambic rhythms of later poetic traditions or the free verse of many modern writers. Occasional modern poets hearken back to the ancient Old English rhythms—for example, Pound in the *Cantos*, Auden in *The Age of Anxiety*, and Tolkien in his poems and songs (see Jones for examples of modern poets using Old English methods). Mainly the strong-stress rhythms remain a medievalist's delight.

Translators deal with Old English meter in different ways. Some attempt to keep to the strict Old English meter and dredge up archaic words to meet the alliterative demands. Some scuttle strong stress for the more comfortable iambic pentameter or free verse or resort to syllabic verse. Some struggle to make compromises. My own compromise represents a cross between the traditional strong-stress meter and a looser form, sometimes approaching a style used by Ælfric in what is called rhythmical prose. It retains the four-stress line in a loosely alliterative pattern. It builds in substantial cross-line alliteration—especially to bind to the rest of the poem an occasional non-alliterative line. It plays with the possibility of assonance and adds the close repetition of words and morphemes. It occasionally uses rhyme or off-rhyme to bind the lines where alliteration seems impossible.

Take, for example, the *Bookworm* riddle (45), which I quote here in Old English, in a straightforward translation (with some indication of the ambiguities in the original), and in my own poetic rendering:

Moððe word fræt—mē þæt þūhte
wrǣtlicu wyrd þā iċ þæt wundor ġefræġn,
þæt se wyrm forswealg wera ġied sumes,
þēof in þystro, þrymfæstne cwide
ond þæs strangan staþol. Stælġiest ne wæs
wihte þȳ glēawra þē hē þām wordum swealg.

A moth ate (devoured, consumed, gobbled) words (speech, sentence, story)—to me that seemed
A strange event (weird fate, odd happening, pun on "strange saying"), when I heard of that wonder (miracle, horror),
That a worm (bug, snake, dragon) should swallow (mentally imbibe, consume, absorb) the songs of a certain one of men,
A thief in darkness (mental darkness, ignorance), his glory-fast sayings (pun on "cud or munchings"),
And their place (intellectual foundation) of strength. That thief-guest
Was no wiser for having swallowed (mentally imbibed) words.

A moth ate songs—wolfed words!
That seemed a weird dish—that a worm
Should swallow, dumb thief in the dark,
The songs of a man, his chants of glory,
Their place of strength. That thief-guest
Was no wiser for having swallowed words.

My poetic translation is written in strong stress meter with four stresses to each line. It contains two primary alliterative stresses each in lines 1, 2, 3, and 6. The stresses of line 4 are linked by the assonance of "man" and "chants"; of line 5 by the assonance of "strength" and "guest" (or "place" and "strength," depending on the individual pronunciation). Lines 4 and 5 are also linked by the cross-line alliteration in "guest" and "glory." All six lines have some form of *s* stress; three lines have a double *w* stress. The sinuous *s* pattern produces some of the ominous overtones of the *wyrm* complex (worm-snake-dragon) in Old English. Verbal repetitions include "songs" (1 and 4), "words" (1 and 6), "swallow"/"swallowed" (2 and 6), and the double "that" of line 2 and triple "of" of lines 4–5. There is also the imperfect rhyme of "weird" and "word(s)," which reproduces that of the original *word* and *wyrd*, even though the meanings are significantly different.

All these devices help to tighten the translation and in some sense compensate for the loosening that takes place with the loss of primary alliteration in lines 4–5. The translation is occasionally iambic as in "A moth ate songs," or "Their place of strength," which sounds more modern (though this Type B half-line pattern of x ′ x ′ is one of the five basic Old English types). But this momentary pattern is almost always followed by the shock of dense stress, as in "wolfed words," and "thief-guest." This clash of accented syllables of a primary or secondary sort is typical of half-line types C, D, and E above, and it may also occur when one half-line ends with a stress, and another begins with a stress. I hope my translation technique produces a rhythm that rolls back and forth between an ancient and modern mode. It is a rhythm that is influenced by Hopkins's sprung rhythm, which is characterized by the primary importance of accentual stress combined with heavy alliteration and assonance, and which was itself probably based in part on his reading of Old English (see Vendler, 9 ff. and Plotkin, 18–19, 149 ff.). This is the method I have used in translating all of the Old English poems that follow, from the smallest riddles to the 3,182 lines of *Beowulf.* Of course, the longer poems have more of a tendency to shift styles, sometimes moving from a looser conversational or prosaic tone to quite dense and compact poetry in a short space of time, and I have tried to capture these tonal shifts in the translations.

Catching the complex meanings and ambiguities of the original Old English poems is often difficult, and sometimes a translator must repeat a phrase with variation to include different semantic possibilities in the original or pick up in one phrase or line what was lost in a previous one. Occasionally it takes two lines to capture the meaning of one especially complex line, and this is why the line numbers in the translations will not always agree exactly with the line numbers in the original texts. The *Bookworm* riddle is a typical example of a poem containing ambiguities that cause difficulties for a translator. Building into any translation what Fred C. Robinson calls the "artful ambiguities" of this riddle proves a challenging task (1975, 355 ff.; I am indebted to Robinson for much of the discussion of this riddle). The word-gobbling *wyrm* that steals man's songs from their vellum foundation may mean "bug, worm, snake, reptile, or dragon" in Old English. The dragon that destroys Beowulf is a *wyrm*, but so is the larva that spins silk. Building the bug into a dragon and bringing him down is part of the mock-epic game of the riddle, but most of this is lost in the innocuous "worm" of modern English. (For more on the parodic devices in the riddle, see Stewart 1975, 227 ff.). Taking the ravenous possibilities of *fræt*, a word that implies unnatural gobbling, I try to recapture the dragon's ferocity with the phrase, "wolfed words" which repeats with variation the initial "ate songs." Thus in order to capture some of the original ambiguity, I've had to use the Old English poetic device of repetition (verb + object) with variation (word choice). Whenever I have to add something to catch a bit of lost meaning in the original, I try to do this in an Old English way, thus imitating the poet's method of composition.

Robinson points out a number of possible puns in the riddle. *Wyrd* is a word whose meaning ranges from "terrible fate" (epic dragons) to "what's happening" (mocking the bug). In the riddlic context, it is also a pun on *ġewyrd*, "speech." The ambiguous tone is echoed by *cwide*, "songs, sayings," a pun on *cwidu*, "what is munched" (*cwidu* or its other forms, *cwudu* and *cudu*, can mean "cud" in Old English). The grotesque irony of this is perhaps conveyed in the "weird dish," since for moderns not only a hard fate but also hot lasagna may be "dished out." Finally modern English "weird" derives from the Old English *wyrd* and has gone from meaning "fact, fate, destiny, Providence" to "strange, uncanny." The addition of "dumb" is also an attempt to catch the bovine level of *cwidu* as well as the unspeaking idiocy of the worm. The word *þystro* means either physical or mental "darkness"; *swealg*, "swallow physically" or "imbibe mentally." These ambiguities are kept in modern English (e.g., "That book left me in the dark." "Don't swallow that old line."). These are just some of the semantic problems any translator must deal with, even in the short space of a six-line riddle. The difficulties in a long, complex poem like *Beowulf* are only compounded (see below for examples).

Some readers may object to the trade of a wolf for a *wyrm* or the intrusion of a dish. And yet, a translator must attempt to reproduce not only primary meanings, but also ambiguities, textures, and tones. St. Jerome says that often "word for word" translation must give way to "sense for sense" translation and notes that "it is difficult, when following the text of another language, not to overstep the mark in places, and hard to keep in the translation the grace of something well said in the original" (Wilcox, 2006, 29–30). A safe translation is often one that does an injustice to the complexity and spirit of the original. My goal in translating these poems has been to recreate faithfully the Old English and to shape modern English poems as beautiful, startling, and compelling as the originals—to bring across the bridge of time something of that original grace.

OLD ENGLISH POETICS AND STYLE

Old English poetry is different from Modern English poetry in a multitude of ways beyond the metrical differences. It's important in any translation to understand the larger modes of composition and then try to build them into the translations themselves. Those modes included in the discussion here are vocabulary (including compounds and kennings), patterns of repetition (including formulas, variation, apposition, parallelism, parataxis, and envelope or ring structure), and the tonal or rhetorical devices of humor, irony, and litotes.

Vocabulary

One aspect of Old English vocabulary evident in the poems is the large number of words for certain common or important concepts such as man, warrior, sword, spear, horse, battle, sea, ship. A seafaring people, for example, will have a greater variety of words for the sea than a landlocked people.

The poems also have a specialized vocabulary with an increased number of poetic or even archaic words, creating a larger *wordhord*, "word-hoard," for the poet to work with. *Beowulf* includes unique words such as *bolster*, "cushion," *cēnðu*, "boldness," and *hæf*, "sea," and compounds like *ǣr-fæder*, "forefather," *mūð-bona*, "mouth-destroyer," and *wīs-hycgende*, "wise-thinking." Mitchell and Robinson note that *Beowulf* has 700 unique words not found elsewhere in Old English (1998, 25). The variety of words enables the poet to make fine distinctions of meaning and meet the alliterative requirements of the poetic lines. It also makes the poetry seem different from everyday prose. It creates a special world by combining the everyday and the unusual—just as *Beowulf* brings us into a world of history and myth, meadhall drinking and monsters marauding. It makes the poetic world both realistic and rare.

Compounds

The Anglo-Saxons loved to shape new meanings out of old words by creating compounds such as *bēag-ġifa*, "ring-giver," *heofon-flōd*, "sky-flood" (rainstorm), *eard-stapa*, "land-stepper," and *hreþer-bealo*, "heart-bale" (distress). The latest editors of *Beowulf* count 903 distinct compounds of which 518 are unique to the poem, observing that "on average there is a compound in every other line" (*Klaeber 4*, cxii; see "Note on Editions" at the beginning of the book for an explanation of this source). Orchard's list of battle compounds in *Beowulf*, from *beado-grīma*, "war-mask," to *wīg-spēd*, "war-success," runs to two pages (70–72). Each compound is a miniature yoking of perceptual worlds. Orchard argues that "in producing such compounds . . . the *Beowulf*-poet is effectively offering a number of snap-shots or perspectives both simultaneously and in sequence, and allowing the audience the chance to savour (or not) the multiplicity of meanings offered" (73). I have kept these compounds in most cases, even when they might seem strange to a modern ear. Such strangeness is part of the act of reading poetry from another language and culture and appreciating the otherness of that perception and poetic vision.

Kennings

A kenning is a special compound that calls a noun something it is not, then modifies it with a contextual clue. Examples of kennings include *bān-hūs*, "bone-house" (body), *hilde-lēoma*, "battle-light" (sword), *hwæl-weg*, "whale-road" (sea), and *hilde-nædre*, "battle-snake" (arrow). Kennings can also be constructed with a genitive modifier such as *rodores candel*, "heaven's candle" (sun), and *homera lāf*, "the leaving of hammers" (sword). In each case, the kenning is like a compressed metaphor. For example, in *bān-hūs*, the unnamed thing (body) is compared to another quite different named thing (house), but modified with a contextual clue (a *bone*-house). Each of these kennings implies a hidden metaphoric analogy:

$$\frac{\text{bone}}{\text{body}} :: \frac{\text{timber}}{\text{house}}$$

This, in turn, sets up four possible kennings: (1) a body is a bone-house; (2) a house is a timbered body; (3) a bone is a body-timber; and (4) a timber is a house-bone. This begins to make each kenning look like a new slant upon the world—a way of crossing categories to reperceive reality. Each kenning is like a miniature riddle which invites the reader to solve the word (or creature or concept) in disguise and to consider reshaping our perceptual lenses to see the world with poetic eyes (for more on kennings and riddles, see Williamson, 1982, 29 ff. and Stewart, 1979, 115 ff.). A related Old English device calls something by one of its typical aspects, then modifies it, such as *wēg-flota*, "wave-floater" (ship), and *bēag-gifa*, "ring-giver" (lord, king). Such constructions are sometimes called half-kennings or *kend heiti* (see Brodeur, 251).

Variation (Parallelism, Parataxis)

The basic construction pattern of Old English verse is built on the syntactic repetition of phrases with semantic variation. A phrase which is repeated exactly constitutes a formula such as the common opening of riddles, *Iċ wiht ġeseah*, "I saw a creature," or the common closing, *Saga hwæt iċ hātte*, "Say what I am called." The formulaic ending might be varied to *Frīġe hwæt iċ hātte*, "Discover what I'm called." In *Beowulf*, there are formulas such as *Hrōðgār maþelode, helm Scyldinga*, "Hrothgar spoke, protector of the Scyldings," which is repeated three times. There are variations on this such as *Bēowulf maþelode, bearn Ecgþēowes*, "Beowulf spoke, son of Ecgtheow" (9 examples). Such formulaic renderings are common in Old English poetry.

They may have first been formulated in an earlier oral tradition and incorporated into the literature, or they may have been simply literary formulas. Other shorter, half-line formulaic examples include *goldwine gumena*, "goldfriend of men," *mēarum ond mēðum*, "with horses and treasures," and *sigorēadiġ secg*, "victory-blessed man." Orchard lists some forty pages of such formulas in *Beowulf* (274 ff.).

The use of repetition with variation can help to define or subtly nuance a description via epithets, such as the poet's description of Grendel as "a hell-fiend / A grim hall-guest called Grendel, / Moor-stalker, wasteland walker" (101b–103). It can also describe an action by stages or degrees, as in the description of Grendel's eating of Hondscio:

> He seized the first sleeper, slit his body,
> Bit open his bone-house, drinking his blood,
> Swallowing flesh, feasting on hands and feet,
> Eating greedily the unliving one. (739–42)

In passages like these, the lines or half-lines move forward, repeating the syntactical pattern of a noun or verb phrase while employing in each case semantic variation. When this occurs without any clear indication of coordination or subordination, it is called parataxis. It produces a pattern of rolling phrases with variations of meaning. The phrases often repeat grammatical patterns, creating formal appositions (see Robinson 1985 for more on this). In the Old English lines for the translation above, the verbs are more directly parallel ("seized," "slit," "bit," "drank," "swallowed," etc.), but in the translation I have varied this a bit by shifting from past tense verbs to participles. This is a useful translator's trick to keep the repetition from becoming overbearing to a modern reader.

The pattern of syntactic repetition with variation can be useful in situations where a single translation of a half-line fails to capture the original ambiguity, no matter what the word-choice in Modern English. For example in the opening line of "The Wanderer," the *ān-haga* or "lonely one" (literally "hedged-in one") is said to *āre ġebīdeð*, which is ambiguous. The verb *ġebīdeð* can mean "waits for, expects, experiences," and the object *ār* can mean "honor, glory, grace, mercy." So then, does the wanderer experience, or merely wait for, mercy? Is it honor he wants or grace? I try to capture some of this ambiguity through the device of repetition with variation by translating, "Waits for mercy, longs for grace." Similarly in the last half-line of *Beowulf,* the poet says of Beowulf that he was *lofgeornost,* which means something like "eager for praise (fame, glory)." There is great debate about whether the hero at the end of the poem is being praised for his proper pursuit of honor or judged for his pride in wanting to fight the dragon alone and his greediness for the dragon's gold. The most recent editors of the poem argue that "the reference is either to glory earned by deeds of valor . . . or to the king's liberality toward his men . . . or both" (*Klaeber 4,* 271). I've tried to keep some of the ambiguity of this concluding half-line by expanding it into a repetition with variation: "Most desiring of praise, most deserving of fame."

The patterned repetition of half-lines can occur with an abrupt caesura between them so as to highlight a stark sense of change or reversal which is called *edwenden.* In *Klaeber 4,* the editors note that this sense of reversal is common in *Beowulf:* "Joy alternates with sadness, good fortune with ill, in what seems like an endless process of reversal" (cx). So, for example, when Beowulf asks King Hrothgar if he's had a pleasant night's sleep after he's cleared the hall of Grendel, Hrothgar responds with great anxiety and sadness because Grendel's mother has entered the hall, killing Æscere. In my translation Hrothgar cries out: "Don't talk of dreams. My life's a nightmare!" (1322). Sometimes this sense of sharp contrast is carried by the phrase *oð ðæt,* "until," which indicates a sudden sense of danger or unexpected outcome such as when the poet says that the thanes in Heorot who are celebrating the newly built hall were "Surrounded by joy until a certain creature / Began to commit crimes" (100–101a), indicating the looming presence of Grendel.

Envelope/Ring

Sometimes the poetic phrases, as they repeat and vary, return to the phrase or motif with which they began. This pattern of circling back by means of repetition and variation is called an envelope or ring pattern. A well-known example comes from "The Battle of Maldon" (25–28):

Þā stōd on stæðe, stīðlīce clypode	A B
Then stood on the shore, fiercely called out	
wīcinga ār, wordum mælde,	C B
the messenger of the Vikings, spoke with words,	

sē on bēot ābēad brimlīþendra   B C
who announced in a vow (boast) of the sea-sailors
ǣrende tō þām eorle þǣr hē on ōfre stōd.   B A
a message to the earl where he stood on the shore.

Lines 25a and 28b repeat the theme of the messenger's location on the shore and enclose or envelop the passage. Lines 25b, 26b, 27a, and 28a all deal with the calling out of the Viking message or vow. Lines 26a and 27b deal with the reference to the messenger's relation to the Viking troops. So the passage opens with ABC, repeats the B pattern twice, and returns home with CBA—a nice tight envelope (for more on this, see Bartlett, 9 ff.).

Humor: Irony, Understatement, Litotes, Bawdy

Old English humor often takes the form of subtle irony, understatement, and litotes (a negative ironic understatement such as saying, "He's not a good singer" when one means "He's a terrible singer"). This is what Frank calls the "incomparable wryness" of the poetry (59 ff.). *Klaeber 4* notes a number of instances of grim humor and litotes in *Beowulf* (cx–cxi). When Beowulf tells of fighting the sea-monsters in his swimming match with Breca, he says he served them with his sword so that they had "little pleasure" (meaning he killed them and they had no pleasure!), and they slept late the next morning, "lulled by [his] sword" (566). When Wiglaf says to the cowardly Geats who fled from the dragon's barrow that their lord had too few defenders, he is indicating by means of litotes that Beowulf had no defenders whatsoever except him. When the poet says of the Danes' great woe from Grendel's nightly visits, "that was no small suffering they endured" (832), he uses litotes to emphasize their endless agony. In the description of Grendel's coming to Heorot for his nightly savagery, there are two related litotes jokes:

> That wasn't the first time he sought
> Hrothgar's home, but he never found
> In his grim days before or after
> Such bad luck, such hard hall-thanes. (718–21)

The first joke is told at the hall-thanes' expense: that wasn't the first time Grendel came there—because he comes every night! The second is told at

Grendel's expense: he never found such hard luck before or after—because following his battle-meeting with Beowulf there will be no "after." Beowulf jokes before he goes to meet Grendel that if he loses the battle, Hrothgar won't have to worry about feeding him at the meadhall table or burying his body since Grendel will have gobbled him up. This instance of Beowulf's joking about his death is a traditional sign of a Germanic hero's bravery. A great hero often indulges in dark humor on his deathbed. When Beowulf is dying, he tells Wiglaf that he would give his armor to his son if only he had one. Of course, this irony also reveals a terrible truth: without a Beowulfian heir to the throne, the Geats are in grave danger, as the Swedes and Frisians will descend upon them.

Another kind of humor occurs in the Old English double entendre riddles when a sexual, bodily element or action is compared wittily with some tool or natural element. The woman-warrior in the bread-dough/penis riddle (Riddle 43) sees something *nāthwæt* (*ne* + *wāt* + *hwæt*, "I know not what") "rising in the corner / Swelling and standing up" (1–2). She knows perfectly well what it is and goes over to grab at that "boneless wonder" (3b–4a) before she covers it up in mock-modesty with a cloth (or a bit of her clothes!). The humor in the butter churn riddle (Riddle 52) mocks the actively engaging male servant who works away at the process of "churning" and is only "sometimes useful," serving well but usually tiring "sooner than she" (7–9). In the sword riddle (Riddle 18), the creature says that his kind of sword, the battle-sword (unlike the implied sexual sword), brings neither bedroom joy nor more children to his lord's wife. At war he has to "stroke in brideless play / Without the hope of child-treasure" (23–24). It may seem odd that Anglo-Saxon humor finds its outlet often in sexual-bed and death-bed jokes, but these are charged moments in any human life, and as Freud argues, humor is often an outlet for submerged desire or fear.

PROBLEM PASSAGES
AND POETIC LICENSE

In any translation there are always words or passages which seem to defy translation. Often these are common words which have a wide range of meanings in the language or are idiomatic to the language, or they are passages which communicate hidden or ambiguous meanings or an emotional force in the original which is difficult to translate. Sometimes these passages demand a degree of poetic license to express their forceful meanings. In this section I want to examine three such passages, the opening lines of *Beowulf*, the *Ēalā* repetition from "The Wanderer," and the enigmatic ending of "Wulf and Eadwacer." In each case I give the passage first in Old English, then in a relatively straightforward translation (with some indication of the ambiguities in the original), and finally in my own poetic rendering.

The opening lines of *Beowulf* look deceptively simple, but they set the tone for the rest of the poem and in some ways encapsulate some of its central themes:

Hwæt! Wē Gār-Dena in ġeārdagum
þēodcyninga þrym ġefrūnon,
hū ðā æþelingas ellen fremedon.

Behold (listen, well, lo)! We, about the Spear-Danes in the old days
    (days of yore, bygone days),
Have heard (learned from asking about) the glory (power, might,
    majesty, splendor) of the people's kings (kings of a wide territory
    or domain),
How the nobles (princes, chiefs, heroes, men) accomplished
    (performed, made, brought about) glory (strength, courage, valor,
    dedication).

Listen! We have heard of the Spear-Danes' glory,
Their storied power, their primal strength—
The kings and princes whose craft was courage.

The opening word *Hwæt* is often taken as a call to attention though it is probably unstressed (on Old English interjections, see Hiltunen, 91 ff). It is translated variously as "Listen," "So," "Indeed," "Lo," "What," "Behold," "Well," and "Ah." None of these work perfectly well, but "Listen!" seems to me the best alternative in terms of its attention-calling quality and meaning, even though it lacks the sharp sound of "Hwæt" and seems a little like a teacher calling a class to order. I could alliterate "So" or perhaps "Say" with "Spear," but this seems a weak, informal opening. Or I could keep "Listen" and alliterate "glory" with the second syllable of "bygone," but this seems unnecessarily archaic. Reluctantly giving up the alliteration in the opening line, I make up for it in the second line by linking "storied" and "strength" with "Spear" in line 1 and by the partial rhyme of "glory" with "storied," which also picks up the sense of tales heard in days gone by. I also strengthen the second line with a double alliteration which was present in the first line of the original. The use of "primal" picks up the sense of the past. In the third line there is a stress on "princes" which makes for an alliterative linkage with "power" and "primal" in line 2. For the primary alliteration in line 3, I've chosen the unusual "craft" to go with "courage" because it picks up the subtle sense of "accomplishing" or "making" in *gefrūnon.* I've kept and even strengthened the technique of apposition with variation in each of the lines. I've tried to communicate the sense of difference between the listening or reading audience and the old story that's being retold in the poem (for more on this theme, see Robinson, 1985, 27–28).

Another difficult passage to translate is the *Ēalā* cry in "The Wanderer" (94 ff. in the Old English and 100 ff. in my translation) where the speaker laments the loss of his lord and hall:

Ēalā beorht bune! Ēalā byrn-wiga!
Ēalā þēodnes þrymm! Hū sēo þrāg ġewāt,
ġenap under nihthelm, swā hēo nō wǣre!

Alas the bright (shining, brilliant, beautiful, magnificent) cup
    (beaker, drinking vessel)! Alas the mailed warrior (fighter with a
    corselet)!
Alas the glory (power, might, majesty, splendor) of the prince (lord)!
    How the time (period of time, age, season) has gone (departed,
    gone out, passed away),
Grown dark (gloomy) under the night-helmet (cover of night, of
    darkness) as if it were not (had never been)!

Gone is the bright cup. Gone is the mailed warrior.
Gone is the glory of the prince. How the time has slipped
Down under the night-helmet as if it never was.

Ēalā is a heartfelt cry imbued with longing and a sense of deep and unrecoverable loss. It is usually translated as "Ah," "Oh," or "Alas," none of which seems adequate to catch the power of the soulful lament, and all of which seem archaic and sentimental to a modern ear. One solution might be to say prosaically "I mourn for" or "I lament the loss of" and then list each of these precious and symbolically laden objects, but I've chosen to use the word "gone" to carry the sense of loss and to repeat it in the manner of *Ēalā* in the original so that it becomes increasingly a ritualized cry. The "g" of "gone" and "glory" provides the alliteration in the first two lines, and the "n" of "never" and "night-helmet" in the last line. The passage from "glory" to "gone" helps to strengthen the sense of loss. I keep the compound "night-helmet," as in the Old English, not only to emphasize the loss of a protecting element but also to pick up the associations of a helmet like the Sutton Hoo helmet which was once grandly decorated but now has lost most of its bright exterior. The slight enjambment of "slipped/Down" hurries the sense of loss along and makes it seem inevitable.

Finally there is the mysterious and enigmatic ending of "Wulf and Eadwacer" which reads like a miniature riddle. In fact the entire poem was once thought a riddle but is now generally accepted as a woman's lament, though it's never quite clear who either Wulf or Eadwacer is, and the dramatic situation is endlessly debated. The narrator, who is lamenting the loss of her husband or lover or son, cries out, "Wulf, my Wulf," mourning his infrequent visits, which may be a litotes for his never visiting. The poem concludes with this enigmatic passage:

> Þæt mon ēaþe tōslīteð þætte næfre ġesomnad wæs,
> uncer ġiedd ġeador.

> One may easily (readily, lightly) tear apart (sever, rend, wound, break
>   open, destroy) what (that which) was never united (joined,
>   assembled, collected, gathered together),
> The song (poem, saying, word, speech, proverb, riddle, tale) of us
>   two together (united).

> It's easy to rip an unsewn stitch
> Or tear the thread of an untold tale—
> The song of us two together.

This ending is both enormously powerful and endlessly mysterious. Questions abound. What is this enigmatic thing that is easily torn and never really together? Is it the speaker's unfulfilled or impossible dream of Wulf's return? Or her long-held but unrealistic romance of reunion with an exiled lover? Why is the storied relationship, their song (or riddle) together, so easily ripped apart? Translators of these last lines must often strain to capture their enigmatic power and meaning in imaginative ways, as I have done here with the image of the unsewn stitch which draws upon the Anglo-Saxon concept of the woman as *friðowebba*, "peace-weaver"—the woman who is married not for love but for an impossible peace-weaving between strife-bound families or warring tribes (as is often the case in *Beowulf*). The word "stitch" makes concrete the final image. Its primary meaning here is "the thread that sews two pieces of fabric together," as the woman and Wulf may have been metaphorically united or "stitched." But the stitch also carries hidden connotations of "a sharp pain" ("a stitch in the side") which catches some of the emotional pain of the narrator's lament. Incidentally, both of these meanings of "stitch" ultimately derive from Old English *stiče*, "sting, prick, pain in the side." The word "thread" also has a double meaning which links the image of sewing with that of the story or song (as in the "thread of a plot"). I've expanded the line and a half in Old English to three lines in the translation. I've used the *s* alliteration in the first line which links up with the "song" of the last line. The *t* alliteration links the last two lines. The use of "un" in "unsewn" and "untold" helps to stitch the lines together in an ironic way. It is important also in that it picks up the sense of difference or undoing in the poem's refrain, *Ungeliċ is ūs*, "It's different for us." The assonant progression from "un" ("unsewn") to "un" ("untold") to "us" binds together ironically the two lovers in an undoing way. What they finally share is an unending separation.

CONCLUSION

The act of translation is a mediation, a human dance between two minds, two languages, two literary traditions, two cultures. The Anglo-Saxons, themselves members of a multilingual community, recognized the complexity of translation. Anglo-Saxon churchmen often translated texts from Latin into Old English (of course to them it wasn't old; it was just *Englisc*). King Alfred describes the act of translation metaphorically in the preface to his translation of St. Augustine's *Soliloquies*:

> So I gathered staves and posts and tie-beams for each of the tools I should work with, and building-timbers and beams for each of the

structures I should make—as much beautiful wood as I could carry. Each time I shouldered the wood home, I wanted the forest, but it was more than I could carry. In each beam I saw something I needed at home. So I urge those who have knowledge and good wagons to go to the woods where I cut my beams and fetch their own beautiful branches so they can weave lovely walls and shape splendid buildings and bright towns and live there joyfully summer and winter as I have not yet been able to do. (Carnicelli, 47; translation mine)

A good translator must be both ambitious and humble. He needs to carry home as much of the beautiful old wood as possible, but the whole forest is always beyond his reach. In my translations I've tried to gather up beams and timbers, posts and staves, from the grand originals and then bring them home to fashion a new building both true to the original form and beautiful in its own right. If this effort succeeds, I hope it will inspire new readers of these poems to think about learning Old English in an effort to return to the originals where the real source of power and grandeur resides.

BEOWULF

INTRODUCTION TO
BEOWULF

PROEM

Over a millennium ago, an anonymous Anglo-Saxon poet—or poets— wrote a long poem about a hero named Beowulf who fought two monsters, Grendel and his mother, ruled a kingdom with courage and wisdom, and killed a dragon in his last battle. Today, in an electronic age when most people cannot read this poem in its original tongue, people still flock to watch movies about Beowulf, read modern retellings of the ancient story in science fiction novels, attend musical versions about the heroes and their monstrous passions, and laugh at a *New York Times* editorial about a political convention in which a past president who can't keep away from the spotlight is compared to Grendel.

This is a story we refuse to forget. John Gardner has recast the tale from Grendel's point of view. Neil Gaiman has written several *Beowulf* parodies and coauthored the script for the *Beowulf* film in which Grendel's mother is a sultry seductress played by Angelina Jolie. Benjamin Bagby travels the world, chanting portions of the poem and playing his reconstructed version of the Sutton Hoo lyre. We have seen a Star Trek Voyager *Beowulf* episode, a Swedish film *Beowulf and Grendel*, an Irish rock recasting, an operatic *Grendel*, and several salacious comic book versions. And this is only a small sample of the modern reshapings (see Osborn for more).

Beowulf still speaks to us across the bridge of time, inviting us to appreciate a foreign culture and to recognize some of our old linguistic and storytelling roots. It reminds us of a shared humanity across a stretch of centuries. The old cultures of the Geats and Danes, celebrated in the poem, are gone.

The audience of Anglo-Saxons who read or listened to the poem centuries later is gone. The scribes who wrote the poem in the manuscript a thousand years ago are gone. The history of *Beowulf* begins to sound like an *ubi sunt* passage from "The Wanderer." *Where have the warriors gone? Where have the monsters gone? Where is the sound of the harp? Where is the joy of the telling?* At the end of the poem, Beowulf's *bānhūs,* his "bone-house," is given to the flames, but his story lives on. Grendel literally loses both life and limb in this poem, but his ferocity is not forgotten. The story has survived the passage of time and the transformation of telling for more than a thousand years. It will probably be recounted in some unimaginably beautiful and terrifying form after another thousand.

DATE, ORIGINS, AUDIENCE

As is the case with most Old English poems, the authorship and composition date of *Beowulf* are unknown. It was composed sometime between 500, when the historical events in the poem occurred, and 1000, when it was written down in a manuscript now known as British Library Cotton/Vitellius A.xv (*Klaeber 4,* clxii; see "Note on Editions" at the beginning of the book for an explanation of this source). There is evidence that it was copied at least once from an earlier manuscript. Most recent editors favor a composition date after 685 and before 800, but some argue for a much later date. The dialect is mainly West Saxon with evidence of other predominantly Anglian forms, which has traditionally argued for an Anglian origin, but the most recent editors note that "seemingly no part of Anglo-Saxon England can be ruled out conclusively" (*Klaeber 4,* clxxix).

The question of the audience of *Beowulf* has often been debated. Some critics favor a court culture, while others support a clerical audience. Some combination of these audiences seems most likely. Mitchell and Robinson surmise that "any of the secularized monasteries in which aristocrats gathered and which had close ties with royal courts would provide the kind of setting where *Beowulf* could be produced and appreciated" (1998, 13). *Klaeber 4* argues for a variety of possible audiences:

> Attempts to identify the poet's audience are complicated by the likelihood that the poem was performed aloud, in one setting or another, in addition to being written down. Even as a written text, preserved (one assumes) in a monastic library, *Beowulf* could have had multiple

audiences, including readers of various degrees of literary competence as regards vernacular poetry. (clxxxviii)

Whatever the real audience, the poem itself assumes and represents an audience of like-minded listeners gathered together around the poet who is sharing the story with them. This implied speaker or singer opens with an invitation or exhortation: "Listen! We have heard of the Spear-Danes' glory/ Their storied power, their primal strength." Like the *scop* or singer in Hrothgar's hall, the poet draws his audience into a scenario of ancient telling and listening, creating for an audience of readers, medieval or modern, a reenactment of this. It is a narrative technique that draws us into a collective audience and transports us back in time.

ANALOGUES AND PARALLELS

There are a number of important parallels to the treatment of both mythic monsters and human heroes in the poem. *Klaeber 4* collects a wide variety of these in their original languages, accompanied by translations (xxxvi ff., 291 ff.). The texts include Anglo-Saxon royal genealogies and charters, a Blickling homily with a description of a countryside that looks like Grendel's mere, excerpts from Scandinavian documents such as the *Prose Edda* of Snorri Sturluson and the Saxo Grammaticus *Gesta Danorum*, as well as sections from chronicles and sagas, passages from various historians, and folktale analogues. I have included a small sample of these materials in the appendices. The tribal feuds and histories, sometimes called "digressive" elements, are summarized in Appendix A, and a genealogical chart of the royal families of the Geats, Swedes, and Danes is included in Appendix B. Two of the most important parallels, the story of Grettir's battles with the monstrous Glamr and with a she-troll in *Grettis Saga*, and that of Sigurd and the dragon Fafnir in *Volsunga Saga*, are summarized in Appendix C along with brief comments about the similarities and differences with respect to *Beowulf.* Other useful parallels may be found in the Old English poems translated in this collection. Elegies like "The Wanderer" help us understand the lament of the last survivor in *Beowulf.* The sense of isolation and mourning in "The Wife's Lament" provides a more articulate analogue to the mourning of the anonymous old woman after Beowulf's death. The religious poem, "Vainglory," offers a context for reading Hrothgar's sermonic advice to Beowulf to avoid the perils of pride. "Cædmon's Hymn" offers a creation song like the one sung in the hall of Heorot. The treatment of loyalty and betrayal in "The Battle of Maldon" sheds light on Wiglaf's loyalty and the Geats' cowardice at the end of *Beowulf*. Even the "monstrous" and unknown creatures of the riddles may offer a playful analogue to the more serious monsters that haunt the Danish hall.

GENRE AND STRUCTURE

Beowulf has often been considered the earliest English epic, though it does not closely resemble classical epics often associated with the term. Tolkien preferred the term "heroic-elegiac poem," emphasizing the movement toward an elegiac tone in the latter half of the poem (1936, 275). Perhaps the poem, like the Danish hall Heorot, moves from building to burning, from epic to elegy. The editors of *Klaeber 4* suggest calling it "a long heroic poem set in the antique past" (clxxxvii), which is an apt, broadly generic description. The poem not only moves back and forth between epic and elegy, between historical materials and mythic elements; it also contains different subgenres. Harris notes that "the *Beowulf*ian *summa* includes genealogical verse, a creation hymn, elegies, a lament, a heroic lay, a praise poem, historical poems, a flyting, heroic boasts, gnomic verse, a sermon, and perhaps less formal oral genres" (236). Paradoxically it both draws into itself a variety of Old English genres and also stands finally as an unmatched genre in itself.

The poem does not have a straightforward chronological structure. Mitchell says that "the poem moves forward, sideways, and backward, in time, but also in a circle, for it begins with a leaderless people who have found a leader and ends with a people who, having lost a leader, face a perilous future" (Mitchell and Robinson 1998, 36). Hill notes that *Beowulf* is a "poem of arrivals and departures," with a narrative structure full of "chiastic structures, envelope patterns, ring patterns, interlace effects or 'digressive' jumps ahead and invited recollections of past kings and events, with both forward and backward shifts" (2008, 3–4). Niles (1983, 181) lists the following kinds of time in the poem:

> Mythic past (Creation, Cain and Abel, Flood)
> Legendary past ("timeless" heroes, such as Sigemund, Weland)
> Historical past:
> > Narrative past (Hrethel, Ongentheow, and so on)
> > Narrative present (Beowulf's adventures)
> > Narrative future (fate of the Geats, and so on)

Present of the poem's performance (real or imagined)
Present of reading the text
Mythic future (Doomsday)

The temporal jumps often emphasize the connection between past history, present action, and predicted future events. Readers often remember the poem primarily as a series of great battles between Beowulf and the monsters, but nearly half of the poem consists of speech acts of various sorts, from the scop's celebrant story of Finnsburg in the Danish court to the messenger's prediction of the great wars to come after Beowulf's death. Orchard notes that over 1200 lines are given over to about forty speeches in the poem (203). In the middle of this movement back and forth between speech acts and direct action, there occurs the singular act of Hrothgar's reading of the runes or images on the sword hilt brought back from Grendel's lair by Beowulf after his killing of Grendel's mother. Lerer argues that "the hilt stands as a figure for the poem itself" (1991, 337) and notes that it points forward in time from the audience of Danes listening to the king and scop in the poem to the audience of readers in Anglo-Saxon England. In the context of the Danish audience in the poem, it is a foreshadowing of a culture to come. In the context of an Anglo-Saxon readership, it is a looking back at the roots of their literate culture.

There are many ways of characterizing the plot structure of the poem. Tolkien postulated a bipartite structure of the rise and fall of the hero and of the Danish and Geatish culture or of young Beowulf in Denmark, successfully fighting Grendel and his mother, and Old Beowulf at home, facing death and the dragon (1936, 271). This structure privileges the hero's age-stages and wraps Grendel and his mother up into a single monstrous package. Some critics see a tripartite structure which focuses on the distinct qualities of the monsters. Niles postulates a ring plot structure, similar to the ring or envelope pattern sometimes found in the verse itself, in which the stages in the first half of the story are mirrored in reverse order in the second half, with battles and celebrations alternating (1983, 158). I use Niles's scheme with some slight modifications to arrive at the following envelope form:

A. Funeral of Scyld
   B. Beowulf fights Grendel
      C. Celebration & story (The Fight at Finnsburg)

B¹. Beowulf fights Grendel's mother
 C¹. Celebration & story (Hrothgar's sermon, & Beowulf's homeland account of Grendelkin battles & prediction about Freawaru & Ingeld)
B². Beowulf fights the dragon
 C². No celebration: Story (Prediction of wars to come)
A¹. Funeral of Beowulf

This scheme indicates the close connection between the substitutional elements in each category (different funerals, monster battles, stories & predictions of human feuds and wars). It also connects the contiguous elements (the relation between the hero battling monsters and the recollection of family or tribal feuds). After Beowulf kills Grendel, for example, and there is celebration in the Danish hall, the court poet sings the song of the fight at Finnsburg, ostensibly to celebrate another Danish victory over its enemies. The story, however, seems to highlight old tribal feuds and the failure of the peace-weaving gesture to marry the princess of one tribe to the prince of another in an attempt to resolve tribal antagonisms. In the story, the feud breaks out again when memories of past hostility and murder lead to present revenge. In the end, the Danish princess Hildeburh is carried back to her original family and people, having lost her husband, her brother, and her son in the carnage. The parallels with the Danish court are an unconscious part of the story, since Queen Wealhtheow seems concerned about the future of her own sons, and Princess Freawaru is about to be married off to the prince of the Heathobards to patch a peace. The latter gesture, as Beowulf later so wisely predicts in his report home to Hygelac, is as usual bound to fail.

The opening and closing bindings of the plot envelope are the great funerals of Scyld and Beowulf. Scyld Sceafing ("Shield, Son of Sheaf") is the legendary founder of the Danish royal line. The poem opens with a description of how he wrestled fate and wrought kingdoms until he died and was given a glorious burial on a treasure-boat set out to sea. What we see of Scyld is a brief, glorious portrait, the image that has persisted over time. We don't know much about his struggles, his conflicts, his battles with ancient enemies or his own impulses. We do know these things intimately about Beowulf by the end of the poem. When Beowulf dies, we mourn with Wiglaf the loss of a great and complicated hero. We know how he has been tested in battle with both monsters and human antagonists. We know that he has only reluctantly come to kingly power after protecting the rights of Heardred and his mother Hygd. We know he has suffered the weakening of old age and the anxiety of wondering whether he is somehow responsible for the dragon's vengeance or the treasure's curse. When Beowulf dies, we see the barrow, the twelve riders, the treasure piled up. We see the myth in the making. We know Beowulf will be celebrated in the manner of Scyld, but we also know the man and see beyond the mythic image. What seems glorious in the funeral of Scyld becomes also a source of great sadness in Beowulf's funeral. We have heard the whole story from the poet, and we understand the magnitude of the loss.

The nameless old woman at the end of the poem, who weeps over the death of her king (whom some see as Beowulf's mother), reminds us of the role of the suffering peace-weavers, the princesses who are married off to secure a truce between warring tribes, only to find themselves bereft of their beloved men after the feud erupts as it seems destined to do. The great funeral in the middle of the poem, which is contained in the story of the battle at Finnsburg, reminds us that while glorious heroes like Scyld and Beowulf may be celebrated for their deeds even as the death ship sails off or the funeral pyre begins to burn, there are women at the heart of this poem whose voices may be muted but not denied. And those voices, quiet as they are, will not leave unexamined the question of whether or not this social system based on the heroic values of loyalty and righteous revenge can sustain the family, the court, and the people. It is finally easier to deal with the monsters without than the monstrous human passions within. (For more on the funerals, see Owen-Crocker.)

THE WORLDS OF MONSTERS
AND HUMANS

The meaning of the monsters in the poem and their relation to the world of the humans has been the subject of endless critical discussion and debate (for an extensive summary of these debates, see *Klaeber 4*, sections III and IV). Tolkien first argued in his seminal essay of 1936 that the monsters were not just some fairy tale element inappropriately brought to center stage in the poem, leaving the more important human and historical elements relegated to the margins. He read the monsters as part of the mythic meaning of the poem and as such, representative of the darker human passions and threats in the worlds of Denmark and Geatland. In his reading, while Grendel is "primarily an ogre," and "approaches to a devil," he is also "an image of man estranged from God" (1936, 279–80). He is related to Cain and at the same time is a representation of savage Death which comes uninvited and "gibbering" to the feast of life (260). The dragon is "a personification of malice, greed, destruction (the evil side of heroic life) and of the undiscriminating cruelty of fortune that distinguishes not good or bad (the evil aspect of all life)" (259). For Tolkien, the monsters represent both human evil and the inevitable cruelty of time itself.

Over time, critics have seen the relation between the monsters and humans in the poem in many different ways. Kaske, for example, draws upon both classical and Christian traditions to argue that the controlling theme in the poem is the heroic ideal of *sapientia et fortitudo,* "wisdom and courage" (423 ff.). In his view, Beowulf represents both wisdom and courage; Hrothgar represents wisdom without courage; and Hygelac represents courage without wisdom. Kaske goes on to argue that Grendel and the dragon each represent a perversion of one of these heroic qualities which leads in each case to *malitia,* evil or wickedness. Grendel represents a perversion of courage, "reckless savagery" or "violent brutality" (438). The dragon represents a perversion of wisdom, "the perversion of mind and will" (450). The Danish lack of courage invites the nightly invasion of savagery in Grendel. The Geatish lack of wisdom accounts for the dragon's cunning attack and the predictable military moves by the Swedes, Frisians, and Franks against them. The reason that the dragon kills Beowulf in the end is not that evil triumphs over good but rather that the "fact of death, of final physical defeat, is inevitable and relatively unimportant; what *is* of desperate importance is having fought the good fight" (454).

In another reading, Hume argues that "the controlling theme of the poem . . . is *threats to social order* [including] troublemaking, revenge, and war—problems inescapably inherent in this kind of heroic society, yet profoundly inimical to its existence" (5). Each of these threats is represented by a monster, and Beowulf stands for humanity's best response to these threats. Hume explains that Grendel embodies both murderous envy and a savagery unbound by social constraint. He is a kin-killer like Cain or Unferth. He is "separated from joy," and the songs of mirth in the hall drive him to madness and murder. Grendel's mother, she argues, embodies the more understandable motive of revenge built into the human, heroic code that governs feuding. She demands an eye for an eye, a life for a life. The irony is that "what makes vengeance so uncontrollable and tragic is the fact that it is directed by the same laudable forces which help create and ensure social order in a violent world—the desire to conserve and protect kin or allies" (7). The dragon represents the need of king and country for gold in the treasury and the necessity for raiding parties and wars to obtain it. Such wars "upset the balance of social order" and in the end bring devastation upon the lordless Geats (9).

Niles also takes up the theme of social order but goes beyond Hume in including the positive ways in which a community can be built and maintained (1983, especially 224 ff.) He argues that "the poem's controlling theme is *community*: its nature, its occasional breakdown, and the qualities that are necessary to maintain it," including such elements as feasting, gift-giving, the exchange of speeches, and the sharing of song (226). Grendel represents the loner, the "creature apart from human community" who cannot enjoy the pleasures of people and play, song and celebration, language and love, story-telling and social bonding (229). Grendel's mere is an anti-Heorot meant to "suggest what human beings could be like in the absence of the joys of the group, in the absence of all obligations except the ties of blood" (231). The elegiac passages toward the end of the poem show us "society breaking down in the face of physical disasters" (231). Ironically, Beowulf's funeral provides an opportunity for his retainers and subjects to mourn together in an attempt to reaffirm their love for their lord and their sense of shared values (234).

The importance of gift-giving and social exchange is also emphasized by Hill, who argues that the monster-human relations must be read symbolically in the larger context of socioeconomic relations with an emphasis on the importance of exchange to cement social ties:

Much of the poem's foreground of monster fights and "background" of feud relations between peoples has a socio-economic context—the context of "exchange," of services and gifts given and received. The outlaw Grendel refuses to exchange with the Danes or to pay for his murders. Grendel, to be sure, is an unusual, serial murderer, perhaps a zombie. But the heroic world produces mundanely human versions of Grendel, along with lesser Beowulfs. . . . Potentially, each warrior, each woman, and each king can turn away from proper exchange, proper service, and proper settlements towards terror, strife and treachery—essentially towards the monstrous. (1995, 113)

The dragon represents the impulse to guard and hoard the treasure which precludes its use as an exchange medium to secure loyalty and trust. The dragon thus threatens to destroy not only Beowulf and the Geats but also the larger culture of human connections.

Tolkien and early scholars tended to group Grendel and his mother together as an undifferentiated monstrous force and to ignore the place of women in the poem, but with the rise of feminist criticism, scholars have begun to examine this issue. Chance, for example, argues that if Grendel is a mock-retainer and the dragon a mock-king, then Grendel's mother must be a mock-mother and mock-queen, a woman who fights her own battles (in Damico and Olsen, 248 ff.). In this respect, she is a perversion of the Anglo-Saxon ideal of the woman as *friðowebbe* or "peace-weaver." She battles heroes, pursues vengeance like a warrior, and places no stock in peace. She's not interested in wergild for the death of her son. What good is gold in a cavern of grief? She is both masculine and monstrous. Chance contrasts Grendel's mother with the women in the poem like Wealhtheow, Freawaru, and Hildeburh, who are married off to patch a peace between warring tribes. They are expected to produce children, pass the cup in the meadhall, mollify feuding men, and keep quiet. Usually their efforts at peace-weaving are doomed from the beginning. They are gifts at their own weddings, pawns in an unwinnable endgame.

These are only a few of the ways in which critics have read the connection between the humans and monsters in the poem. The fact that such interpretations continue unabated is a sign of the complex vision and vitality of the poem.

BEOWULF'S GLORY OR GUILT

Another highly debated topic is the question of Beowulf's possible pride and greed in wanting to battle the dragon alone and in desiring the dragon's gold. In 1953, Tolkien raised this question in an article on "The Battle of Maldon" in which he accused the two heroes, Byrhtnoth and Beowulf, of being too rash or proud in their pursuit of glory, rushing into battle with Vikings or monsters when more pragmatic caution would have been in order (1953, 1 ff.). He argues that both heroes are guilty of *ofermōd*, "excessive courage, overweening pride," which ends up destroying not only themselves but the warriors and cultures they are meant to protect and sustain.

He charges the aging Beowulf with rashly charging into battle with the dragon with insufficient troops and says that the "element of pride, in the form of the desire for honour and glory, in life and after death, tends to grow, to become a chief motive, driving a man beyond the bleak heroic necessity to excess" (14).

Many critics have taken up this thread. Goldsmith, for example, argues that Beowulf "possesses that arrogant self-confidence which is the special trait of the supremely noble and courageous fighter," and that his "insistence on challenging the dragon alone destroys the Geats" (1962, 73). In the first half of the poem, she notes that Beowulf is given the opportunity to see the dark side of Heorot revealed—its hidden feuds and hostilities, its failure of kinship bonds and of peace-weaving marriages, its lack of courage. In his sermonic advice to Beowulf, Hrothgar warns him of these dangers. The second half of the poem shows Beowulf succumbing to the sins of pride and covetousness that Hrothgar warned him about earlier. Goldsmith says that "Hrothgar, whose own spiritual sloth had let envy and murder into Heorot, has seen his error, and so could beg Beowulf to guard himself against pride and covetousness, when the testing time should come" (83). Hrothgar's early advice provides both a warning and a foreshadowing of Beowulf's fate. Finally, Goldsmith argues that Beowulf is "a man fighting his personal devil . . . supremely brave, supremely heroic in suffering, and supremely wrongheaded" (83).

On the other hand, many critics have viewed Beowulf as an ideal hero in heroic or even religious terms. Malone argued early on, for example, that the Christian poet of *Beowulf* found much to admire in the Germanic heroic tradition of the poem and that "his hero in all he says and does shows himself high-minded, gentle, and virtuous, a man dedicated to the heroic life, and the poet presents this life in terms of service: Beowulf serves his lord, his people, and all mankind, and in so doing he does not shrink from hardship, danger, and death itself" (1948, in Nicholson, 140). Alexander, in a similar vein, calls Beowulf "a peaceable man who is cast in the role of a slayer of monsters and dragons [who] is (by the standards of Germanic heroes) exceptionally modest, gracious, generous, and magnanimous . . . an ideal rather than an actual historical figure" (79).

Finally, how we read Beowulf's guilt or glory in the poem depends in large part on how we view his fight with the dragon, his calling for the treasure, and the poet's description of him as *lofgeornost* at the end of the poem.

READING THE END OF *BEOWULF*

Beowulf is bound to fight the dragon. He cannot do otherwise after the unnamed slave steals a cup from the dragon's hoard, and the dragon unleashes his unnatural, inordinate revenge on the Geatish hall and countryside. Beowulf is both his people's protector and their most celebrated fighter, so he must meet the challenge. He is also an aging warrior, so there is not much question about the battle's outcome, as the poet reveals before the conflict:

> An old man's fate was closing in,
> When a grizzled king must seek his soul-hoard,
> Separate life from living, body from being.
> He had not long to linger in flesh—
> His soul was ready to leave the bone-hall. (2420–24)

Beowulf would like to meet the dragon unarmed as he did with Grendel, but considering the dragon's fire-power and scaly protection, he goes wisely armed with sword, mail-coat, and iron shield. He tells his retainers to await the outcome by the barrow door because this is not their battle. He predicts that he will kill the worm or be hauled down into death. As it happens, both predictions prove true. The critics debate whether Beowulf's going to meet the dragon alone is a mistake or an act of pride. Perhaps he thinks he is as strong as his younger, Grendel-fighting self. Perhaps he sees this battle as a one-on-one mythic struggle between monster and hero. He does not seem particularly glory-hungry in his decision. There is a sense of fatefulness hanging over the encounter. Beowulf himself seems to sense this, and yet he enters the barrow determined to destroy the old destroyer.

After Beowulf engages the dragon in battle, Wiglaf urges the Geats to come to their lord's aid, but they flee in cowardly fashion to the safety of the nearby wood. Wiglaf alone enters the "shared strife" of lord and retainer together, urging Beowulf to keep up his courage. Together they kill the dragon, but only after Beowulf is mortally wounded. What destroys the worm is the warriors' combined efforts, the *sibb* or "loyalty of relationship" between them. This is the loyalty so often signified and sustained by the giving of treasure. Beowulf directs Wiglaf to go into the barrow and bring out the treasure so that he can see the gold he is leaving behind for the

Geats. What he doesn't know is that his Geatish retainers have proved cowards, and the Geats will predictably fall prey to the Swedes and Frisians after Beowulf's death. The treasure is now useless and will be returned to the earth in Beowulf's barrow at the end of the poem.

The cowardly Geats troop up to the headland to gaze on the awesome sight: their gift-giver next to the serpent at his side, "a loathsome mate" (3041b). Beowulf and the dragon represent a dialectic of attitudes toward the treasure. A good man, a good king, seeks treasure not for itself but to give to others to signify trust and to build the bonds of loyalty and community. A dragon simply hoards treasure as a useless material possession. One gives his gold charitably; the other hoards it in his cave of cupidity. One translates material wealth into spiritual bonds and a place in memory. The other erases memories by burying objects associated with human culture in the darkness and dirt. The dragon's treasure was sheathed in a spell for a thousand years so that no man could touch it without God's permission. The owner who hid the treasure, the sole survivor, got nothing from it, moving on till "death's hunger / Devoured his heart" (2268b–69a). The treasure holds an ancient curse: anyone who digs it up before doomsday (here superimposed on the doomsday of Beowulf and the Geats) will be guilty of sin and tormented by demons unless he sees or recognizes in it something not easily seen before.

The lines about the treasure's curse (3068 ff.) are probably more highly debated than any other lines in the poem (see *Klaeber 4*, 266–67 for a summary of the possible readings). Is Beowulf being accused of some sin? Has he become the chosen one to lift the treasure, even at the cost of his life? Has he seen something in it, some grace of giving, that has heretofore eluded all treasure-seekers? Critics cannot agree about this, and the reading depends partly on whether one sees Beowulf as the best of heroes in the world of this poem or as a man touched by pride and covetousness at the end. My own view is that we could not find a better hero than Beowulf in this world and that he sees something miraculous in the treasure at the moment of his dying. I translate the central passage literally as: "Any man who dug up the treasure would be guilty of sin . . . unless he saw more readily (or clearly) than (anyone) before, the gold-giving munificence (or grace) of the owner (the Lord?)." I believe that Beowulf recognizes what the poet has been implying throughout the poem: that treasure is only truly valuable when it is given from one person to another to strengthen the bonds between them.

A treasure hoarded is worthless—worse than worthless actually—because it not only destroys the possibility of giving but also attracts equally greedy enemies. A treasure is meant to be given, to be passed along, just as Hrothgar rewards Beowulf with treasure, and Beowulf, in turn, gives the treasure to Hygelac and the court, and then Hygelac turns around and gives him great gifts in return. Beowulf wants the treasure not for himself but as a gift to the Geats. What he realizes is that it is not the gold that counts but the giving of it. He sees not so much the treasure as the love and loyalty which the treasure-giving signifies. By sharing the gold, a hero or king shapes a meaning beyond materiality, a gift beyond greed, a quality (not a quantity) of meaning worthy of memory. This is the key to unlocking the curse. You can bring the treasure up out of the ground if you don't want to keep it and hoard it. You can only escape the jaws of the dragon or the entropy of the earth if you transform your material goods, your material life, into something of spirit, something of memory. What this something is in the world of this poem is complicated by the fact that we have a pre-Christian, heroic culture here articulated by a Christian poet for an Anglo-Saxon audience. But the act of giving, of reaffirming the *sibb,* is the greater treasure, something of lasting value, no matter how we choose to characterize it.

The Geats build a barrow to house their lord's ashes high on the sea-cliff as a sign to seafarers. In Beowulf's barrow the Geats hide the haul from the worm's hoard, returning the ancient treasure to the earth, where the gold in the ground will remain "useless, unloved, unliving" (3169b). In a final gesture of respect and admiration, twelve warriors ride around Beowulf's barrow, "keening for the king, shaping their praise/For a precious man" (3172–73a). They sing of his great deeds of courage and lament his fall,

Keening and claiming that of all the kings,
He was the kindest of men, most generous and just,
Most desiring of praise, most deserving of fame. (3180–82)

There is great debate about the final line in the poem, *lēodum līðost ond lofgeornost,* literally "kindest (mildest, most gracious) to his people and most eager for praise (repute, fame, glory)." Shippey argues that "*lof* in practice covers 'generosity' as well as praise" (1978, 20), and *Klaeber 4* notes that *lofgeornost* here may be a reference "either to glory earned by deeds of valor . . . or to the king's liberality toward his men" (271). Some critics like

Tolkien take the ending to mean that Beowulf was too eager for fame or was vainglorious (see, for example, Robinson 1985, 80–82). These are the critics who often fault him for the sins of pride and covetousness in the second half of the poem and who blame him for taking on the dragon by himself and calling for the cursed treasure. Other critics, myself included, believe that Beowulf is the best that the heroic world of the poem has to offer—brave, wise, and generous in gift-giving—and that he not only desires but deserves the fame he has justly earned. He has shown both courage in battle and wisdom in his understanding of the impotent gesture of peace-weaving in marrying off women to enemy tribes to patch the peace. He has been generous and good to his people. He protected the young Heardred instead of taking the throne from him. He has seized no throne; he has killed no kin. He has destroyed Grendel and avoided his sin of savagery unbound by social order. He has destroyed Grendel's mother and at least understood in part the frustration and anger of peace-weavers. He has not been entirely free of the Geatish feuds, but he has tried to rule wisely and well in spite of them. He hasn't solved the terrible riddle of how to weave a secure peace and resolve the brutality of the revenge code, but then no one in the world of this poem is able to do this. Not even the poetic narrator seems to know how to accomplish this task; this subtle evil is too much woven into the warp of the social fabric. Beowulf has killed the dragon and understood the deeper meaning of the treasure—that gift-giving is the real gold. He hasn't escaped the jaws of the dragon or the drag of time, but no earthly hero can escape these banes. He has established a lasting *dōm* or "reputation" which should stand the test of time. He has been a man worth remembering, worth singing about, worth taking as a heroic model. The fact that we are still reading and translating and thinking about this poem over a thousand years after it was written is testament to that. He is after all in Hrothgar's judgment *Bēowulf lēofa, secg betesta,* "beloved Beowulf, best of men" (1759b–60a).

THE ENIGMA OF *BEOWULF*

The great critical debates about the poem are bound to continue. Ultimately we must recognize that *Beowulf,* like any great work of literature, both invites and resists interpretation. This accounts for the great variety of critical readings of the poem, of which I have sketched only a small portion above. The wisest of editors and critics must finally agree to disagree about the poem, sometimes even in the same space, and it seems fitting to close this introduction with the voices of two great *Beowulf* scholars, Bruce Mitchell and Fred C. Robinson, who in their edition of the poem arrive at different conclusions. Mitchell says:

> For me *Beowulf* is a poetic exploration of life in this world, of the blind forces of nature and the dark passions of humans against "our little systems [which] have their day and cease to be." This contest is seen in terms of the system within which the poet lived but of whose inevitable weaknesses he makes us aware through both the story and his own comments. But I believe that the poet meant us to admire, not to condemn, Beowulf and that the poem ends on a note of hope not of despair. Today, in this nuclear age, with man's inhumanity to man daily more apparent on all levels and the powers of darkness in seeming ascendancy throughout the world, we may see *Beowulf* as a triumphant affirmation of the value of a good life: as the poet himself says *Brūc ealles well*, "Make good use of everything" (Mitchell and Robinson 1998, 37; quote from Tennyson's "In Memoriam")

Robinson draws a somewhat different conclusion:

> According to the strictest clerical spokesmen of the day, there was no room in the Anglo-Saxon Christian world for pagan ancestors, but a nation needs a past and pride of ancestry. This is what the *Beowulf* poet gives to his people. Through deep thought and high art he finds a place in his countrymen's collective memory where their ancestors can reside with dignity even as the Anglo-Saxons acknowledge that those ancestors were pagan and lost. It is this accomplishment of the poet that gives to his narration of warrior courage, exultant triumph, and honour in defeat its tinge of sadness and conflicted nostalgia. It also gives the poem its unforgettable gravity and makes it more than an exuberant telling of mighty exploits in bygone days. (Mitchell and Robinson 1998, 38)

Perhaps *Beowulf* is like a great literary riddle which each reader must solve for himself or herself. Perhaps the poem is an invitation from the hero to "Say who I am" and from the poet to "Say what I mean."

BEOWULF

Listen! We have heard of the Spear-Danes' glory,
Their storied power, their primal strength—
The kings and princes whose craft was courage.
Often Scyld Sceafing denied dinner
To his arch-foes, wrecked meadhall benches,   5
Stealing joy so that all his enemies
Drank terror instead. Their cups were cold.
At first a foundling, he wrestled fate,
Made that misery his own slave
Till the whole world over the whale-road   10
Yielded power, lifting tribute,
Offering gold. That was a good king.
To him was born a boy of promise,
A young prince for court and country,
A gift from God, an heir and comfort,   15
For the Lord of life saw such suffering
So often inherited in a kingless hall,
Such great violence, such grim sin,
Such deep need, that he brought Beow,
Son of Scyld, to end the anguish   20
And establish honor—his name was known.
So should a young prince make a friend of power,
Learn the grace of giving in his father's house,
Gather courage and hearth-companions

Who will stand by him in savage battle   25
In later years. A warrior thrives
Through glorious deeds and generous gifts.
Great Scyld left life in God's keep.
His comrades bore his body down
To the sea's curl as he'd commanded,   30
The land-leader for many years.
The ring-necked ship stood ready,
Icy and eager to embrace the king.
They laid their tall treasure down
Next to the mast, the gift and the giver,   35
With gold and gems, swords and mail-shirts:
No ship ever sailed in such grave beauty.
On his breast lay a clutch of arms—
What men crafted and the sea claimed,
A tribe's treasure for the king's crossing,   40
His last gifts not less than the foundling's first,
When unknown parents put the baby boy
Into a plain boat like a poor beggar
And offered their gift, cold and friendless,
To the endless sea. Who came with nothing   45
Left with gold. Who sailed alone
Was mourned by many. His men set up
A bright banner to proclaim his coming,
Then let the long waves take their treasure—
No sound but the ship's sliding into water   50
And the heart's keening. No man knows,
Whether wise counselor or world-traveler,
Who received that gift of cargo and king.

Then the son of Scyld ruled wisely
After his father went from the world—   55
Beow grew up, a beloved king,
And also sired a warrior prince,
Healfdene the great, brave and battle-fierce,
Who ruled the Scyldings, siring sons,
Princes of power—Heorogar, Hrothgar,   60
And Halga the good—and a daughter Yrse,

Who stories say was Onela's queen,
Bed-gem of that battle-Swede.
Then Hrothgar won great battle-glory,
Found worth at war, till his young troops   65
Swelled with power and pride, obeyed orders,
Supported their king. Hrothgar's dream
Was a meadhall built for his mighty band,
The work of craftsmen, worth remembering,
Where a king could share with the sons of men   70
His gifts from God in his hall of glory—
Stories, treasures, everything except
The common land and the lives of men.
The word went out—the craftsmen came
From all over middle-earth to shape beams   75
And raise up the glorious people's hall.
They quickly finished this finest of buildings,
This show of strength, and King Hrothgar,
Whose fame had spread, named it Heorot
After the ancient Hart. The king kept promise,   80
Giving gold from the treasure-table,
A feast of rings. The raftered hall,
High, horn-gabled, was doomed to wait
For battle-flames, the fierce sword-hate
Of family feud, when oaths of in-laws   85
Might mean less than murderous rage.

Then the monster who lived in shadows,
The dark's demon, suffered pain
When he heard the harp's sweet songs,
The poet's music in the hall of joy.   90
The shaper sang the world's creation,
The origin of men, God's broad grandeur
In sun-bright fields and surrounding waters.
That greater Shaper set sun and moon
As land-lights and adorned all earth   95
With leaves and limbs, created each
Green gift, each living thing,
Each walking wonder of this bright world.

The listening warriors lived in the hall,
Surrounded by joy until a certain creature   100
Began to commit crimes. A hell-fiend,
A grim hall-guest called Grendel,
Moor-stalker, wasteland walker,
Demon of the fens, he dwelled in marshes,
In monstrous lairs, unhappy, unhoused,   105
After God the Creator had rightly condemned
The race of Cain, that murdering kin,
When the Lord of life took vengeance
On Abel's bane, that slaughtering son.
No one found joy in that long feud,   110
That banishment for family-killing.
Out of Cain's crime what woke was evil,
A brutal borning of orcs and elves,
Gibbering giants, the living dead,
Who fought God, finding a hard reward.   115
In black night came the hall-marauder,
To see how the beer-drinkers soundly slept,
A feast of dreamers who'd forgotten sorrow—
They locked out misery, this mess of men.
Unwhole, unholy, the monster came,   120
Grim and greedy, ready, ravenous—
A stalking mouth, he quickly seized
Thirty thanes, hauled them home,
His precious plunder, his proud slaughter—
King of the lair, exulting in dinner.   125
A dark cry woke before dawn,
A wail of Danes long after dinner,
Grendel's bloodbath their breakfast greeting,
His war-craft the morning's misery.
The glorious king had cold joy,   130
Suffered for his thanes, drank sorrow,
When he saw the bloody tracks
Of the grim guest, the ravenous ghost.
That strife was too strong, that loathing too long—
He even invited himself back the next night   135
For more murders and no mourning!

He was bent on vengeance, savage in sin.
Then it was easy to find a hero who sought
A hall removed from the ravenous beast,
A separate bed, once the blood-feud was known,   140
The grim crime of the murderous hall-thane.
Only those who left the hall escaped the hate!
So Grendel ruled the greatest of halls,
Sabotaged the right, a monster unmatched
Against many men, till the meadhall   145
Stood empty, unguarded, an idle house—
Twelve winters long, the time of grief
That Hrothgar became king of nothing,
Ruler of agony, lord of woe.
Then the shaper's song to the sons of men   150
Was of blood-feud and baleful sorrow,
Grendel's stalking and Hrothgar's suffering:
His night-hatred was no secret—
His plan was to devour peace with the Danes.
He offered no payment for past crimes,   155
No gold for his gnawing. No hall-counselor
Hoped to see shame's wergild in that claw.
That hall-bane, fierce and relentless fighter,
That death-shadow, moved against men.
Out of the mist, up from the moors,   160
He ambushed and ate, drank and devoured
Both young and old, both able and feeble.
He shaped the fens into endless night.
No one knows where the hell-shades walk.
The enemy of men, that lone horror,   165
Brought endless shame home to the hall,
A bed of terror to bright Heorot,
A night-demon in the dark hall,
But he was barred from the king's throne,
Kept from the gift-seat and God's love,   170
Separated from grace. That was wrack and ruin
To Hrothgar, ravaging his brave heart.
Wise men in secret counsel considered
What brave men might best do

To turn back terror. They offered sacrifices   175
At heathen shrines, prayed that some soul-slayer,
Some demon might ease their dark distress.
Their hope was dire—they prayed to hell
Instead of heaven. They knew no God,
No Great Shaper, no Judge of Deeds.   180
They laid praise at the mouth of hell,
Sang no songs to the greatest Lord,
Asked no favors of the Glory-giver.
Woe to those who in terrible affliction
Must offer their souls to the flame's embrace;   185
Well to those who on death's day
Can seek their Lord's protecting power,
Wrapped in the welcome of his embrace.
So Hrothgar brooded, Healfdene's son,
On seething sorrow. The wise king   190
Could not stop that killing, ward off woe.
That strife was too strong, that feud too fierce—
That hall was home to the grimmest of night-woes.

Then the story spread so that Hygelac's thane,
The greatest of Geats, heard about Grendel   195
And his hateful crimes. Beowulf was a huge hero,
Strongest in battle, mightiest of men
Alive at the time. He ordered his ship built,
A great wave-walker, and said he would seek
Over the long sea, the swan's road,   200
That well-known king needing brave new men.
Beowulf was beloved at home, but counselors
Laid no claim to his staying—they urged him on,
Observed omens, figured the fates,
Called his quest good. He picked out the bravest   205
From the Geatish ranks. The group of fifteen,
Gathered for glory, sought the wave-wood,
Followed their sea-skilled battle-lord
Down to the shore-mark, the edge of land.
The ship waited, a wave-floater,   210
Under the tall cliffs. Time passed.

Warriors prepared to climb the prow.
Sea-currents shifted against the sand.
Men bore bright war-gear
To the ship's belly, smith-crafted armor.   215
The ship shoved off, warriors willing—
The sea lifting the well-braced wood.
They went over water, driven by wind,
The foam-necked floater like a great bird,
Until the next day at the augured hour,   220
When the proud bird with a twisted prow
Swooped toward land, as seafarers saw
Bright sea-cliffs, high headlands,
The stony shores. Sea-warriors knew
The waves were crossed, the journey done.   225
The Battle-Geats climbed down,
Secured the boat, rattled their mail-coats,
Bright war-shirts, and thanked God
That they had found safety in the sea-crossing.

Then the cliff-guard, watchman for the Danes,   230
Whose duty it was to survey the sea,
Saw bright shields borne over the gangway,
The glint of war-gear ready for the road.
Curiosity burned: who were these men?
Hrothgar's lookout leapt to his horse,   235
Rode to the shore, brandished his spear,
Spoke to the strangers, offering a challenge:
"Who are you? What are you,
War-bright, mail-coated men,
Bringing your tall sails over the sea-streets?   240
Long have I held this high lookout,
Watching the waves for a threat to the Danes,
So no ship-army, no enemy threat,
Might sail up and sack us unawares.
No shield-warriors have marched more openly   245
Onto our shore than yours, nor did you count
On the consent of my kinsmen for safe passage.
Never have I seen a more splendid warrior,

A mightier man, than one who walks with you.
That's no mere retainer but a man of lineage,   250
No mere warrior but an armored lord—
Nothing belies such greatness. Now let me know
Your lineage before you ride quietly forward
Like spies on our land. Here's my plain thought:
Tell me quickly where you come from."   255
The greatest of Geats answered the coast-guard,
The leader of war-men unlocked his word-hoard:
"We will give you the gift of our lineage—
We are known as the nation of Geats,
Hearth-companions of King Hygelac.   260
My father was known at home and abroad—
Ecgtheow, a great lord and leader.
He lived long, endured many winters
Before he went walking on his last road,
An old man leaving hearth and home—   265
No wise man now living has forgotten him.
We come with true hearts and trusty swords
To greet your king, the people's protector.
Be courteous and give us good counsel.
We come on an errand, a warrior's mission   270
To the lord of the Danes. Let's all agree:
Nothing should be secret, nothing hidden.
The only thing hateful we've heard—you know:
Something of darkness walks among the Danes,
Some evil enmity, who knows what,   275
A secret scourge, a shade of slaughter—
An unknown malice moves among men,
A shaper of corpses in the shadow of night.
I am the healer who can help Hrothgar—
I bring a remedy for the sickening foe.   280
I offer counsel to the wise, good king,
A remedy for ravaging, an end to woe,
If he's to escape evil, reverse his fate—
If he's ever to trade his seething sorrow
For a cooler heart, or a hall's blessing   285
For the hot rage of a tormented house."

The coast-guard spoke, high in his saddle,
A fearless follower: "A smart shield-warrior
Who thinks clearly with a keen mind
Should know the difference between words and deeds.   290
What I see is this—a brave troop bound
To aid and sustain the king of the Danes.
Go forth with your chain-mail and war-gear.
I will guide you and order my men
To guard your ship, tarred and ready,   295
Against all enemies, till it bears back home
Over the sea-streams its beloved warrior,
Carrying a hero with its curve-necked prow,
And the good Geats who survive unharmed,
Home whole, safe through this battle-storm."   300
The men marched out, the ship stayed still,
A broad-bellied boat, rope-tethered
And anchor-bound. Bright boar-shapes
Gleamed over cheek-guards, high over helmets
Fire-hardened, variegated, inlaid with gold,   305
War-masks guarding the grim warriors.
The men moved as one, a fell formation,
Till they saw the hall, timbered, tessellated,
Adorned with gold, the most beautiful building
On middle-earth, the best-known hall   310
Under heaven where the mighty one dwelled,
Its gold light gleaming long on the land.
The battle-brave coast-guard pointed to Heorot,
The bright hall of men, showed them the way,
Then wheeled his horse, speaking to the Geats: 315
"I must go back to my post. May God the protector,
The father of men, keep you whole.
I return to the shore and my sea-watch
To sound the alarm against enemy invaders."

The street was stone-paved, the road straight,   320
The walkway clear to the ranks of men.
Their war-coats gleamed with bright chain-mail,
Hard and hand-locked as they neared the hall—

The rings of their corselets singing to Heorot.
The sea-weary warriors set broad shields,   325
Their round body-guards, against the wall—
Brave men came boldly to bench-seats,
Battle-gear ringing; spears stood together
Like an ash-gray troop, the craft of smiths,   330
A sharpness of shafts. That mailed troop
Was an energy of armor, a worth of weapons.
Then Wulfgar the hall-guard asked the warriors,
Those grim house-guests, about their ancestry:
"Where do you come from with decorated shields,   335
Gray-iron mail-coats, grim-masked helmets,
And a stand of battle-spears? I am Hrothgar's
Herald and hall-guard. I've never seen
Such bold faces on seafaring strangers.
I think pride brings you—not anger or exile—   340
With heart's courage to seek Hrothgar."
The proud one answered, prince of the Geats,
Unlocked words, hard under his helmet:
"We are hall-thanes and hearth-companions   345
Of noble Hygelac. Beowulf is my name.
I would speak with the son of Healfdene,
Glorious Hrothgar, lord of the Danes,
If the king in his goodness would grant me leave."
Wulfgar considered—his wisdom was known,   350
His courage, clear: "I will ask the king,
Lord of the Scyldings, giver of rings,
Glorious prince, what you request,
Regarding your journey, and as seems fit,
Bring back his reply, whatever it is."   355
Then Wulfgar hurried to where Hrothgar sat,
Gray and grizzled, surrounded by thanes,
A brave messenger before the Danish lord,
Addressing his king as custom demanded.
Wulfgar spoke to his beloved leader: 360
"Here are travelers from a long crossing,
Seafarers, wave-warriors, men of the Geats—

The bold, battle-scarred thanes name
The greatest one Beowulf. They seek permission
From you Prince Hrothgar to trade words,   365
Mix wisdom. May you choose wisely
And give them counsel, a good hearing.
They are worthy in war-gear, esteemed in armor,
And the leader who brought them here is good,
Truly a war-gift, mighty among men."   370

Hrothgar spoke, protector of Scyldings:
"Young Beowulf was a boy I knew well.
His famous father was called Ecgtheow.
Hygelac's father, King Hrethel of the Geats,
Made him a marriage-gift of his only daughter.   375
Now has his hard, strong son come here,
A mighty warrior to sustain old friends.
Seafarers said, who carried precious gifts,
Gold to the Geats, that his hand-grip
Held the strength of thirty men—   380
It was battle-tested. Holy God
In his great mercy has sent this savior
To the beleaguered Danes to give Grendel
The gift of his grip. That's my hope.
I will give him treasures for courage,   385
Gifts for tearing that terror from life.
Order them in to meet our kinsmen—
Bid them welcome to the Danish hold."
Then Wulfgar went to the hall door,
Offered these words to the waiting warriors: 390
"My lord of victories, leader of the Danes,
Commands me to say he knows your lineage,
And you seafaring warriors are welcome,
You brave-hearted men, to our Danish lands.
Now you may enter in battle-armor,   395
Approach Hrothgar under war-grim helmets,
But let your shields and slaughter-shafts rest
By the wall, waiting the outcome of your words."

Up rose the warrior, around him his men,
A splendor of thanes; some stayed behind   400
To guard their gear, as their chief commanded.
The troop rolled in under Heorot's roof,
Warriors behind their battle-commander.
He stood on the hearth, hard under helmet,
His corselet crafted by clever hands,   405
A ring-net sewn by skillful smiths.
Beowulf spoke, offered a greeting:
"Hail Hrothgar, may you always be well.
I am Hygelac's kinsman and thane.
I have done deeds, gathered youthful glories.   410
This story of Grendel has spread to the Geats—
Seafarers say this greatest of halls
Stands idle and useless, without warriors,
When the day's late light fades,
Hidden under heaven. Wise ones counseled   415
That I should come to King Hrothgar.
They knew my cunning and battle-craft—
They saw me come home from bloody combat,
Stained with slaying a family of fiends—
I challenged and crushed five fierce giants—   420
Slaying night-monsters riding the waves.
Their pain was my pleasure—they asked for trouble.
I avenged the Geats, grinding the grim ones.
Perhaps I might hold a private meeting
With your monster, give a gift to Grendel,   425
Settle his endless feud with the Danes.
I entreat you now, great Lord Hrothgar,
As I've come so far, to grant me this favor,
Protector of Scyldings, prince of the people—
Let me, alone with my band of hard warriors,   430
Purge Heorot, clean out this hall.
I have heard that the awe-striker,
That skulking atrocity, wields no weapons.
So, let's be fair. I'll scorn the sword,
Meet that monster's reckless abandon   435

With my fist. I'll fight tooth and nail
With no broad shield, no yellow wood,
Foe upon foe, talk terror with my hands.
Let the warrior whom Death decides to take
Trust in God's judgment, his fair doom.   440
I expect if Grendel rules the day
In this battle-hall, he'll ravage us all,
Devour the Danes, eat some Geats.
If death claims me, no need to cover
My missing head, my bloody body!   445
He'll haul home my bones and blood,
My savory shroud, devour without sorrow
My ravaged body, stain his lair.
There'll be no need to feed my gobbled form,
No need to mourn, no cause to grieve,   450
No body to bury—but send home to Hygelac,
If the battle takes me, the best of my war-clothes—
What's left of them—the chain-mail
Protecting my chest, Hrethel's heirloom,
The work of Weland. Let the fates fall."   455
Hrothgar spoke, Lord of the Scyldings:
"For our old favors to your father Ecgtheow,
You have come to fight, Beowulf my friend.
Your father slew Heatholaf with his hard hands,
Struck up a feud with the warlike Wylfings.   460
Then the Geats could no longer keep him—
They were harried hard by the fear of war,
So he sought the South-Danes' protection,
Sailing over the sea-surge, the rolling waves,
When I was a young king, ruler of the Danes,   465
Keeper of the treasure-hoard of heroes.
My older brother Heorogar, Healfdene's son,
Was newly dead, my own dear kin,
An unliving man—he was better than I.
Afterwards I settled your father's feud   470
With a wergild of treasures sent over waves,
Ended his troubles. He swore me oaths.

Now it's my shame and sorrow to say
To any man what evil the monster Grendel
Has wreaked in Heorot, his brooding hatred,   475
His sudden ferocities, his unbound feud,
His steady slaughter. My troop is depleted,
My war-band shrunk. Fate has swept them
Into the claw and clutch of Grendel's rage.
God may easily separate that mad ravager   480
From his foul deeds. Often my warriors,
Have boasted over beer, angry over ale-cups,
That they would wait to meet that terror,
Greet Grendel with their grim swords.
Then in the morning, the meadhall was stained   485
Bright with blood, shining with slaughter
When the day dawned, mead-benches broken
And drenched with gore. I had fewer followers,
Since death carried my dear men off.
But now, Beowulf, sit down to feast,   490
Unlock your thoughts, share stories
Of great victories as your heart desires."
Then benches were cleared in the meadhall
For the gathering Geats. The bold-hearted sat,
Proud in their strength. A thane served mead   495
Shimmering in ale-cups. The shaper sang,
His clear voice in Heorot. There was joy in the hall,
The camaraderie of warriors, a keep of carousing.
That was no small company of Geats and Danes.

Unferth spoke, Ecglaf's son, who sat at the feet   500
Of the Scylding king, unlocked battle-runes—
Devious thoughts and unfriendly words.
Beowulf's undertaking was an ache to him,
For he hated to hear that any man's deeds
Might hold more glory than his. He offered gall: 505
"Are you the great Beowulf who challenged Breca
In swollen pride, to swim the sea,
To risk your lives for a foolish boast?
No one could stop you, not friend or foe,

From your swimming match on the open sea,   510
Your death-diving in deep waters,
Your proud journey over ocean roads.
Your hands churned up the sea-streets,
Those winter-waves for seven nights,
But Breca was better, a winner over waves.   515
The smarter warrior overcame your strength,
Gathering glory. On the eighth morning,
The sea washed him up on the Heathoreams' shore.
From there he sought his own homeland
Where he ruled the Brondings, beloved by all,   520
To sleep in his stronghold and deal out treasure.
He had strength in swimming and a wealth of rings.
That son of Beanstan fulfilled his boast,
Got the best of you. I think worse things
Await you even though you've endured   525
Grim battles before, if you dare to keep
The night-watch here to greet Grendel."
Beowulf replied, the son of Ecgtheow,
Measured out meanings, mixed words:
"Well, Unferth my friend, you said a mouthful   530
About Breca's bravery, on a belly full of beer.
I'll tell you the truth—I had greater sea-strength,
More hard riding on the heave of waves
Than any man. We were just boasting boys
When we risked our lives in the roiling sea,   535
Two alone at the edge of youth.
We did what we said, made good our words.
We took our bare swords swimming,
Hard blades in hand, to ward off whales.
Breca failed to swim faster or farther   540
Beyond my strength in the surging sea,
And I stayed by him. We swam together,
Suffering the surge for five nights
Till the coldest of sea-storms, heaving water,
Tore us apart in the darkening waves,   545
And the battle-grim north-wind
Savaged our bond, split us apart.

The waves were rough. Sea-beasts roused.
There my body-mail of hand-locked rings
Protected my life—the battle-jacket,   550
Woven of iron and worked with gold,
Covered my chest. A savage sea-fiend,
Monster of the deep, dragged me down
To the sea-bed in his cruel grasp,
Till I touched him with my sharp sword,   555
A burial greeting, a gift for his chest.
Battle-rush took the sea-beast's life
Through my hard hand. Time and again
The terrors attacked, monsters moved in.
The fierce ones found me, diving for dinner.   560
I served them well with my good sword—
It was fitting for fish. I don't think
They enjoyed that feast at their sea-bed table.
Their dead mouths weren't able to eat me.
The morning after, they slept late,   565
Lulled by my sword, dozing on sand,
Swept up by waves, so that never again
Could the monsters hinder seafarers' sailing.
Light lifted from the east, God's bright beacon,
The sea calmed, the swells subsided,   570
So I could see headlands, wave-walls,
Windward shores. Fate often protects
The undoomed man if his courage holds.
I was offered nine sea-monsters
To slay with my sword. I've never heard   575
Of a harder battle in wind or water,
Nor of a man more pressed in the sea-rush;
Yet I survived the monsters' grasp,
Swam home alive, weary from the work.
The sea-streams bore me far from home   580
Into the arms of the Finns, the land of the Lapps.
I've never heard, Unferth, of your exploits,
Tracking terror, matching wits with monsters,
Slinging courage with a swinging sword—
I don't mean to boast—though I heard   585

You were a kin-killer, a bane to your brother.
For that family ravage you'll rot in hell—
Your soul is damned though your wit is keen.
You want the truth? I'll tell you Unferth,
Son of Ecglaf, if your spirit had been strong,   590
Your mind on monsters instead of memories
Of killing kin, that awesome terror,
That savage Grendel might have slain fewer
Of Heorot's heroes, left the hall unhaunted.
He's found this feud a little one-sided—   595
He knows no need to fear your swords,
The battle-blades of the Victory-Scyldings.
He takes his toll in terror from the Danes—
Your life's the tribute he needs. The monster
Shows mercy to no one. He lusts and feasts,   600
Kills and carves up dinner with his claws,
Invites the Scyldings to an endless sleep.
The Geats will give him what the Danes have not—
Strength and courage, a sword's grim greeting.
Then men may wake unafraid, drink   605
Morning mead, saunter under the southern sun,
Their world clothed in light, find their fellowship
And forget fear."
                    Then the treasure-giver,
Gray-haired, battle-famed, knew joy.
The Lord of Bright-Danes had heard Beowulf,   610
Counted his courage, his strength of spirit.
Then laughter lifted in the great hall—
Words were traded. Wealhtheow walked in,
Hrothgar's queen, clothed in gold.
Careful of custom, mindful of manner,   615
She greeted each hall-thane in turn.
The noble woman served the first cup
To the Danish king, keeper of the land,
Beloved by his people, bade him rejoice
In the beer-feast. He enjoyed the banquet,   620
Raised up his cup, the victory-king.
Then the lady of the Helmings went through the hall,

Carrying the jeweled cup to young and old,
Generous of mead and her gracious mind,
Sharing her spirit, till the courteous queen,   625
Adorned with rings, brought Beowulf the cup,
Welcomed the Geat with wise words,
Thanking God for granting her wish
That some warrior might offer defense
Against the darkness and an end to woe.   630
The battle-fierce warrior took the cup
From Wealhtheow's hand. Beowulf spoke,
Son of Ecgtheow, eager for battle:
"I knew when I boarded the boat with my men,
Sat down in the ship with my brave band,   635
And sailed the sea, that I would fulfill my oath
And the Danish hopes or discover death
In Grendel's claws, his fierce grasp.
Here in Heorot I will stop this savagery,
Cleanse this hall or cancel my days."   640
The queen cherished that plain boast,
Sitting with Hrothgar, adorned with gold.
The talk rose up, the hall-troops rejoicing
Over old victories. The son of Healfdene
Sought his night-rest in another hall.   645
He knew the monster was bending his mind,
Mulling since morning on attacking Heorot.
Dark shapes were gliding, shadows sliding
Under cloud-cover. The dark rim-walker,
Fierce ravager, was writhing toward Heorot.   650
The company rose—the leaders paid regards.
Old Hrothgar wished young Beowulf well,
Gave him control of the hall with these words:
"I've never entrusted my people's hall
To anyone since I could lift hand and shield;   655
Now I yield its keep to you—
Control it. Guard this greatest of halls.
Remember glory, reveal your strength,
Watch out for that walking wrath,
Confound the wraith. Whatever you dream   660

Will be yours if you survive the onslaught."
Then King Hrothgar, protector of Danes,
Left the hall with his close companions.
The war-king wanted to find Wealhtheow,
His bright queen in her bed-chamber.   665
The King of Glory, as men would learn,
Had set a hall-guard to greet Grendel,
A dangerous man on a special mission
To stand night-watch for the monstrous guest,
The great giant. The lord of the Geats   670
Trusted his strength and God's grace.
He stripped off his chain-mail, unlaced iron,
Unlocked his helmet, lifted it from his head,
Gave his sword to a servant, his best iron blade.
Beowulf of the Geats spoke the quiet boast   675
Of a good man before getting into bed:
"I don't claim any lesser strength,
Any poorer power, any weaker will,
Than Grendel, so I'll give him this gift:
I won't put him to sleep with my sword,   680
Steal his life with iron, though I might.
In spite of his strength, his violent fame,
His clawed hand can hold no sword
To hew my shield, to hack my life.
Let's fight as equals—I'll forgo the sword,   685
If he dares to fight me without weapons,
And let wise God give out glory
Wherever he wants to the one who wins."
The battle-brave earl put his head on his pillow,
Lay back to rest with his seafaring thanes.   690
None of them expected to see home again,
Family or friends, kith or kin,
The light of day or their land of birth.
They knew night-slaughter had stricken the Danes,
A curse of killing in a hall of corpses—   695
But God gave them fortune's weaving,
The warp and weft of war-victory,
A gift to the Geats of craft and comfort

Through the savage strength of one warrior
To seize the shadow, catch the killer.   700
This is the truth of time's long telling—
A mighty God rules over all mankind.

Out of the darkness a shadow-walker
Came writhing, sliding toward sleepers
Unaware in the gabled hall—except one   705
Who watched, waiting for the wraith.
Men know that God the Creator
Will not let a demon, a savage stalker,
Drag us into shadows. Beowulf waited
In waking anger, rage in reserve,   710
Aching for action. Grendel came gliding
Out of the moors, up from the marshes,
Bearing God's wrath. The monster meant
To stalk and kill a mouthful of mankind.
Under a shroud he slid to the door—   715
Under dark clouds he crept to the hall,
The house of giving, the home of feasting.
That wasn't the first time he sought
Hrothgar's home, but he never found
In his grim days before or after   720
Such bad luck, such hard hall-thanes.
The unholy warrior reached the door,
Separated from joy. The door burst open,
Its iron bonds snapped with a touch of hands—
A mindful of evil at the mouth of the hall.   725
The fiend stalked the floor, swollen with anger,
Fierce in his fury. Out of his lurid eyes,
Leapt like a flame, an unfair light.
He saw in the feast-hall a pile of men
Sleeping together. His heart exulted,   730
His mind bent—he meant before daybreak
To separate life from limb for each man—
An awesome terror up to old tricks.
He was driven to find a fulfilling feast—
His fate was one last feeding on mankind.   735

The mighty one watched how the other moved,
The kinsman of Hygelac saw his killing attack.
The monster never thought of holding back—
He seized the first sleeper, slit his body,
Bit open his bone-house, drinking his blood,   740
Swallowing flesh, feasting on hands and feet,
Eating greedily the unliving one.
One power moved unwarily up
To the body of the other, a warrior at rest,
Seized the strong-hearted thane with his hand,   745
Reached for a clutch of flesh with his claw—
But Beowulf was hatching his battle-plan,
Snatched up the creature's nailed hand,
Shook his claw in a monstrous greeting,
Grabbed his grasp. The cold keeper of sins   750
Had never met a harder handgrip
In all his dark marauding in middle-earth.
His wretched heart discovered fear—
He wanted to flee back home to the marshes,
But his hand was locked in a terrible fist.   755
His spirit spooked, his heart heaved for home,
A host of demons, a haven of fens—
But this time his only hold was in Beowulf's hand.
That was a new way of life for him.
Hygelac's thane remembered his boast   760
Earlier in the evening, stood up strong,
Held the fiend fast, fingers bursting.
One tried to bolt—the other crushed him back.
One wanted the fens—he got cold fingers.
That was a bitter journey the demon-walker   765
Made to Heorot. The hall resounded—
The building shook like a wild ale-party!
The proud Danes panicked, their hearts in shock,
With two fierce hall-guards feasting on rage.
The building roared with battle-shrieks   770
As both warriors were bent on slaughter.
It's a wonder the wine-hall withstood
The ravaging warriors, their fierce rage.

It was braced and bound, inside and out,
With iron bonds, hammered by smiths.   775
I heard it said that many mead-benches
Were ripped from the floor, splintered seats
Of inlaid gold, while the grim ones grappled.
No wise one of the Scyldings ever thought
That Heorot could be wrecked by any means,   780
That antler-boned hall, by crash or craft,
Unless fire should reach out ravenous
And swallow it whole. The sound of slaughter
Rose in the hall, a strange new song.
Fear seized the North-Danes who heard   785
For the first time there through the wall
A dirge of terror, mad music
Sung or screeched by the foe of God,
A song of no victory, a depth of wailing
From the clutch of hell. He was held fast   790
By the strongest man in living memory.
The protector of men had a plain purpose—
To keep in his clutch the uninvited killer
Whose useless days would serve no one.
Beowulf's retainers raised their swords,   795
Old heirlooms, to protect their prince,
To save the life of their mighty leader.
When they leapt into the fray, they little knew—
Hard-hearted warriors hacking at Grendel
From every side, seeking his soul—   800
That no iron on earth, not the sharpest sword,
Could harm that demon, cut through flesh,
For he had woven a spell against wounding,
A protection against weapons made by man,
A secret skin so nothing could touch him.   805
His life-parting was painful, unexpected;
That alien spirit, that savage shadow
Would travel far to the keep of fiends.
The demon discovered, who had always sought
To bring his murderous heart to mankind—   810
He was at war with God—that his body

Would not travel on that last road
Because the kinsman of Hygelac, bold Beowulf,
Held him by the hand. Each was anathema
To the life of the other. The awesome creature   815
Finally felt pain in a body-wound:
His shoulder-bone was seen, his sinews torn,
His tendons ripped, his bone-locks broken.
Battle-glory was given then to Beowulf.
Grendel fled, life-lost and spirit-sick,   820
Into the fens to his joyless home,
A clutchless wraith. He knew his days were done.
For the Danes, it was a dream come true
After the blood-rush. He had purged the hall—
The warrior who was battle-wise and heart-strong,   825
Cleaned out Heorot, Hrothgar's home,
Delivering it from darkness. He rejoiced in his night-work,
In the doom of his deeds—they were worth remembering.
The leader of the Geats made good his boast
To the East-Danes, brought an end to evil,   830
An ease to suffering, a last look at grief.
That was no small sorrow they'd endured.
It was a plain sign when the battle-brave man
Nailed the monster's arm—shoulder to fist—
Under the eaves of Heorot's roof.   835
A welcome-home was Grendel's claw.

The next morning many great warriors
Gathered in the gift-hall, as I heard tell;
Folk-leaders came from far and near,
Traveled long roads to Hrothgar's home   840
To marvel at the monster's tracks. His leave-taking,
His life-going, brought sorrow to no one
Who saw the footprints of the ungloried guest,
How the weary one dragged himself off defeated,
To the lake of demons, fated, fleeing,   845
Leaving his bloody life-tracks behind.
The lake-water boiled with blood—
The fiendish waters swirled with gore,

The red roil of battle, the hot clutch of blood.
Death-doomed, deprived of life-joy,   850
He laid down his life in the murky fen,
His heathen soul in his stronghold. Hell seized him.
Hall-thanes tracked him to the foul mere,
Then turned back joyfully, traveled home
To Heorot, young and old on their horses,   855
Speaking in high spirits about Beowulf,
Praising his deeds, spreading his fame.
Time and again they talked of his power,
Saying that no one between the seas,
Under the expanse of heaven, the sky's sweep,   860
Was a bolder shield-bearer, a braver warrior
More worthy of a kingdom to rule—
But they didn't blame Hrothgar, unpraise him,
Find fault with their dear lord and friend—
He was a good king. Sometimes they spurred   865
Their horses on, galloping on good roads,
Sometimes held back their bridling bays
While the king's song-shaper, story-teller,
The one who remembered old songs,
Who could weave old rhythms with new words,   870
Chanted Beowulf's story, securing his glory,
Weaving courage and wisdom in a weft of song.
He sang too of Sigemund, son of Wæls,
His wide travels and great glories,
Strange stories known and unknown,   875
His crimes and feuds craftily hidden
From the children of men, except Fitela,
His nephew and friend to whom he talked,
For they fought together, battled like brothers,
Blood-companions in countless battles,   880
Slaying a swath of giants with their swords.
No small glory sprang up for Sigemund
After his death-day. Hardened by battle,
He killed a dragon, destroyed the worm,
The old treasure-hoarder, guardian of gold.   885
Under the gray stones, into that cold cave,

The prince's son went without Fitela,
Alone in his courage, daring the dragon.
What fate offered, he took—shook his sword,
Stabbed the scaly worm to the wall,   890
Pinned the bright beast to the stone
With his edge of iron, its skin shining.
The dragon was dead, the serpent skewered.
The awesome striker, son of Wæls,
Sigemund had sought the ring-hoard alone.   895
He brought treasure to the boat's belly
Where he could rejoice over gems, fathom gold.
The old worm melted in its own heat.
He was the most hailed hero after Heremod—
Whose strength and daring, whose battle-courage   900
Was finally drained in a twisted war.
He was betrayed by giants into enemy hands—
His end was quick. His surging sorrows
Beat his spirit till he became a source of sadness,
A gathering of grief to his thanes and people.   905
Wise men mourned then their lost lord,
For they had hoped from the oldest days
That this stout-hearted warrior might prevail,
Offer an end to affliction, relief from ruin,
A remedy for evil. A king's son should prosper,   910
Take the role of his father, rule wisely his people,
Protect the land and its treasure-hoard,
Shaping a shelter-hall for the Scyldings.
Beowulf was dearer to all his people, a better
Friend than Heremod, who was seized by sin.   915
Sometimes they spurred their horses, racing
Down sandy roads. The morning sun
Also hastened across heaven. Warriors walked
Bold-hearted back to the high hall Heorot
To see the strange wonder. The king came   920
From the queen's bed, the guardian of gold,
Keeper of ring-wealth, fast in his fame,
With his company of men, and his queen too
With her wealth of women on the meadhall path.

Hrothgar spoke, stood on the porch steps,   925
Staring at the eaves under the roof,
Glistening with gold and Grendel's claw.
"Thank God for this saving sight!
I've endured evil, a bundle of grief
At Grendel's hand. May the Guardian of heaven   930
Keep working wonders. Not long ago
I never expected relief from my sorrow,
When the greatest of halls stood stained
With bright blood, shining with slaughter,
A stretch of woe to all wise counselors   935
Who despaired of defending the people's place
Against demons, sprites, and dark shadows
Haunting Heorot, a nightwork of woe.
Now a great warrior has wrought relief,
And through God's hand, healed Heorot,   940
Found out evil and cunningly fixed it,
Where we failed with our unsound plans.
Your mother may say—whoever she was
Who bore such a son among mankind—
That God was gracious to her, kind in creating   945
A boy, a blessing. Now Beowulf, best of men,
I hold you humbly in my heart like a son,
And cherish your coming. Keep well this kinship.
No treasure I own cannot be yours.
Often I have given gifts to honor   950
Weaker warriors, a trust of treasure.
Now you have done such glorious deeds
That your fame will never falter."
Then Beowulf, son of Ecgtheow, spoke:
"With kind hearts and cold courage,   955
We have entered this struggle against the unknown,
Ungrasped power, and snapped its strength.
I wish you might have seen him yourself,
The feast-weary fiend, scales dragging,
Falling in the hall, dead-tired.   960
I wanted to catch him quick, hold him
Hard with a hand-grip, cradle him

In a death-bed, a slaughter-couch,
So he might find a savage sleep,
His ghost lifting from the body-bed;   965
He was bound to stay in my unyielding grip
Unless his flesh could flee. I wanted
Him dead, no bones about it—
But I couldn't hold him, the restless enemy,
Against God's will. He slipped my grasp.   970
To save his life he left his hand behind,
His arm and shoulder—a nice touch!
The token claw gave him cold comfort,
No hope of life, that loathed spoiler,
Tortured by sin; but pain grabbed him   975
In a hard grasp, a wailing wound,
A misery-grip. There he must wait,
Stained with crime, till bright God
Brings judgment for his dark deeds."
After this, Unferth son of Ecglaf,   980
Boasted less of his battle-works,
His courage quiet, while all warriors
Gazed on the claw, the fiend's fingers,
Nailed near the roof by Beowulf's strength.
Each claw-nail, each hand-spur   985
In the heathen's banged up death-grip,
Was stiff as steel. The old talk was dead—
Men claimed no hard thing could pierce him,
No ancient iron, no trusted blade,
Could cut his bloody battle-fist.   990
Then Heorot was ordered adorned by hands.
Men and women readied the wine-hall,
Decorated for guests. Gold-threaded tapestries
Draped the walls, bright weavings,
A web of wonder for the eyes of men.   995
The beautiful building had been blasted,
Its iron hinges shattered by terror's touch,
When the monster, stained by sin,
Outlawed from men, jerked into flight
To run for his life. Only the roof stood   1000

Untouched, unharmed, unbloodied in the end.
Death offers no easy escape to anyone
On the road from birth, no matter the need:
Earth-dwellers, world-walkers,
Soul-bearers, the sons of men—   1005
Each of us seeks the place prepared
Where after feasting in the pleasure-hall,
The flesh lies down in death's bed,
With a blanket of earth for a long unwaking.

That was the time for a victory-feast—   1010
King Hrothgar, Healfdene's son,
Hailed the warriors in. I've never heard
Of a greater group of kinsmen and thanes,
Gathered about their treasure-giver,
With such noble bearing. Glorious warriors   1015
Feasted at mead-benches, drinking their fill,
With Hrothgar and Hrothulf, bold-minded men.
The heart of Heorot was filled with friends—
That was before some of the Scyldings,
Betraying their brothers, took treachery in.   1020
Then Hrothgar gave Beowulf a victory-banner,
Woven with gold, a helmet and mail-coat,
Healfdene's jeweled sword, ancient to onlookers.
Beowulf drank mead with no need for shame
Before his bowmen with such rich gifts.   1025
Not many have given four finer treasures
As a sign of friendship, gleaming with gold.
The helmet's rim, a costly crown,
Was wrapped with wire, wound in wealth,
A guardian roof-ridge for a warrior's head,   1030
So that no keen sword, no hammered leaving
Of a smith's sharp files, no battle-hardened blade,
Could cut him down, pierce his protection,
When the shield-warrior met his fierce foe.
Then the gift-giver, protector of men,   1035
Ordered eight horses onto the hall floor,
Bridled in gold. One of the saddles

Was crafted with gems, cunningly wrought—
That was the battle-seat of the great king,
When glorious Hrothgar, Healfdene's son,   1040
Sought sword-play. His war-mood never faltered—
His fame was tested and forged in battle
Where men fought in a field of corpses.
The lord of the Danes, in the line of Ing,
Their ancient king, offered ownership   1045
To Beowulf of both horses and weapons,
Urged him wisely to use them well.
That gift-giver repaid his battle-rush
With horses and treasure so no truth-teller
Could find fault. He also gave seafarers sitting   1050
On mead-benches who came with Beowulf
Heirloom treasures and ordered wergild
Paid for the Geat that Grendel killed
In vicious sin—surely he might have slain
More men if wise God and a man's courage   1055
Hadn't hindered his desire, forestalling fate.
God rules the race of men, both then and now,
So understanding is always best, the soul's seeing.
Whoever lives long through days of feud and strife
Will come to endure both love and loathing,   1060
Get an eyeful of both good and evil on this earth.

Then sound and music were mixed in the hall,
Harp-songs before Hrothgar, battle-son of Healfdene;
The joy-wood was touched, a tale spun out,
As the king's shaper, the song-weaver,   1065
Wove strands of story to men on mead-benches
Of days when Finn, surrounded by his sons,
Slid into slaughter, a surprise attack,
And how Hnaef of the Half-Danes fought and fell
In that Frisian strife. His sister Hildeburh   1070
Could not praise the faith of those Finnish giants.
Blameless she lost both brother and son
In that shield-play—they fell to their fates,
Slain by spears. She was struck with grief.

Hoc's daughter mourned that shaft of fate   1075
When morning came, and under the sky
She saw the slaughter of kith and kin,
All those she loved most, her family joy—
Cold corpses. That fight seized
Finn's thanes, all but a remnant,   1080
So the Frisian prince could not continue
To battle the Danes or Hengest their leader
Who survived Hnæf—or even protect his own men.
So Finn and Hengest fixed a truce:
A hall-space would be cleared for the Danes,   1085
Ruled jointly, so that mighty King Finn,
Son of Folcwalda, from its high seat
Might share the gift-giving with rings to each,
And treasure to the two tribes, gold to Frisians
And Danes alike; he might honor the others   1090
As well as his own, bring joy to both,
However hard in the shared beer-hall.
Both sides pledged peace, secured a settlement.
They swore oaths. Finn promised without fail,
Without feigning, to honor all survivors   1095
On both sides, as his counselors advised,
So that no warrior by words or works
Should break the truce, destroy the treaty,
Undermine the peace. No one would mention
Out of malice that the princeless Danes   1100
Had to follow Finn in the Frisian hall,
The slayer of Hnæf, their own ring-giver,
Since fate forced this truce upon them.
If any Frisian warriors wanted to remember
The murderous feud or recall it with words,   1105
Then the sword's edge should settle it.
Hnæf's funeral pyre was prepared
And ancient gold hauled from the hoard.
The best of the Scylding battle-warriors
Was laid on the pyre. He was not alone.   1110
In plain sight were plenty of mail-coats,
Bloody and stained, iron-hard helmets

With boar-images bathed in gold and gore.
Retainers from both sides lay ravaged,
Warriors at rest with their gaping wounds,   1115
The cringing dead in a pile of slaughter.
Then Hildeburh asked that her son be borne
Beside her beloved brother, his uncle Hnæf,
On the funeral pyre. Their bones and flesh
Blazed and burned. She keened over corpses,   1120
Grieving in song. The dead drifted up
In sound and smoke; the ravaging flame
Raged over the barrow, reaching heaven.
Heads melted, wounds burst, blood sprang out,
Sizzling from sword-bites. The flame gobbled all,   1125
Greediest of ghosts, war-heroes on both sides—
Their glory was gone, their strength sapped.
Some of Finn's warriors went home without friends,
But Hengest and Finn lived in the hall unwillingly
With their own retainers, with their own memories   1130
Of summer-slaughter through the savage winter.
Hengest dreamed of his homeland, unable to sail
His ring-prowed ship over storm-wind roads,
Winter-waves locked in the bond of ice—
Until spring came to the halls of men   1135
As it still does today, unlocking light,
A wonder of weather biding its time.
Winter was gone, the earth was fair.
The exile was eager to seek his homeland,
Yet he dreamed more of revenge than return,   1140
More of settling grief than sailing home—
If only he could fight Finn, answer with iron
That unending feud. So he did not refuse
The world-wide custom of hard revenge
When Hunlafing laid in his lap that intimate edge,   1145
That flashing sword known to the Frisians.
So Finn too felt the sword's touch,
A cruel death in his own hall—
After Guthlaf and Oslaf, Hunlaf's kin,
Reminded Hengest of that grim slaughter   1150

After the sea-voyage, in that guest-hall,
Fixed the blame for that family feud
On the Frisians. The blood's revenge
Cannot be contained in a restless heart.
Then the hall was decorated red   1155
With the blood of foes. Finn was dead,
His company killed, his queen taken
Home to the Danes. The Scyldings
Took all the hall-treasures, heirlooms,
Tapestries and gems, home with Hildeburh,   1160
Over the sea to her own people.
The shaper finished his song of victory,
Of family feud. Joy rose up,
Bright bench-sounds; cup-bearers
Brought wine in beautiful jugs.   1165
Then Wealhtheow walked in with her gold crown,
Sat down between two good men,
Uncle and nephew, Hrothgar and Hrothulf,
Each true at the time, their trust unbroken.
Also Unferth was there, admired by many,   1170
The king's mouthpiece. Men knew his heart
Held courage and cunning—he'd killed his kin
Without mercy. Wealhtheow spoke:
"Take this cup, my noble king,
Giver of treasure, gold-friend of men.   1175
Be kind in your words, generous to the Geats
With gifts and treasures from all the tribes.
I've heard you would treat Beowulf like a son.
Heorot is purged, the ring-bright hall.
Use well your gifts and give rewards   1180
While you may, but leave your kingdom
To kinsmen when you go, to folk and family.
I know gracious Hrothulf will honor our sons,
Keep the kingdom for them if he outlives you,
Lord of the Scyldings. I hope he'll give them   1185
Back the good that we've given him here,
The joy and honor he's had since childhood."
Then she turned to the bench where her sons sat,

Hrethric and Hrothmund, with other brave boys,
Next to the good man, Beowulf the Geat.   1190
Beowulf was brought the welcome cup
Of words and wine, feasting and friendship,
And twisted gold, arm-bands and rings,
Chain-mail and the world's greatest
War-collar worn by any man on earth—   1195
No finer treasure, no greater gift
Under heaven since Hama carried off
The neck-ring of the Brosings to that bright city,
The beautiful jewel and its rich setting.
He wanted silver instead of strife, gold not gore.   1200
He fled from the killing craft of Eormenric
And found in the feud his last reward.
This collar was the one that Hygelac wore,
Grandson of Swerting, when he rallied his troops
Under his war-banner to protect his hoard   1205
And bring back booty, the spoils of slaughter.
Fate took him for his pride in provoking
A feud with the Frisians and the savage Franks.
He wore that neck-gem with precious stones
Over the bowl of the sea. His body fell   1210
Beneath his shield, a king in the clutch
Of the dreaded Franks, his chain-mail,
His neck-ring and life in their last embrace.
Then common warriors plundered the bodies,
Harvesting gain from the ground of slaughter,   1215
Reaping treasure in the field of corpses.

The hall resounded. Then Wealhtheow rose
And spoke to the company: "Enjoy this collar,
My beloved Beowulf, this beautiful neck-ring,
My lucky young warrior, the mail-coat   1220
And treasures, war-shirts for strength.
Be crafty, courageous—be proud and prosper—
Be kind in counsel to my precious sons.
I'll reward you for that. You've earned the praise
Of generations across windy seas and cliff-walls.   1225

May you thrive and enjoy these treasures.
Be gentle to my sons, bringer of joy—
Here warriors hold true to each other in the hall,
Loyal to the lord, devoted to duty,
Gracious in heart, their minds on mead.   1230
Downing their drink, they do as I ask."
Wealhtheow went back to sit by her lord
At this best of banquets. Warriors drank wine
Which tasted finer than the dark fate
Destined again to stalk the hall   1235
At the end of evening when King Hrothgar
Retired to his rest in a separate room.
Countless men cleared the benches,
Spread out their pillows and padded bedding,
Just as before. One beer-drinker,   1240
Unsuspecting, sank into bedrest,
Doomed to die. Each sleeper set at his head
His war-shield, bright battle-wood,
And above on the bench, his high-ridged helmet,
His ring-mail shirt woven with iron,   1245
And his sharp-shafted war-wood.
Their custom was clear: be ready to strike
In bed or in battle, at home or away,
Whenever their lord looked in dire need—
That was a loyal band, a trusted troop.   1250

So they sank into sleep. One paid a high price
For his night's rest, a monstrous replay
Of times when Grendel haunted the gold-hall,
Unleashing evil until his end,
Crushed in sin. Too soon it was clear   1255
He had an avenger bent on killing—
Her hatred teeming at the loss of her son—
Grendel's mother, a monster-woman,
Awesome, appalling, a walking dread,
Who lived in the lake's liquid terror,   1260
In the cold currents after Cain killed
His only brother, the sword-slayer

Of his father's son. So Cain was outlawed,
Marked for murder, fleeing from joy,
Wandering the wasteland. Then monsters woke   1265
From that demon seed, ghosts and ghouls—
Grendel was one, a savage outcast,
A fierce foe, who found in Heorot
A waking warrior, watchful, warlike,
Waiting for battle. Each reached out   1270
With a savage grip. One was ready
With his yawning strength, a gift from God.
He trusted the Lord, his Maker's mercy,
And his powerful grip. He finished the fiend,
Humbled the hall-guest, the hell-ghost.   1275
Grendel fled, separated from joy,
Seeking his death-home, the bane of men.
His greedy mother, grim as the gallows,
Rushed ravenous to avenge her son.
She came to Heorot where the Ring-Danes slept,   1280
Handing twisted fate to trusting warriors.
Grendel's mother made her way in.
Her terror was only less than Grendel's
By this much—as the terror of a woman-warrior
Might be less than a man's, the shock of a war-wife   1285
As her hammer-forged blade stained with blood,
The red-sweat of battle, severs the ridge
Of a man's boar-helmet and splits his head.
Suddenly in the hall, hard swords were drawn,
Shields grabbed with hands, too late for helmets,   1290
Too late for corselets. She snatched a man!
She was in and out, quick on the take,
In a rush to revenge and return home.
She fled to the fen. He was Hrothgar's man,
His favorite retainer between the seas,   1295
A beloved shield-warrior. She savored him too,
A man ripped from bed, stripped of his sleep.
She touched his heart, feeding on his fame.
Beowulf, the honored Geat, was gone.
After the great feast and the gift-giving,   1300

He had been offered another lodging.
Cries rent the hall, an uproar in Heorot.
She had seized her son's claw, his blood-crusty hand—
That was no slaking of sorrow but a bad exchange
With brutal payment of kith and kin on both sides.   1305

Then the grizzled king, a once-great warrior,
Was fiercely troubled, torn by grief,
When he heard his chief thane, his dearest friend,
Was dead. Beowulf was brought to the high hall
For vengeance and valor. In the dawn light   1310
He and his seafarers came to the hall,
Where the wise king waited, wondering
Whether God Almighty would ever grant
A better fortune, a chance at peace,
After he heard the wail, reliving old woe.   1315
Beowulf the worthy warrior walked across
The bloody floor with his band of men.
The hall-slats resounded, the boards shook.
He approached the wise king, asking
If he'd had a restful night with pleasant dreams.   1320
Hrothgar responded, protector of the Scyldings:
"Don't talk of dreams. My life's a nightmare!
Sorrow haunts this hall again, stalking the Danes.
Æschere is dead, Yrmenlaf's brother,
My rune-reader, wise counselor,   1325
Shield-warrior, and shoulder-companion.
We guarded each other's back in battle
When troops clashed, blade against boar-crest.
He was all an earl should be, from start to finish,
Always good. Now some unsteady spirit,   1330
Some restless, ravenous hall-beast
Has been his slayer. Who knows
Where the savage feeder has taken his body,
Feasting on flesh. She's avenged her son,
Finished the feud you started with your grip,   1335
Hard hands on the monster who'd winnowed
My people too long. His life languished

In your hands. Now another has come,
The second night-stalker, hall-wrecker,
Borne by feud, bent on vengeance,   1340
And many may feel who grieve for their king,
Their generous gift-giver, and mourn his counselor,
That her coming follows hard upon your killing—
It galls our hearts. She's stolen my right-hand man
Who supported your coming and sustained your dreams.   1345
I've heard rumors, what land-dwellers
And hall-counselors say, that they've seen
Two monsters on the moors, wasteland wanderers,
Ghastly spirits or grim beasts,
And one has a shape most like a woman,   1350
While the other's like a man, a miserable wretch,
Outlawed in exile, except bigger than a man—
That one they've called Grendel from distant days.
No one knows of his father, if some man-dark shape
Begot the fiend, the spore and sport   1355
Of savage lust. The two roam a remote land,
A cruel country, wolf-slopes, wild headlands,
Windswept roads, fen-paths in the marsh,
Where a mountain stream slithers under hills,
Not many miles from here where the mere   1360
Hunkers down under trees, under frost-covered wood,
With roots snaking down in dark water.
There you can see a stark wonder each night—
Fire walks on water, flame on the flood.
No wise man living can fathom its depths,   1365
Sound its source. Though the heath-stepper,
A stag with strong horns is harried by hounds
To flee through that forest, he would rather die,
Lay his life on the shore, than plunge in that lake
To protect his head. That's no gentle place,   1370
No shielding strand. Surging waves
Roust black, ravenous storms,
Raising dark waters to the heavens,
When the wind howls, stirs up evil,
Marsh-mist, and the sky weeps.   1375

You're the only help for this horror,
Our hope and protection. It's a dread land
Beyond your knowing, a place of peril
Where you might find our evil enemy
Who stalks in sin. Seek her if you dare.   1380
I will give you a reward for revenge,
Fair recompense for the feud, twisted gold
From the treasure-hoard, if you return."
Beowulf spoke, son of Ecgtheow:
"Grieve not, wise warrior and good king.   1385
It's better to avenge a friend than endure
Headlong mourning. Each man must discover
His own death someday. A good man gathers
Glory before he's gone, a warrior's tribute.
Arise great guardian of the Danes' kingdom—   1390
Let's go look at the tracks of Grendel's kin.
I promise you this: she can't hide
In the earth's embrace, a deadly den,
In mountain-woods, or ocean caves,
Wherever she flees. Have patience,   1395
Bide time, and bear sorrow as a man should."
Then the old Danish lord leapt up,
Thanking God for that great speech.
Hrothgar's horse, his braided steed,
Was saddled and bridled. The wise prince rode   1400
In stately splendor with a band of shield-warriors
Marching behind. The monster's tracks were plain
On the forest paths; they followed her going
On the marked ground. Over the murky moor,
She carried the corpse of Hrothgar's thane,   1405
The lifeless counselor, the best retainer
Who shared with Hrothgar home and hall.
The noble prince rode over rocky slopes,
Steep stone-paths, narrow one-man roads,
Into the unknown moor-homes, marsh-lairs   1410
Of water-monsters and sea-snakes.
He went with his counselors, crafty men,

Scouted the land till they found some trees,
A stunted grove leaning over gray cliffs,
A joyless wood. Water was below,   1415
Bloody and roiling, a turmoil of gore;
To the Danes it was terror and torment,
A goad in the mind, a grief in the heart,
When they found Æschere's head
Sitting on the sea-cliff. The lake boiled with blood,   1420
Surged with hot gore as the warriors looked on.
The war-horn sounded a surging battle-song;
The foot-troops sat down, gazing in wonder.
They watched in the water strange worm-shapes,
Sea-serpents swimming, exploring the lake,   1425
And water-monsters lying on the headland shores
Like beasts of the deep who wake in the morning
And wander the sea-roads, sorrowing ships,
A wilding of worms. The fierce ones fled,
Thrashing with rage at the bright, sudden sound   1430
Of the battle-horn. A bow-bearing Geat
Cut one of them off from his life with a shot—
A stitch of iron in his monstrous heart.
He swam a little slower as death stroked by—
Shortly he was hard-pressed and hampered by spears,   1435
By barbed boar-shafts, like a pig in the waves,
Riding the pikes, assailed by enemies,
Hauled to the shore—that wave-walking worm,
Alien beast, wonder of the water.
Men gazed at that guest, that grim horror.   1440
Then Beowulf put on his battle-clothes
Without fuss, without fear of losing his life.
His chain-mail—hard, broad, hand-woven—
Would breach the sea—it knew how to keep
His bone-house whole so his fierce foe's   1445
Hand-crush could not reach his heart,
Or the anger of enemies tear out his life.
A shining helmet guarded his head—
It could slice dark water, strike the depths,

Lunge for the lake-floor. It was cunningly made,   1450
Crafted by smiths, adorned with gold,
Encrusted with gems, with emblematic boars,
So no sword or blade could bite through its iron.
Not the least of his strengths, his battle-aids,
Was what Unferth gave him in his time of need—   1455
Hrunting was the name of that ancient sword,
That iron-edged blade and heirloom treasure—
It was engraved with waves, serpentine swirls
Like deadly snakes, tempered with gore.
Never had it failed any warrior wielding it   1460
Who greeted terror with his battle-hand
In a meeting of monsters in their unholy home.
This was not the first time it carried courage.
Surely Unferth, Ecglaf's son, crafty and strong,
When he lent this sword to a better warrior,   1465
Beowulf the Geat, was not thinking much
Of what he had said, boasting in the hall
And drunk on wine, a cowardly slanderer.
Unferth was a taunter who took no risks.
He never wanted to walk under water.   1470
He never thought to brave broiling waves.
He gave up glory for loathing at the lake,
Unlike the other who carried courage to the edge.
Beowulf spoke, son of Ecgtheow:
"Remember, great Hrothgar, son of Healfdene,   1475
Wise king, gold-friend of men,
What we agreed, now that I'm ready to go:
If I should leave life, discover death in this dive,
You would stand as my father, guardian and shield
Of my thanes and retainers, if slaughter takes me.   1480
The gifts you've given me, gracious Hrothgar,
Rewards for the hall-strife, send on to Hygelac,
So the lord of the Geats, son of Hrethel,
Will know from that gathering of gold and wealth
That I found here a good ring-giver   1485
Whose favor I enjoyed. And let Unferth,
Known for sharp words, take home my sword,

The hard-edged heirloom with its serpentine stain,
Its wave-patterned blade. With his sword Hrunting,
I will gather glory or die in death's clutch."   1490

After these words, the man of the Geats,
Without waiting for an answer, dove down—
The sea-surge welcomed the warrior,
Seized and swallowed the brave swimmer.
He drifted down, the daylight fading,   1495
As he touched lake-bottom. Soon that sea-creature
Who ruled the realm for a hundred years,
Grim and greedy, ravenous for slaughter,
Saw that warrior winding through water,
Pushing down from the land-light above,   1500
Seeking her strange home. She seized the intruder
With her fierce claws, but she broke no bones,
Pierced no hide—the warrior was whole,
Protected by mail from the monster's hand,
Shielded by rings from those savage fingers.   1505
No claw could cut that coat. When Beowulf came
To the murky floor, the sea-wolf seized him,
Dragging him home to her desperate lair,
So despite his courage, he could not swing his sword,
Wield his weapon. He was battered by sea-beasts   1510
Who tore at his mail-coat with terrible tusks,
Attacking the alien warrior. Then Beowulf saw
He was in a hall-cavern which held back water;
The cave-roof held up the floor of the sea
So the warrior would not suffocate in the waves,   1515
The fierce grip of the flood. He saw a fire-light,
Pale and blazing, both bleak and bright.
Then the good man greeted the mere-woman,
Monstrous, mighty, outlaw of the deep.
He gave her a sword-gift, thrust and stroke,   1520
Held nothing back from his sharp greeting,
So that ring-patterned blade was swinging
Straight for her head, singing a war-song,
Greedy for battle. Then the cave-guest saw

That his lightning blade would not bite her body,   1525
Slice through her life. The battle-edge failed
Where before it had split both helmet and head,
Sailed through chain-mail, fixed a man's fate.
That was the heirloom's first failure.
Resolute and keen, the kinsman of Hygelac,   1530
Seeking glory, cast off the sword
With the serpentine swirls and inlaid gems,
Dropped the useless steel to the ground.
He trusted the strength of his fierce hand-grip,
As a man must do in his quest for fame   1535
And lasting glory—he must risk his life.
The prince of the War-Geats feared no feud,
Refused no strife. He seized the shoulder
Of Grendel's mother, swollen with fury,
Battle-hard with rage, threw that life-foe,   1540
That grappling grim-wife to the ground.
She came back for more, gave him a gift
Of harrowing hands, a clench of claws.
Then war-weary, the strongest of foot-warriors,
Hardest of heroes, stumbled and fell.   1545
She sat on her hall-guest, gripping her knife,
Broad and bright-edged, lunging in his lap,
Embracing revenge for the loss of her son.
His corselet clung, a woven war-web,
Guarding his heart against stab and sting,   1550
Protecting his body against penetration.
Then the son of Ecgtheow might have perished,
Ended his life there deep under ground,
If his hardened chain-mail, a web of rings
Had not held strong, and if holy God,   1555
Guarding the right, had not shaped victory
For the greatest of Geats who rose up again.
Then Beowulf saw a battle-rich blade,
Boding bright victory among some armor,
An old sword of giants, a warrior's glory,   1560
Heavier than any man's hand-play,
Forged in fire, invincible and adorned.

The Scyldings' hero seized the ringed hilt,
Lifted its length, heaving its heft.
Fierce in fighting, savage in strength,   1565
Desperate for life, he struck the furious
Blade at her body—it bit through her neck,
Broke the bone-rings, shattered her life.
The edge cut through her fated flesh.
She fell to the floor, the sword sweating blood,   1570
And the warrior rejoiced in a good day's work.
The pale light flared like heaven's candle,
An indoor sun brightening the cave.
He gazed round the chamber, circled the hall,
Raised up the old sword, hard by the hilt,   1575
Hygelac's thane, angry and resolute.
This blade was useful, unlike Unferth's.
Beowulf had a battle-gift for Grendel—
He wanted to repay his vengeance in the hall,
His devouring of Danes in their witless sleep,   1580
Night after night, sometimes a few,
One time fifteen, a monstrous gift—
He'd dragged them away like delicious prey.
Beowulf repaid him with swift revenge
As he saw him lying, war-weary, lifeless,   1585
Drained on his death-bed from hall-wounds
At Heorot. Suddenly his blade swung,
Cutting the corpse. The body burst open
In a handful of gore from that hard stroke.
With a sword-slice to his dead body,   1590
Beowulf severed Grendel's head.

Then wise men watching up on the shore,
Gazing with Hrothgar at the churning waves,
Saw the roiling water stained with blood.
The grizzled elders talked together,   1595
Counseled sagely that no one could come
Out of that lake a conquering hero,
Proclaiming victory to their glorious king—
Surely the sea-wolf had slaughtered him.

Then came the ninth hour. The Scyldings forsook 1600
Their headland watch—Hrothgar went home,
The gold-friend of men. The Geats sat still
Like loyal strangers on the alien shore,
Stared at the water, sick at heart,
Hoping against hope to see their lord. 1605
Meanwhile below, the great battle-sword
Began to melt like a bloody icicle
From the sweat of battle, as the wonder after winter,
When the Father who rules all times and seasons
Unlocks the ice-bonds, the chains of frost— 1610
He is the true Creator. The prince of the Geats
Took no treasures from that cavernous hall
Except the head and the jeweled hilt.
The sword-blade had melted, burning away
Its damascened beauty. The blood was too hot, 1615
The poison of the alien spirit too strong,
The gore of the cave-dread who died too great.
The Geat came swimming who killed the monster,
Slaughtered the she-worm—he plunged up through water.
The currents were cleansed, the lake and its lair, 1620
The liquid roads where the monster played,
Leaving her days of life-loan in the deep.
Then the lord and protector of seamen swam,
Stroking toward shore, rejoicing in his haul,
The burden of the blade he was bringing home. 1625
The Geats leapt to greet him, thanking God
That their hero was whole, safe and sound.
Then was the mail-coat of the conqueror loosened,
The helmet of the hero untied. The lake drowsed,
The waves calmed, the water subsided, 1630
Stained with blood. The men marched back,
Their spirits unburdened, their hearts rejoicing,
Following the footpaths, the old known roads.
The thanes were bold and proud as kings.
They bore Grendel's head from the mere-cliffs, 1635
A weight for the warriors—it took four to haul
Grendel's head to the gold-hall stuck on spears,

A toil of trouble. Straightway they came,
A gathering of Geats, a strength of retainers,
Toward Hrothgar's hall, fourteen warriors, 1640
Their great lord with them, who moved across fields,
A troop together, home to the meadhall.
The prince of the Geats, bravest of battle,
Gathered in glory, surrounded by thanes,
Came to the hall to greet King Hrothgar. 1645
They bore Grendel's head by the hair
To the hall floor where the Danes drank,
Dragged that left-over flesh to the table,
A ball of terror to the men and the queen—
A dead gaze, a stark sight. 1650

Beowulf spoke, son of Ecgtheow:
"Now—son of Healfdene, Lord of the Scyldings,
See what we've brought—a gift from the mere,
A token of glory to gaze upon.
I did not walk readily under water, 1655
Battle calmly in the monster's cave,
Keep my life easily in that lake-lair.
I'd have perished if not for the power of God.
That great sword Hrunting, gift of Unferth,
Was not much good, though famous enough, 1660
But the Ruler of men, who often guides
A warrior alone, gave me eyes to see
An heirloom on the wall, an old sword of giants,
So I found a better weapon to wield.
When the time was right, I slew those demons, 1665
Monstrous house-mates. Then that battle-blade,
The serpentined sword, melted down to the hilt,
As the blood spewed out, hottest of battle-sweats.
I brought back the hilt from the cave-hoard,
Paid the monsters in kind for their killing, 1670
The slaughter of Scyldings, the death of Danes—
It was only right. I promise you this:
Tonight you can rest without fear in Heorot,
Thanes all together, both young and old,

Prince of the Scyldings, lord of your people.   1675
Death will not haunt you as it did of old."
Then the golden hilt, the old work of giants,
Was given to the hand of the grizzled king.
It passed that day to the prince of the Danes
From the hoard of demons after their fall,   1680
Created by craftsmen, shaped by smiths.
When that grim-hearted foe of God,
And his monster-mother, guilty of murder,
Left this world, the beautiful hilt
Came to the best of earthly kings   1685
Between the seas. Hrothgar spoke.
He gazed at the hilt, an heirloom treasure,
On which was engraved in images and runes
The origin of strife, the first feud,
When the sea surged and the flood slew   1690
The race of giants—they knew suffering,
Always alien to eternal God.
He gave them the deep water's reward.
So rune-staves told this ancient story
On the gold hilt, once grip and guard   1695
Of the greatest sword, the sharpest steel,
Naming its owner with serpentine shapes,
Worm-like runes. Then wise Hrothgar spoke,
The son of Healfdene—the thanes listened.
"Now a man who knows truth, acts rightly,   1700
And rules with justice, a protector of the land
And all its people, recalling the past,
Will say that this is the best man ever born.
You have harvested glory, great Beowulf—
Your name is renowned to the ends of earth.   1705
You keep courage tempered with wisdom,
The surest of strengths. Your fame spreads far.
A king keeps his promise—I honor my vow.
You will be your people's pride and joy,
Comfort and keep, for a long time.   1710
You're not like Heremod, the king before Scyld,
Who slew the sons of Ecgwela, nurturing slaughter,

Not justice and joy. A plague to the Danes,
Quick to anger, he killed his mates,
His hearth-companions. He turned notorious,   1715
Trading hall-mirth for murder, though God alone
Gave him power to rule, sustained his strength.
The heart in his breast was blood-thirsty—
He gave no rings for honor and glory
To his people the Danes, serving only himself.   1720
He lived without joy, an ache and affliction
To his own people. Learn from his story:
Be manly and munificent—shape worth from wealth.
I give you this story from my treasure of years.
It's a wonder how God with his great heart   1725
Deals out to mankind wisdom and land,
Nature and nobility, in his all-wielding power.
Sometimes he lets a good man's mind dwell
In desire or delight, gives him hearth and home,
A kingdom to rule, prosperous and proud,   1730
Subjects to govern, a stronghold to guard,
Till lost in unwisdom, driven by folly,
He cannot imagine an end to joy.
He lives in fullness, so the fool believes
That nothing can touch him, no turning of fate,   1735
Neither sudden illness nor old age,
Neither sword-strife nor ancient sorrow.
Neither heart's hatred nor dark dread
Can twist his comfort—the world is his will—
Until his pride puffs up, his arrogance increases,   1740
So the soul's guardian sleeps, the watcher wanes.
His sleep is too sound, bound up by care,
And the soul-slayer wakes with his treacherous bow.
The man's heart is shot with a bitter shaft,
His mind poisoned without protection,   1745
The savage suggestion of a dark demon,
An insidious evil. He's without defense.
He thinks he owns too little and rules too few.
His grim mind is bent toward treasure.
He hoards everything, gives nothing,   1750

Honors no one but himself, forgets fate—
Forgets that his glory was given by God
Who offers honor. Finally he falls.
His flesh-house crumbles—it was just a loan.
His end approaches. Another succeeds him,   1755
A generous king who never hoards,
A ring-giver who rules without fear,
Who hands out treasure without mourning.
Guard against the soul's bowman, beloved
Beowulf, best of men. Avoid evil,   1760
Seek eternal gain, pursue no unyielding pride,
Be great and giving. Power is fleeting.
For a time you may have might and glory,
Yet soon illness or the edge of a sword
Will sap your strength, or the fire's clutch,   1765
Or the flood's surge, or the sword's reach,
Or the spear's flight, or the horror of old age,
Or the dimming of eyes, the coming of dark.
Then death will suddenly seize you, my warrior.
I've ruled the Ring-Danes for fifty years,   1770
Kept them safe from swords and spears
Throughout middle-earth, ruling under heaven,
Till I thought no enemy could touch me.
Well, fate's twists and turns have found me—
Sorrow turned out joy from my homeland   1775
When that old foe invited himself in,
The dreaded Grendel with his unexpected gift
Of sorrow to my spirit, suffering to my soul.
I thank God that I've come to see,
After such long strife, his bloody head,   1780
His gaping gaze with my own eyes.
Come now to the seat of joyous feasting,
War-worthy hero of the Geats—
We'll share many treasures before morning."   1785
The Geat was heart-glad, accepted his seat
As the wise king suggested. The food was served
To the brave warriors sitting down to feast
For a second night—just as before.

Night's dark helmet dimmed the hall; 1790
The retainers rose, the gray-haired Scylding
Sought his bed. It pleased the Geat,
The glorious shield-warrior, that he could rest.
A hall-thane came, attended to his needs
With awe and reverence, led the weary warrior 1795
And sea-crosser who was far from his country
To a separate lodging and a well-deserved sleep,
As was the tired sea-traveler's due.

Then the warrior with a great heart rested;
The hall towered over him, vaulted with gold. 1800
The guest slept till the blithe-hearted, black raven
Sang in the sun, declaring the dawn,
Heaven's joy. The bright light hastened,
Shining over shadows. Warriors rose,
Eager to travel home to their people. 1805
Bold-hearted Beowulf longed for his ship.
He ordered Hrunting, that precious blade,
Returned to Unferth, son of Ecglaf,
Said thanks for the loan, calling the sword
A good battle-friend, war-crafty. 1810
He found no fault with that good weapon,
No blame with the blade: he was generous with praise.
The warriors in armor prepared to depart,
Eager for home. Dear to the Danes,
The Geatish prince approached the high seat 1815
Of Hrothgar, greeted the great king.
Beowulf spoke, son of Ecgtheow:
"Now we seafarers, guests from afar,
Ask leave to speak: we must return to Hygelac.
You treated us well, provided properly. 1820
If I can accomplish any more on earth
To earn your heart's love, your people's praise,
Than the battle-deeds I've already done,
Just send for Beowulf—I'll be back.
If over the sea-roads, I hear that any neighbors 1825
Or even hall-thanes, those hanging around,

Threaten to harm you, I'll bring you war-heroes,
A thousand thanes, to stifle that strife.
I know that Hygelac, lord of the Geats,
Guardian of his people, though young as a ruler,   1830
Would support my coming in words and works,
Declarations and deeds, so I can keep my promise,
Continue to help and honor the Danes
With power and protection, and a forest of spears,
When you need good men. If your son Hrethric,   1835
Heir apparent, wants to visit the Geatish court,
He'll find many friends there. Foreign lands
Are best sought by sons who stay strong!"
Hrothgar spoke, answering his friend:
"A sage God sent these words to your spirit;   1840
I've never heard a young warrior speak so wisely.
You are strong in might, sharp in mind,
Wise in words. If in fortune's twists,
Your king Hygelac, son of Hrethel,
Should ever be slain by a grim war-spear,   1845
A battle-sword, or some unknown sickness,
And your lord is gone, the Geatish prince
And people's protector, yet you remain alive,
The Sea-Geats could not find a better man
To select as king to hold their land,   1850
To guard their hoard and protect the kingdom,
Should you consider ruling the land of your kinsmen.
The longer I know you, the better I like you,
My beloved Beowulf—your heart pleases me.
You have brought us together, Geats and Spear-Danes,   1855
Built a common kinship, a bridge between nations,
A tying of tribes, so that strife may sleep,
And old hostilities may be put to rest.
While I live and hold this kingdom together,
We will share treasures with your seafaring people,   1860
Greet them with gold over the sea-bird's bath.
The ring-necked ships will carry this sharing
Of gifts as tokens of honor and friendship.
I know our peoples will act honorably

In the old way toward friend and foe." 1865
Then king Hrothgar, Healfdene's son,
Protector of thanes, gave twelve treasures
To Beowulf in the hall, bade him go safely home
To his own people and come back again.
Then the king from a long Danish line, 1870
Lord of the Scyldings, old and wise,
Kissed and embraced that best of thanes,
Holding his head while the tears ran down
His grizzled face. He was of two minds,
But it seemed unlikely he would ever greet 1875
This Geat again or keep his counsel.
So dear was Beowulf, his mood was keening—
He could not hold back the heart's surges,
The waves of sorrow, the spirit's longing
Deep in his breast for this beloved man— 1880
It burned in his blood. Then Beowulf left,
Glorious with gold, strode over the green,
Proud of his gifts. The wave-walking ship
Waited for its owner, tethered on its anchor.
On that sea-journey, the gifts of Hrothgar 1885
Were hailed by all. He was a blameless king
Until old age sapped his strength,
Stole his joy as it does with so many.

Then young warriors walked to the shore,
Bearing mail-coats, ring-locked battle-shirts, 1890
Woven steel. The coast-guard met them again.
He offered no taunts from the top of the cliff
But rode down to greet them, glorious guests—
Said that their return would be richly welcomed
At home by the Geats when the men in bright armor 1895
Disembarked from their boat. Then on the strand,
The sea-bellied ship was loaded with armor,
The ring-prowed craft with horses and treasure.
The mast towered up over the gathering of gifts,
From Hrothgar's hoard. Beowulf gave the boat-guard 1900
A sword wound with gold—he was always honored

Afterward in the meadhall for that heirloom gift.
The ship sailed out, plowing deep water,
Leaving Danish lands. The mast was rigged
With a swath of sail, a great sea-cape, 1905
Bound by ropes. The sea-wood groaned,
Timbers creaked; the wave-winds did not hinder
That sea-craft from its course. The foamy-necked floater
Rode the swells, walked over waves—
The boat with the bound prow crossed deep water 1910
Until seafarers could see the cliffs of the Geats.
The ship sprang forward, driven by wind,
Strode for the sand, stood up on the shore.
The Geats' coast-guard who gazed at the sea,
Watching for warriors to welcome them home, 1915
Hurried down to the shore, eager to greet them.
They moored the wide-bellied ship to the shore
With an anchor-rope, so the surging waves
Would not bring wrack and ruin to the wood.
Beowulf ordered the prince's treasure— 1920
Armor, trappings, gems, and gold—
Borne from the ship. Soon they saw Hygelac,
Son of Hrethel, their own gift-giver,
Whose hall of thanes nestled near the sea-wall,
A beautiful building. The king sat proudly 1925
On his high throne. His young queen Hygd,
Wise and well-taught, courteous and accomplished,
Hæreth's daughter, had dwelled in his hall
Only a few years. She was generous to the Geats,
Not grasping of gifts or hoarding of hall-treasures. 1930
She was not like Fremu, the queen of crime,
Who served up terror. No one except her lord
Dared look at her directly in the light of day.
Whoever stared received the sword's edge—
Whoever gazed got seized and shackled— 1935
Whoever looked had a shortened life.
After any arrest, the case was soon settled
By the stroke of a sword, the shadow of justice,
The wail of slaughter, the blood of sorrow.

That was not a queen's proper custom— 1940
A precious woman should be a peace-weaver,
Knitting trust not terror. She should not steal
A man's life with a trumped-up insult.
Marriage to Offa put an end to that.
Men shared her story at the mead-benches, 1945
Said she caused less harm, cursed fewer lives,
After she was offered, sheathed in gold,
To the young warrior, a prince to his people,
When she sought Offa's hall with her father's blessing,
Followed his counsel across the waves, 1950
Found a wedding in her husband's wielding.
There on the throne of Offa's hall,
Her fate turned—she enjoyed a better life.
She was generous, glorious and good,
Useful to all, kind and loving 1955
To her husband the king, the lord of warriors
And prince of men—the best, I believe,
Between the seas, of all mankind.
Offa was honored far and wide
For his keen courage and generous giving. 1960
He was sharp in battle, wise in ruling.
He held his homeland till Eomer was born,
Grandson of Garmund, kinsman of Hemming,
Mighty in battle, a comfort to men.

Then the brave Beowulf with his band of warriors 1965
Walked along the shore, strode across the sand.
The world-candle shone, the sun rising high
In the southern sky. The warriors went eagerly
To the hall of Hygelac, protector of men,
Slayer of Ongentheow in the Swedish feud, 1970
A young battle-king, generous with rings.
Hygelac heard of Beowulf's coming:
Men said there in his homestead near the sea
That the guardian of warriors, his shield-companion,
Had come back alive to the Geatish court, 1975
Safe from the strife and sport of battle.

The hall was prepared with a place for the men.
The battle-survivor and the proud king,
Kinsmen together, traded talk,
Both formal greetings and shared stories.   1980
Queen Hygd, Hæreth's daughter,
Moved with mead-cups through the hall,
Carrying kindness—she loved the people—
Offering spirits to the outstretched hands
In the high hall. Hygelac was curious—   1985
He began to question his brave companion,
Wondering what marvels the Sea-Geats had met:
"How was your journey, beloved Beowulf,
As you swiftly resolved to ride the seas,
Stalking battle over salt water   1990
In the hall of Heorot? Did you bring a remedy
For Hrothgar's woe, his well-known grief?
My heart welled up with care and sorrow—
My spirit quailed at your dangerous quest.
I urged you to leave that slaughter-fiend alone,   1995
Let the Danes do battle with the monster Grendel,
Deal with the dread of their own demon.
I thank God you survived, came home sound."
Beowulf spoke, son of Ecgtheow:
"It's no secret, my lord Hygelac,   2000
What happened at that monster-meeting,
The clash and combat of two mighty creatures.
I grappled with that grim beast Grendel
Who had long torn Heorot apart with terror,
Tormenting the Scyldings, devouring the Danes.   2005
I avenged them all, finished that feud,
So that Grendel's kin, any savage creatures
Who may stalk the earth to the end of time,
Snared in sin, will have no reason
To boast of that battle, that clash at dawn.   2010
I traveled to Heorot to greet Hrothgar
In his ring-hall to make known my mission.
When the son of Healfdene heard my purpose,
He gave me a seat with his own sons.

The hall-troop was happy—I never saw more   2015
Joyful mead-drinkers under one roof.
Sometimes Wealhtheow, the wondrous queen,
The peace-weaver of peoples, walked the hall,
Cheering up warriors, offering the gift of rings
To young retainers before she sat down.   2020
Sometimes Freawaru, Hrothgar's daughter,
Carried an ale-cup or gold-rimmed horn
Around to retainers, offering a drink
From the jeweled vessel, the communal cup.
Draped in gold, she is promised to Ingeld,   2025
Son of Froda, prince of the Heathobards,
Enemies of the Danes. This peace-weaving plan
Is Hrothgar's hope to settle the feud
And buy off strife with the gift of his daughter,
But princes perish and slaughter sneaks back   2030
In the slayer's spear, even if the bride is good.
It may irk Ingeld, lord of the Heathobards,
And his proud thanes, when he enters the hall
With his foreign bride, that her retinue of Danes,
Aliens and enemies, rejoices at the feast.   2035
They'll see Scyldings bearing their ancestral heirlooms—
Bright treasures, battle-gear, sharp swords.
At one time their fathers wielded these weapons
Until bitter sword-swing and shield-play
Led to death and the loss of heirloom treasures.   2040
An old warrior will remember, while drinking beer
With a fierce heart, his ancestor's hilt-ring,
And the slaughter of Heathobards, his close kin,
At the hands of the Danes. His heart is grim.
He unlocks sorrow, unpacks hatred,   2045
Tests the resolve of a fierce young warrior,
Stirs up savage strife with these words:
'I wonder if you recognize your father's sword,
That dear family blade he bore into battle
His last time in armor, when the Danes slew him,   2050
Fierce Scyldings seized the battlefield,
And Withergyld lay dead among Heathobards.

Now some slayer's son sits in our hall,
Drinking our mead, boasting of that battle,
His mouth full of murder, bearing your treasure, 2055
The family honor which you rightly own.'
He rakes up the past with proud, bitter words,
Pricking his conscience over family killing,
Till the time comes when the queen's retainer,
Who is wearing that sword of stolen honor, 2060
Lies sleeping in death-rest, slain by the sword,
Drenched in blood for his father's deeds.
The avenger escapes—he knows his homeland.
Then the oath will be broken, the promise of peace,
And Ingeld's love for his wife will be cooled 2065
By seething sorrow. Some deceit bedevils
The tenuous trust between Heathobard and Dane.
Theirs is not a friendship or a marriage to last.
Only the bond of bitterness will hold true.

But I was speaking of Grendel. You should know, 2070
Great Hrothgar, my giver of treasures,
What became of the hard hand-fight of heroes.
After heaven's gem, the glorious sun,
Had slipped past earth, the night-stalker came,
The savage spirit seeking Hrothgar's hall 2075
And its heap of yet unscathed warriors.
Hondscio was fated to be the first hall-guard
Nearest the door, a monster's dinner.
Grendel was mouth-slayer to that armored thane—
He swallowed the life of that dear man. 2080
But the bone-biter, tooth-slayer, flesh-eater,
Had no intention of leaving the gold-hall
Empty-handed. He paid me a visit
With his fierce hand-grip, a clutch of claws.
He had a pouch like a great glove to put me in— 2085
It was made of devil's craft and dragon skin.
The demon beast exulting in dark deeds
Intended to stuff my flesh and innocence in,
Pile me up with a pack of warriors in his pouch.

He found this impossible when I stood up. 2090
I stopped his stuffing, filled with fury,
Driven by rage. It would take too long
To recount the battle, tell how I repaid
The people's bane, the enemy of mankind.
There with my works I honored the Geats, 2095
And all of our people, my glorious prince.
He slipped away, enjoying his life
For a little while, but he left a gift,
His right hand, a token of the terror
He found in Heorot that horrible night. 2100
The miserable wretch left for his lair,
Sinking to the lake-bottom like a stone.
For that slaughter-rush, the king of the Scyldings
Gave me plated gold, a good reward,
A trust of treasures, when morning came, 2105
And we shared together both talk and table.
There was song and story, a hall rejoicing;
A wise old warrior unlocked his word-hoard,
Sometimes singing with hands on harp-wood
Songs of truth and sorrow, sometimes shaping 2110
Strange stories. The great-hearted king,
A battle-warrior bound in years, began to recall
The strength of his youth. His heart surged
As his mind reached back over many winters.
We were happy in the hall, sharing pleasures 2115
All day long till the dim night drew down.
Then the slaughter-ghost, the grief-slinger,
Grendel's mother came to the death-hall
Where her son was slain, where the boy-beast
Discovered the battle-grip of the Geats. 2120
That monstrous wife, that horrid hag,
Avenged her son, ate Æschere whole,
A wise counselor—his life departed.
There was no body to burn on the pyre
When morning came, no death-bed fire 2125
To ease his rest. She had borne his body
In her fiendish arms, her evil embrace,

Beneath the brackish mountain streams,
Back home to her lair under a loathly lake.
That was for Hrothgar the greatest of griefs.   2130
He implored me out of loyalty to you
And deep-hearted grief to do a warrior's work,
Risking life and limb in the tumult of waves,
To finish the feud and find glory.
He promised the Geats a great reward.   2135
I swam to the slaughter—that's widely known—
Discovered the cave-guard under deep waters.
We locked arms—the lake boiled with blood.
In the grim hall of Grendel's mother,
I severed her head with a great sword.   2140
I barely managed to escape with my life,
But fate was with me. The lord of the Danes
Gave me many rewards, magnificent treasures.
So King Hrothgar kept proper customs,
Held nothing back in the way of riches.   2145
The son of Healfdene opened his hoard,
Gave me treasures of my own choosing,
A generous meed for my fierce might.
I offer them to you, my warrior-king;
I count on your kindness—I've few kinsmen left."   2150
Then Beowulf ordered his rewards brought in—
A war-standard with a boar's head,
A battle-helmet with a beautiful, high crest,
A gray iron mail-coat, a great battle-sword.
He also offered this gift of words: 2155
"Hrothgar gave me this battle-gear—
The wise king counseled me to convey to you
Both treasure and story, to recall their history.
He said that Heorogar, his elder brother
Who was king before Hrothgar, held this armor,   2160
Treasured it so highly that he firmly refused
To give it up to his own son Heoroweard,
Though he was loyal and loved. Use it well."
I've heard there were four horses,
Swift and similar, apple-fallow,   2165

Brought in next. Beowulf gave his gifts,
Steeds and goods, to his beloved king,
As a kinsman should do—not weave a web
Of greed and malice, craft and cunning,
A gift of death to comrades and king.   2170
Hygelac's nephew was loyal to him;
In hard battles each helped the other.
I've heard that he gave the neck-ring to Hygd,
The gold-wrought treasure from Queen Wealhtheow.
He gave the king's daughter three fine horses,   2175
Supple and saddle-bright. Hygd wore the necklace,
A gift of gold, gleaming on her breast.
Beowulf was brave in battle, honorable to all—
His glory was woven of good deeds.
He killed no kinsmen, no hearth-companions   2180
In feuds or drunken fits. His heart was fierce
But not savage—his strength was God's gift,
The greatest of mankind. He was slow to start,
So the Geats never thought him great as a boy,
Nor would the lord honor him with gifts   2185
In the meadhall. He seemed unstrong.
No one knew how to take his measure.
But the Geats were wrong—his time came.
Fate often turns, offers the unexpected—
He found fame and glory after an unsung youth.   2190
Then the guardian of earls, Hygelac the king,
Ordered in the heirloom of Hrethel his father,
A glorious sword adorned with gold.
No blade was more treasured among the Geats.
He laid the sword in Beowulf's lap   2195
And gave him also a grant of land,
Seven thousand hides' worth, a hall and throne.
Each had inherited his land by birth,
But the king's was greater by royal right.

Time passed. In the strife-filled days   2200
Of the Swedish wars when King Hygelac
Lay dead and the Geats lost many lives

In battle-clashes, when the savage Swedes,
Those terrible warriors, hunted down Heardred,
Hygelac's son, Hereric's nephew, 2205
And slew him bitterly behind the shield-guard,
Then the kingdom passed into Beowulf's hands.
He ruled wisely for fifty winters,
An old warrior, a respected king—
Until a dragon came in dark terror, 2210
A savage worm who ruled the nights,
Who sat on treasure in a steep stone-barrow.
There was a hidden path under his cave,
An entry-burrow unknown to men,
But a certain slave stole quietly in, 2215
Crept up to the worm-hoard, seized a cup,
Glazed with gold. It gained him nothing
But the dragon's rage, the worm's wrath.
His shrewd stealing caught the serpent
Unaware, unready—but neighbors would know 2220
His dread revenge, his swollen rage.
Not for himself did he disturb the dragon,
Not for his own gain. This desperate slave
Robbed the dragon because he was homeless,
Outlawed from men, fleeing their feuds, 2225
The judgment of their swords, guilty of sin.
When the unwelcome guest gazed at the hoard,
He saw bright terror, a sleeping dragon.
He stole the cup, taking quick advantage
Of the worm's rest. The cave was filled, 2230
The old earth-house, with twisted treasures,
Ancestral gold, ancient heirlooms,
Hidden by the last of a lost race,
The sole survivor of a fallen tribe.
Death took them all in the embrace of time, 2235
Except for one, the last guardian
Who mourned his people, remained waking
For a stretch of years, walked alone,
Expecting to enjoy the hall-gifts
By himself in his last brief days. 2240

A barrow stood ready, an old earth-hall,
On the high headland near the surging sea,
Secure because of its secret entrances.
The ring-guardian bore the hoard to the barrow,
Placed the ancient gold and gems   2245
Back in the ground, speaking these words:
"Hold now, earth, what heroes cannot,
The treasures of men, the gifts they took
From your mines and quarries. Battle-death
Has drawn them down. Savage strife,   2250
The terror of time, and endless evil
Have seized all my people who knew the hall-joys,
Claiming their lives. I've no one left
To carry the sword or polish the cup—
The tribe is gone. The hard helmet,   2255
Plated with gold, has lost its edge,
Stripped of its skin. The polishers sleep
Who could make it shine, the bright war-mask.
The mail-coat that endured blade-bites
Over the crash of shields decays like its wearer.   2260
The corselet cannot ride to war with its rings,
Cannot sing its battle-song. No longer the harp-joy,
The song of the wood, no longer the good hawk
Swinging through the hall, no longer the swift horse
Striking the court-stones. Savage death   2265
Has sent forth the races of men on a dread road."
Sad in spirit, the survivor mourned,
Moved like a lone wraith down life's road,
Keening day and night until death's hunger
Devoured his heart.
                        Then the night-demon,
The old dragon, discovered the hoard-joy   2270
Unguarded, unprotected, a worm's want.
The serpent stole in, the furious flamer
Who seeks barrows, the naked slayer
Who flies by night, sheathed in fire.
Earth-dwellers desperately dread this dragon,   2275
Who guards heathen gold in earth for eons.

His unused gifts bring him no good.
So the enemy of men, heirloom-crafty,
Guarded the hoard for three hundred winters,
Gold in the ground, until one angered him,   2280
Enraging his heart. The thief carried
The cup to his lord, garnished with gold,
Encrusted with gems. He asked his owner
For a peace-promise to heal their feud.
The hoard had been raided, its riches drained   2285
By a precious cup. His lord relented,
Seeing the heirloom for the first time
With longing eyes. The worm had awakened—
Strife was renewed. He sniffed along stones,
Sensing the man-spoor, his enemy's tracks.   2290
The thief had crept too near the dragon—
Yet an undoomed man may survive exile
And suffering with good fate and God's grace.
The hoard-guard sought eagerly along the ground
To greet the thief who had caught him napping,   2295
Harmed his sleep. Fierce and flaming,
The savage worm searched near the barrow—
No one skulked in that barren wasteland.
On the scent of battle, he was keen for killing.
Sometimes he crawled back in the barrow,   2300
Searching for the cup. The dragon discovered
That a man had disturbed his beautiful treasure.
He waited with hot patience until evening,
A barrow-guard swollen with fury.
He would trade death-fire for the drinking cup,   2305
The taste of rage. The daylight dropped down
As the worm wanted—he would not wait long
Near the cave-wall but would soar in the air
With savage fire. The onset was ominous
To Geats on the ground; the end would be agony   2310
To their treasure-giver, their beloved lord.

Then the earth-guest began to vomit fire,
Scorching bright halls. The blaze spread

Like a burning light, a terror to men.
The spitfire left nothing living, 2315
Nothing quick among the dead. The worm's rage
Was alive in the dark, his cruel killing,
His slaughter-flames, both near and far,
His feud of fire with the neighboring Geats.
Then he fled to his cave-hall—secret, secure— 2320
Hiding at dawn. He had circled and slain,
Sheathing houses and men in a glaze of flame.
He trusted his cave and his courage, his barrow
And battle-rage, but he was sorely deceived.
He holed up under stone. Then the terror was told 2325
To Beowulf, the grim truth made known,
That the flames had feasted on his own hall,
Devoured his home, the best of buildings,
The gift-throne of Geats. His heart burned
With rage and regret, the greatest of sorrows. 2330
The wise king feared he'd offended God,
Maddened his Maker by breaking old laws.
His heart was hot with some dark thought,
Some quiet despair—strange and unsettling.
The fire-worm had ravaged his ancient hall, 2335
The heart of his people on the sea's headland.
For that crime, the war-king devised a wrack
Of misery for him—he would waste the worm.
He ordered a battle-shield made of iron,
Knowing wood was worthless against dragon-flame. 2340
The old king was coming to the end of his days,
His last loan of life, just as the worm
Was fated to die, though he grasped at gold,
Held desperately to goods, as dragons will do.

The prince of rings proudly scorned 2345
To meet the dragon with his full troops,
Disdaining aid. The king feared no conflict
With a cave-dragon, thought no worm's courage,
Strength, or savvy worth worrying about,
Because he had survived battle-crash and fury, 2350

Sustaining great victories in Hygelac's army
Many times after crushing Grendel's hand-grip
And purging Heorot of his savage kin.
That was not the smallest of combats
When Hygelac was slain, lord of his people, 2355
Greatest of Geats, son of Hrethel—
He died of sword-drinks, slain by blades
Thirsty for blood, at the hands of the Frisians
In the battle-rush. Beowulf escaped the slaughter
Because of his swimming strength in the sea; 2360
He carried in his arms the precious armor
Of thirty warriors while he rode the waves.
The Frisians and Franks who bore war-shields
Had no need to boast of their battle with Beowulf—
Few came back from that grim meeting. 2365
The son of Ecgtheow swam home to his people,
Sad and alone, a wanderer on the waves.
There Queen Hygd offered him the kingdom,
Trust and treasures, gift-throne and gold.
She knew her young son could not sustain 2370
The Geatish kingdom against its enemies
Or hold the throne now that Hygelac was dead.
But the Queen and the counselors could not convince
Beowulf to take the kingdom from its rightful heir,
Heardred, son of Hygelac and Hygd— 2375
He valued honor and friendship, not pride and power.
Beowulf served Heardred with wise counsel
Until the boy grew into a good Geatish king.
Then Swedish outcasts came over the seas,
Eanmund and Eadgils, sons of Ohthere, 2380
Seeking sanctuary in Heardred's court.
They had rebelled against their uncle,
King Onela, greatest of sea-kings,
A glorious prince and giver of gold.
For Heardred that was a hard stroke— 2385
His sheltering those sons cost him his life
When Onela brought his hard war-troops
To battle the Geats, killing Heardred

For high treason with a righteous blade
And installing Beowulf to rule the Geats
And guard the throne. That was a good king. 2390
But Beowulf remembered Heardred's killing:
In later days he supported the outcast Eadgils,
Making a friend of the man in his misery.
He gave him the gift of warriors and weapons
To sail home to Sweden with an icy heart 2395
To take his vengeance and kill the king.

So Beowulf had survived each of his enemies,
His beastly battles, the family feuds,
The endless strife and slaughter of men,
Until the day he fought the dragon, 2400
Until he waged war with the worm.
Righteous with rage, the lord of the Geats
Sought the serpent with eleven of his warriors.
He knew of the dragon's feud and fury,
Its malice meant for the race of men. 2405
The cup had come to the king from the hand
Of the thief, the thirteenth man in their band,
The sorrow-bound slave who began the feud.
He led them down to the dragon's lair,
Against his will—he walked to the earth-cave, 2410
An old stone barrow near the sea-wall,
Bulging with treasures, ornaments and rings.
The terror-guardian who held the hoard,
Ancient under earth, was bent on battle.
That gold was no man's cheap bargain. 2415
The battle-hard king, gift-lord of Geats,
Sat on the headland, saluting his thanes,
Wishing them luck. His spirit was sad,
His mind restless, his heart ripe for death.
An old man's fate was closing in, 2420
When a grizzled king must seek his soul-hoard,
Separate life from living, body from being.
He had not long to linger in flesh—
His soul was ready to leave the bone-hall.

Beowulf spoke, son of Ecgtheow: 2425
"In youth I endured battle-storm, war-clash,
Many warriors' meetings—I remember them all.
I was only seven when King Hrethel of the Geats,
The guardian and giver of treasure took me in,
Received me gladly from my father's hand,   2430
Fostered me with treasure and feast-hall joy,
Mindful of caring for kith and kin.
I was no less loved than his own three sons,
Herebeald and Hæthcyn, and my dear Hygelac.
For Herebeald the eldest, heir to the throne,   2435
A death-bed was savagely spread by Hæthcyn,
Who killed his brother with his horn-tipped bow,
Shot him dead with an accidental arrow
That missed its mark, a bloody point,
Killing his own kin with a slip of the hand.   2440
That feud could not be fixed with vengeance
Or wergild, grim swordplay or life-gold.
That bloody deed baffled his father's heart—
One son unavenged, the other his slayer.
In the same way it's sad for an old man   2445
To see his son riding the gallows,
A boy on a bitter tree. He sings a song
Of sorrow, seeing his son hanging high,
A hungry raven's ravenous joy,
And he knows of no help for the hanged man,   2450
Wise as he is. Each morning he remembers
That his son is gone—he mourns the dawn.
He has no care for another heir in the hall,
No joy in the next son when his dear first one
Has discovered death. He sees his son's   2455
Empty room, deserted hall, joyless bed,
A home for the winds. The gallows-rider
Sleeps in his grave—no joy of the harp,
No song or storied life for him.
The old man mourns, slips into sorrow's bed,   2460
Rests his grizzled head on a painful pillow,
Thinks everything is empty, hall and homeland.

Likewise the guardian of Geats, King Hrethel,
Bore heart-sorrow for his own son Herebeald.
He could not find vengeance or settle the feud   2465
With his younger son, his brother's life-slayer.
He had no revenge, no remedy for murder.
He couldn't kill his own unloved son.
That sorrow was too great—he gave up his life,
Left the joys of men and chose God's light.   2470
To his sons he rightly left hall and land,
His kingdom a gift to his living kin.

Then there was grim savagery and strife
Between Swedes and Geats over the seas.
When Hrethel died, old feuds flared up.   2475
The sons of Ongentheow, Onela and Ohthere,
Were battle-hungry; they attacked at Hreosnabeorh,
Brought slaughter not friendship to the Geats.
We pursued the Swedes at great price
As Hæthcyn our king was killed in battle,   2480
But the next morning his brother Hygelac
And all of our warriors avenged that crime.
When Ongentheow attacked Eofor the Geat,
The boar-warrior answered back with his blade,
The revenge of kinship on a cold morning—   2485
The Swede dropped down from the sword's swath,
His war-helmet split. Eofor's hand withheld nothing
From the sword's fury, spared no strength
In the death-swing. He remembered that feud.
I've repaid Hygelac for his trust and treasure   2490
With my bright blade, my loyal sword.
I gave him my battle-strength for those gifts.
He granted me land, both hearth and home.
He never had reason to hire mercenaries,
To seek with gifts among Swedes, Danes,   2495
Or East-Germanic tribes for a weaker warrior.
I was always his leader on the front line,
Greeting his enemies, guarding his life.
While my sword and strength endure, I'll always

Protect my people in the crush of battle, 2500
As I did slaying Dæghrefn, champion of the Franks
With my bare hands. He brought no booty home,
No bright neck-ring back from the battle,
But fell with his standard, a proud prince.
My blade was no slayer—I crushed and killed him 2505
With my hard hand-grip, broke his bone-house,
Opened his heart. Now must sword-edge,
Hard hand and blade, again seek battle,
Bringing the gift of a fist to the dragon's hoard."
The prince proclaimed his battle-boast, 2510
His last promise to the Geatish people:
"In my youth I have fought many battles,
Surviving by strength. In my old age
I will slay this serpent, seek out glory,
If the worm will come out of his earth-hall." 2515
Then he turned to his dear companions,
Bold shield-warriors and helmet-wearers,
Spoke for the last time to his own troops:
"I would not bear my sword against the serpent,
Wield a weapon against the awesome worm, 2520
But will meet the dragon as I greeted Grendel,
Alone with my arm-strength, my death-grip—
But who knows how to grab a dragon
Or fend off fire with his bare hands?
Here I expect bitter breath, spit-flame, 2525
Deadly venom, so I must wear a mail-coat,
Carry an iron shield. I will not back off
One foot from the barrow, but trust to the Lord
Of fates among men. I will forego boasting
And beat old battle-wing. Wait here at the barrow-door, 2530
Protected by armor, to see which of us survives
The slaughter-rush, weathers his wounds.
This is not your battle—I'm the only warrior
Who can test his strength, share this strife,
Do manly deeds against this death-dragon. 2535
With courage I will kill the evil worm,
Gather his gold and ancient heirlooms,

Take his life, or his hatred will haul me down—
That life-bane breaking your lord's bones."

Then he rose up, hard under helmet,   2540
With battle-coat and shield, went to the worm
Under the stone walls, in no way a coward.
There by the cave-wall, the man who had conquered
Many monsters, coming through battle-clashes
With his great heart and warlike will,   2545
Saw a stone arch standing with bitter steam
Bursting out of the barrow. What he saw
Was a stream of fire, a blaze of hatred
Like burning bile—he could not reach the heart
Of the hoard, unscathed by dragon-fire.   2550
Then the king of the Geats, swollen with fury,
Sounded a challenge with fierce words,
Daring the dragon—his war-cry resounding
Under gray stone. Hate was renewed—
The hoard-guard recognized in a man's cry   2555
The voice of vengeance. That was no peace-promise.
First came a fierce breath out of the cave—
The serpent's fire shot out from the stone,
A raging steam. The earth screeched.
The lord of the Geats, bold man in the barrow,   2560
Swung his shield against that fiery terror,
That alien awe. The coiled creature
Heaved its hot heart into the battle.
Beowulf brandished his sharp sword,
An ancient heirloom, an undull blade.   2565
Each killer saw cold terror in the other.
The strong-hearted man stood with his shield
And war-corselet while the serpent coiled
In flaming fury. The cave-snake
Came gliding, a fire-worm toward its fate.   2570
The shield protected Beowulf's life
For a short time, but less than he needed,
And he feared there for the first time
Since wielding weapons—uncertain, unsure

If fate would offer him a share of glory.   2575
The lord of the Geats raised his hand,
Slashed with his sword through scales and skin—
The blade bit bone, the edge broke,
The cut less keen than the king needed.
After that savage stroke, the serpent fumed.   2580
The barrow-guard's heart was kindled for killing—
He spit forth fire. The battle-flames flew—
Fire leapt in air. The gold-friend of the Geats
Could claim no victory. The bare blade failed.
That was no easy journey to give up ground,   2585
To find a home in another place, no painless road
For brave-hearted Beowulf, son of Ecgtheow.
So each man must travel when his days are spent,
Winding a long road beyond walking,
Learning the hard way that his life is lent.   2590

Not long after, the fierce fighters,
Awesome creatures, clashed again.
The hoard-guard took heart—his breast heaved,
His breath steaming. The guardian of Geats
Was sheathed in fire, engulfed in pain.   2595
His noble companions did not keep courage—
They crept from the cave, fled to the wood,
Deserting their prince, protecting their lives.
Only one stayed—his heart was true,
Surging with sorrow. Nothing can undermine   2600
The claim of kinship in a moral man.
Only Wiglaf stayed, son of Weohstan,
A worthy shield-warrior and beloved retainer,
A proud prince who came from the Swedes,
From the Wægmunding tribe, Beowulf's clan.   2605
He saw his lord sweltering under his helmet,
Tormented by fire, and remembered the rights
And rich homestead given to his father by the Geats.
He could not hold back, but seized his shield,
The yellow linden-wood, unsheathed his sword,   2610
An ancient heirloom, the death-gift of Eanmund,

Son of Ohthere, when Wiglaf's father Weohstan
Was Eanmund's slayer with his deadly blade,
His bane in battle. The sword changed hands,
And Weohstan was a wanderer, exile and outcast—   2615
He killed his kin. He took the spoils
To Eanmund's uncle, the fierce Onela—
The burnished helmet, ring-bound corselet,
And ancient sword crafted by giants.
Onela gave the booty back to Weohstan,   2620
As gifts for vengeance. There was no feud
For killing his nephew—he condoned that crime.
Weohstan passed the sword and corselet on to Wiglaf
So his son could do great deeds like his father.
They lived with the Geats; then Weohstan died.   2625
This worm-strife was young Wiglaf's first battle
Beside his lord. His heart did not melt—
He kept courage. The sword of his kin
Was undaunted, as the dragon would discover!

Wiglaf reflected, said the right words   2630
To the Geats who'd fled, his heart sad:
"I remember well when we all drank mead
In the beer-hall, promising Beowulf,
Our beloved lord, who gave us arm-rings,
That we would honor his gifts of armor,   2635
Helmets and hard swords, if his need came.
We were hand-chosen from his host of troops
To follow him into battle. He believed in us,
Thought us battle-worthy, bound to glory.
He gave me treasures, tokens of his trust.   2640
He counted on us to be good spear-warriors,
Bold helmet-bearers, the best of Geats,
Even though our lord intended as leader
To meet that creature alone with his courage
Because he's achieved such daring glory,   2645
Such audacious fame. Now the day has come
When our lord needs the might of warriors,
The strength of arms. Let's help our battle-hero

Through this heat, this grim terror.
God knows I would welcome the flame's embrace   2650
To battle beside Beowulf in the fiery flesh.
It seems dead wrong for retainers to flee,
Bearing shields back home before we feel
The fearful flame or strike down our foe,
Defending the life of the lord of the Geats.   2655
It would not be fair with all his proud deeds
For Beowulf to fall alone, undefended—
To endure terror and treachery together.
We should all enter this shared strife
With sword, helmet, corselet, war-clothes."   2660
Then he braved the fire, wading through smoke
To support his lord, hailing his king:
"Brave and beloved Beowulf, battle well!
Remember your vow since the days of your youth:
You would never let your glory fade,   2665
Your name go unremembered. Now, noble warrior,
You must trust to your strength to save your life.
Keep up your courage—I am coming to help you."

After these words the worm grew fierce,
An alien evil, blazing in rage—   2670
The serpent came seeking his human foe,
Sheathed in flame, a fiery bane—
He hated mankind. The flame surged out,
The shield burned down to its metal boss,
And the mail-coat did not serve well—   2675
So the young warrior ducked down,
Sought the protection of his kinsman's shield,
An iron shelter. Beowulf the battle-king,
Mindful of glory, striking with strength,
Drove his blade with a righteous rage,   2680
Thrust his sword into the dragon's head,
Stuck his skull. The ancient iron,
Whose name was Nægling, broke at the bone—
An aging blade that failed in the fight.
The iron edge was not fated to save Beowulf   2685

In this burning battle. I've heard his hand
Was always too strong—it strained his sword.
That blood-tempered blade was not much help.
Then the scourge of mankind, the dread dragon,
Attacked for the third time, flaming in feud,   2690
Blazing with bile. He seized Beowulf's
Neck with his claws, struck with his fangs,
Death-biting bones. Beowulf's blood surged
From his open wounds like waves of gore.
Then, as I've heard, at the Geatish king's need,   2695
Wiglaf showed strength and skill beside him,
A keenness of courage natural to him.
He took no heed of the dragon's blazing head—
His hand burned when he helped his kinsman.
The mail-coated warrior struck lower down   2700
In the dragon's belly, the demon's bulge,
Shoved in his sword with its serpentine blade,
So the fire subsided. The dying king,
Conscious again, drew out his battle-knife,
Deadly and dangerous, that he kept on his corselet—   2705
The guardian of Geats sliced open the worm's belly.
Their courage and kinship destroyed the dragon—
Comrades together, noble warriors in need.
So men should share strife, keep camaraderie,
Honor their kin. That was bold Beowulf's   2710
Last victory, the end of his life's work.
Then the deep wound that the dragon made
With its fierce fangs began to swell and burn.
Beowulf found a bitter evil festering in his breast,
A poison licking at his heart. Then the prince sat   2715
By the stone wall at the edge of the barrow.
He gazed at the old work of giants,
Saw how the ancient earth-hall was held up
By pillars of stone. Then his peerless thane
With his own hands washed him with water—   2720
Wiglaf tended his battle-weary lord,
His blood-stained leader, lending him comfort.
Tenderly he took off his helmet.

Then a dying Beowulf began to speak
In spite of his wounds. He knew deep down   2725
His life-days were done, his joys on loan.
Death was drawing inexorably near:
"Now I would give my good battle-clothes,
Sword and armor, to my heir and son,
Flesh of my flesh, if only I had one.   2730
I've ruled the Geats well for fifty winters.
None of the neighboring people's kings
Dared to greet me with battle-song,
Sword-shouts, or the slash of war.
None of them touched me with terror.   2735
I've held my own, endured my fate,
My allotted time, a treasure of years,
Sought no feuds, sworn no devious oaths.
Now sick with life-wounds, I celebrate this—
My times of joy, my treasure of memories.   2740
The Ruler of men will not blame me
For the murder of kinsmen, the misery of feud,
When life leaves my body. Go quickly,
Wiglaf my friend and battle-companion,
To seek the hoard under the gray stone,   2745
Now that the dragon sleeps, the unwaking worm,
Deprived of his treasure. I want to see
The ancient wealth, the gifts of gold,
The beautiful gems, skillfully wrought.
I want to see what the worm has guarded,   2750
The gifts in the ground, so I can leave life,
Knowing the treasures I've left behind
To a land and nation I've long ruled."

I've heard that Wiglaf, son of Weohstan,
Obeyed his battle-wounded lord,   2755
Went into the barrow, wearing ring-mail,
Walked by a stone seat, saw gems and jewels,
Gold on the ground, rich wall-hangings,
In the dragon's den. In the night-flier's cave,
Ancient cups stood, unused for eons,   2760

Without their polishers, bereft of gems.
Wiglaf saw hundreds of helmets
Gnawed by rust, people's arm-rings
From tribes gone by, once artfully adorned.
Gifts in a barrow, gold in the ground,   2765
Will easily overcome or eventually outlast
Any man—no matter who hides it!
Wiglaf also saw a strange gold standard,
Hanging high in the hoard, a hand-work
Delicately woven. Out of its unearthly web,   2770
A light shone so he could see the treasures
Of wall and floor. No sign of the worm,
Of the serpent, could be seen. The keen blade
Of two warriors had taken him. Then I've heard
That Wiglaf alone plundered the hoard,   2775
The old work of giants, robbed the barrow
Of cups and plates, gems and jewels,
And the old standard, brightest of banners.
His old lord's blade with its stout iron edge
Had already wounded the guardian of the hoard,   2780
The treasure-terror and flame-breather,
The dragon who blazed in the dead of night,
Till his life was cooled by sword-cuts.
Wiglaf hurried, eager to return
With his glittering treasure, anxious to know   2785
Whether his brave lord would still be alive
Where he left him, his life-blood fading.
He carried the treasure to his glorious king,
His dear lord whose life was draining,
His body-wounds leaking blood.   2790
Wiglaf once again wiped his lord's face,
Sprinkling water on him till his words
And spirit revived from a deep source,
Welling up through his breast-hoard.
Beowulf spoke, wrapped in grief,   2795
Gazing at the gold: "I thank God,
The King of Glory, the Ruler of all,
For this ancient treasure, this trust of gold

I gaze on here, a gift to my people,
As I leave life, departing on death's road.   2800
I have bought this hoard with my elder days
To sustain our people. Lead them now—
I can't hold out. Command the brave Geats
To build a bright barrow after my funeral fire
On the high sea-cliff of Hronesness   2805
As a reminder to my people, so that seafarers
Will guide their ships by what they call
Beowulf's Barrow through dark waters."
He took off his collar, the gold neck-ring
And gave it to Wiglaf, the young spear-warrior—   2810
Also his mail-coat, gold-plated helmet,
And a gift of rings, telling him to use them well:
"You are the last remnant of our race,
Wiglaf of the Wægmundings. Fate has swept away
All of our kinsmen, earls and their courage,   2815
Warriors and their sword-wielding strength.
They have braved a way that I must follow."
These were the old warrior's last words,
A gift from his heart's hoard before he climbed
The funeral pyre to embrace the fierce flames.   2820
Out of his breast the soul flew seeking
A righteous doom, the judgment of the just.
Then young Wiglaf sorrowed to see him suffer
In his last moments, the man he loved most,
Who lay by his slayer, the evil earth-dragon,   2825
In unwaking sleep. No longer could the coiled worm
Guard the ring-hoard, rule his treasure.
The flame-forged, battle-notched sword,
Hammered by smiths, had stolen his life.
The bitter serpent, the wide-flying worm,   2830
Stilled by his wounds, had fallen by the barrow,
Tucked beside Beowulf and the ancient treasure.
He could no longer glide through the dead of night,
Alone in his arrogance, pleased with his blaze,
Proud of his treasure. He'd dropped down to earth   2835
Through Beowulf's heart and hand-work.

I've heard that hardly anyone on earth,
No matter how strong or daring of deeds,
Could disturb the ring-hoard with his hands
Or run through the worm's bitter, blazing breath,   2840
If he found the barrow-guard awake and watching.
Beowulf bought the hoard with his life.
Each of them traveled on a treasured road,
Awesome at the end of their loan-days.

It wasn't long before the ten battle-slackers,   2845
Weak-willed traitors, left the woods.
They dared not bring their spears to battle
When their liege-lord needed them most.
Now they bore their shields to the barrow,
Ashamed and late, their armor to where   2850
Their old king lay. They looked at Wiglaf,
A weary foot-soldier bent by his lord,
Washing him with water, trying to rouse him
Without success. The gesture was fruitless,
Though he wished dearly to wake his warlord,   2855
Preserve his prince's life on this earth.
He could not alter the flow of his fate,
The judgment of God, whose doom rules all deeds,
Both then and now, never alters, never ebbs.
Then young Wiglaf gave a grim response   2860
To the cowardly Geats who'd lost their courage.
Wiglaf, son of Weohstan, looked at the unloved ones,
Spoke these dark words, sad in his heart:
"A man who speaks the truth may well say
That your liege-lord who gave you gifts of trust   2865
Like the war-gear you're wearing as you stand here,
When he handed out gifts to hall-thanes
Drinking at mead-benches—helmets and mail-coats,
The finest of treasures far and near—
That lord threw away his war-trappings and trust,   2870
For they proved useless when the battle broke out,
And the great worm wanted to take his life.
The people's king had no need to boast

Of the good courage of such battle-companions.
Yet the Ruler of victories shaped the strife   2875
So that Beowulf alone might slay the worm,
Destroy the dragon, wield vengeance with a sword
In his time of need. I had little power to protect him
But was able to help beyond my means.
The deadly dragon grew steadily weaker   2880
After I struck him with my sword. The fierce fire
That flamed from his head died down.
No crowd of defenders came to the king's aid
In his darkest hour. Now your inheritance
Of ancient treasure and homeland joy,   2885
The giving of swords, receiving of rings—
Your future has fled with your lost courage.
You and your kin must lose your land rights
When neighboring nobles hear of your flight.
Your hall-joy is gone—your glory is buried.   2890
Death is better for you than a life of shame."

Then Wiglaf commanded the battle-outcome
Proclaimed in the camp over the sea-cliffs
To the band of sad-hearted shield-warriors
Who'd waited the long morning to discover   2895
If their dear lord was alive or dead.
The messenger galloped off with harrowing news,
Held back nothing from the people's hearing:
"Now the joy-giver and hall-guardian,
The lord of the Geats, sleeps in his death-bed,   2900
With a blanket of slaughter wrought by the worm,
The ancient serpent who lies beside him,
The dragon struck down by his deadly dagger.
His sword could not slice through worm-scales.
Wiglaf son of Weohstan sits beside Beowulf,   2905
The living warrior keeping his heart-weary
Watch over the dead, keening for his lost lord,
Guarding them both—the loved and the loathed.
Now the Geats are in for a terrible time,
The sure threat of war from the Franks and Frisians,   2910

When the neighboring nations hear the news
Of Beowulf's death, the fall of the king.
The old strife between us is no great secret.
Our feud with them began when Hygelac
Sailed to their shores with a seafaring army,   2915
Where the enemy assailed him, attacked quickly
With a stronger force, made the man of the Geats
Bow down in his mail-coat, clutching the ground.
That king gave no more gifts in the hall,
Trust and treasure to his loyal retainers.   2920
The King of the Franks was never our friend.
And let's not expect any peace from the Swedes,
Any keeping of promises from old enemies.
Everyone knows how Ongentheow their king
Robbed Hæthcyn of his life near Hrefnawudu,   2925
The son of Hrethel, when the Geats in their pride,
Their battle-arrogance, attacked the Swedes.
Ohthere's father, Ongentheow the king,
Old but terrible, fiercely struck back,
Killing Hæthcyn, the sea-raiders' king,   2930
Rescuing his wife whom the Geat had seized,
The old queen bereft of her family gold,
Mother of Onela and Ohthere, her sons.
Ongentheow followed his deadly foes
Who fled leaderless to the refuge of Hrefnawudu.   2935
The Swedes laid siege to the war-weary Geats,
The remnant of the sword-fight, threatening them
Throughout the night with savage vows,
Saying they intended to slice them with swords,
Greet them with slaughter when morning came,   2940
Hang them on gallows for the ravens to eat,
A breakfast for birds. Relief for the grieving
Came at dawn when the Geats gratefully heard
Hygelac's horn trumpeting that help was coming,
The sign of an army advancing on the road.   2945
The Swedes and Geats left a trail of blood
In that rush to slaughter. Everyone saw
The tracks of blood, stoking the feud.

Ongentheow the brave began to back off,
Weary with his kinsmen, to his own stronghold.   2950
He had heard the horn sound a warrior's warning,
Knew the power of the proud Geatish prince,
His strength and savvy in waging war.
He doubted his weary troops could resist
The new onslaught of savage sea-warriors   2955
And worried for the safety of his wife and sons,
So he pulled his war-troops back to a shelter,
An old king holing up behind an earth-wall.
The Geats gave pursuit, dogging the heels
Of the Swedes, overrunning the camp,   2960
Raising the standard of Hygelac over the field.
Then the grizzled Ongentheow was laid low
By the sword of Eofor, son of Wonred,
After being wounded by Wulf, Eofor's brother,
Who struck him first with his hard sword   2965
So that blood-streams surged from his head,
From under his hair. The old Swede was not afraid,
But paid Wulf back with a harder battle-blow,
When the king gave Wulf his sword's greeting.
Wulf, son of Wonred, daring destruction,   2970
Could not answer Ongentheow with a counter-blow
Because the king had cut through his helmet,
Hacking his head. He was streaming with blood
And had to lie down. He fell on the earth.
He was not doomed to die but fated to recover   2975
From the Swedish wound. When Wulf swooned,
His brother Eofor, Hygelac's thane,
Lifted his broad sword, an old blade of giants,
Slashing the helmet of the giant Ongentheow
Across the shield-wall. The king fell,   2980
Guardian of the Swedes, his life severed.
Then many of the Geats gathered Wulf up
When fate turned the battle in their favor
With a slaughter of Swedes and a field of corpses.
Eofor then plundered Ongentheow's body,   2985
Stripping the king of his war-corselet,

Hard-hilted sword, and huge helmet.
He brought that war-gear back to Hygelac.
The Geatish king accepted his trust and treasure,
Promising him rich rewards among the warriors.   2990
The lord of the Geats, the son of Hrethel,
Gave Wulf and Eofor, when they came home,
Untold treasures for their battle-prowess—
A hundred thousand in land and rings,
In gifts and gold. No man on middle-earth   2995
Could fault the rewards that the brothers reaped
For their battle-deeds. And the king gave Eofor
His only daughter as a marriage-pledge,
A peace-weaver to grace his home.
That's the history of hatred and hostility,   3000
Of savagery and feud, between Swedes and Geats,
That will spur their shield-warriors to seek us out,
Once they learn that our lord is lifeless,
Who guarded our kingdom, land, and treasure
Against all enemies, keeping us safe   3005
As a hero should, protecting his people.
Now we must hasten to see our king,
Bring back the ruler who gave us rings,
Tokens of trust, carry our lord
To his resting place on the funeral pyre.   3010
Let's not begrudge him gold, offer only
Some small share to melt with the brave man,
For we have here a dragon's hoard,
An untold treasure, dearly bought,
Grimly paid for with our lord's life.   3015
The fire shall devour this gold, these rings,
A web of flame embrace the giver.
No man may wear these rings in remembrance—
No woman can wrap her neck in this collar,
These links of gold. Sad-hearted, the Geats   3020
Must now wander new worlds,
Stripped of inheritance in strange countries,
Now that their leader has laid down laughter.
Now our hands must wake to morning spears

And battle-beasts, not sweet harp music. 3025
The dark raven shall sing its feasting song,
Tell the ravenous eagle how men tasted,
When he and the hungry wolf plundered corpses."

So the messenger brought back dire news,
A hateful speech. He didn't hold back 3030
About their past or future. Tearfully the troop
Of cowards rose up, walked without hope
To Earnaness, the high headland,
Where they gazed in wonder on the strange sight.
They saw on the sand their lifeless lord, 3035
A gift-giver lying in endless bed-rest.
That was the last day of Beowulf their lord,
Battle-warrior, king of the Geats.
His death was awesome, uncanny.
What was stranger was the serpent with him, 3040
The worm at his side, a loathsome mate.
The grim fire-dragon was glazed by flame,
Coated in colors, fifty feet long.
Sometimes he'd soared in the joyful wind,
Sometimes dived down to his secret lair, 3045
The last of his earth-caves where he met death.
Beside him lay piles of cups and pitchers,
Swords and dishes, gnawed by rust,
As if blighted by a thousand years
In the earth's embrace. The ancient treasure, 3050
Heritage of the hoard, was sheathed in a spell—
So that no man might enter the ring-hall,
Touch the treasure through time,
Except through God's gift, the King of victories,
Who is man's protector. Only He could choose 3055
The man who could open the hoard at last.
It's clear that the one who unrightly hid
The glittering treasure, rings and riches,
Gold in the ground, got nothing from it.
The scaly hoard-guardian slew the warrior, 3060
The rarest of heroes who avenged that feud.

No one knows how or where or when
A glorious warrior will meet his end,
No longer dwell in the meadhall with his kin.
So it was with Beowulf when he sought strife   3065
And the barrow-guard, not knowing
He was lifting his sword on his last day.
The great princes who first buried the hoard
Laid on that treasure a timeless curse
That any man who dug it up before doomsday   3070
Would be guilty of sin, chained in hell,
Tormented by demons at their heathen shrines,
Unless he saw more readily than before,
The grace of the owner's charmed gift—
Gazed at the giving instead of the gold.   3075
Wiglaf spoke, son of Weohstan:
"Often many must suffer for the will of one,
As we do now. Nothing we said
Could persuade our prince, defender of our kingdom,
Not to seek the dragon, the guardian of gold,   3080
But to let him live, lie where he was,
In his old barrow till the end of time.
He held to his high destiny with the dragon.
The hoard is here, grimly gained.
The fierce fate that drew our king here   3085
Against our counsel was too strong.
I've been in the barrow, seen the serpent's
Beautiful gems under the earth-wall,
When the way was opened uneasily to me.
I seized as much as a man could carry   3090
Of that burden of gold in my hands and arms,
Bore them beyond the cave to my king,
Who was still alive, conscious and alert.
He spoke out of sorrow, out of old age,
Asked me to greet you. The king commanded us   3095
To build a high barrow in the place of his pyre,
To honor our hero and his glorious deeds—
A grand monument like the man himself.
He was the most worthy of men in this world

As long as he lived in the wealth of hall-joy. 3100
Let's go see the treasure again, the serpent's hoard
Of gold and gems, jewels and heirlooms,
In the heart of the cave. I'll lead the way
So you can see the precious rings and stones,
Bright trappings and broad gold. 3105
Let Beowulf's bier be quickly built,
So when we come out, we can carry our king,
Our beloved prince to a place of peace
Where he can rest in the protection of the Lord."
Then the brave warrior, Weohstan's son, 3110
Ordered warriors to announce the message
That powerful men, leaders and land-owners,
Should bring firewood from far forests
For Beowulf's pyre. Wiglaf spoke:
"Now darkening flames must devour the prince 3115
Of warriors who long withstood war-storm,
Iron-rain, the sharp wind of arrows shot
Over shield-walls, driven by bow-strings,
When shaft served barb, death-feathers whistling."

Then Wiglaf, wise son of Weohstan, 3120
Summoned seven warriors from the troop,
Collected the best to enter the cave,
Under the earth-wall, the evil roof,
Following the torch-bearer to the treasure.
No lots needed to be drawn to loot the hoard— 3125
They all rushed to plunder the treasure-cave
When they saw it unguarded, unused,
Wasting away. No man mourned
The loss of that treasure. They plundered the hoard
And pushed the dragon over the sea-wall, 3130
Plunging the worm to a watery grave,
So the sea could embrace the body of the serpent,
The fiery dragon in the clutch of waves.
They loaded the twisted gold on their wagons,
Untold treasure of every kind, 3135
And bore their king to Hronesness,

The old battle-warrior. The Geats prepared
His funeral pyre, a splendid hoard
Hung with helmets, battle-shields,
Bright mail-coats, as Beowulf had asked.   3140
In the middle they laid their battle-lord,
Lamenting their leader, mourning the man.
There on the barrow they woke the flame,
The greatest of funeral fires, stoking the pyre.
The wood-smoke rose to the sound of wailing   3145
In the curling fire. The blaze was fierce,
Its fury twisted with the sound of keening.
The wind died down—the fire had ravaged
Beowulf's bone-house, hot at the heart.
Sad in spirit, they mourned their prince;   3150
Likewise a lonely old woman of the Geats,
With her hair bound up, wove a sad lament
For her fallen lord, sang often of old feuds
Bound to fester, a fearful strife,
The invasion of enemies, the slaughter of troops,   3155
Slavery and shame. Heaven swallowed the smoke.
Then the Geats built a barrow, broad and high,
On the sea-cliff to be seen by seafarers.
It took ten days to build that beacon,
A hero's monument. The pyre's remains,   3160
The fire's offering of ashes and dust,
They wrapped in walls for the great warrior,
As beautiful as craftsmen knew how to build.
In that best of barrows, the Geats buried
Rings and gems, ornaments and heirlooms,   3165
All they had hauled from the worm's hoard.
They returned to earth its ancient treasure,
The gifts of men now gold in the ground,
Where it still lies useless, unloved, unliving.

Then around Beowulf's barrow twelve   3170
Battle-warriors rode, mourning their prince,
Keening for the king, shaping their praise
For a precious man. They spoke of sorrow,

They sang of courage, of great words and deeds,
Weaving glory with a weft of power.   3175
When a lord's life lifts from its body-home,
It's only fitting to mourn and remember,
To lament and praise. So the Geats recalled
His great heart and lamented his fall,
Keening and claiming that of all the kings,   3180
He was the kindest of men, most generous and just,
Most desiring of praise, most deserving of fame.

OTHER
OLD ENGLISH
POEMS

A NOTE ON GENRES

The shorter Old English poems that follow are grouped by genre, as is common in collections of this sort. The caveat here is that the poems are not identified by either genre or title in the manuscripts. Genres can sometimes be identified by formal motifs such as riddles opening with "I saw a creature" and closing with "Say what I mean," or charms opening with medicinal instructions such as "Boil feverfew and plantain and the red nettle." Other genres can be identified by thematic motifs such as the presence of an elegiac speaker who laments his or her misfortune and attempts find some consolation, or the heroic concern with battlefield loyalty to one's lord.

Poems sometimes show characteristics of different genres. The vellum creature of Riddle 24 laments in elegiac fashion the loss of its life as the hide of a living animal, and the shield and sword creatures of Riddles 3 and 18 detail their heroic battle-field lives. "The Dream of the Rood," an important religious poem, shows formal similarities with the riddles as the cross recalls its own life, as well as an elegiac tone as it laments being torn from its natural family and turned into an instrument of destruction.

A few poems have changed their generic category over time as critics have reinterpreted them. "Wulf and Eadwacer" was once thought to be a riddle because of its paradoxes and enigmatic language, especially its ending, but now is generally classified as an elegy spoken by a woman, similar to "The Wife's Lament." "Deor" has been variously categorized as a heroic poem, an elegy, and a charm.

At the beginning of each generic section, I point out some of the essential characteristics of the genre, but it is important to remember that such generic groups are defined by post-medieval readers and not by the original poets, and that a certain amount of generic cross-over or ambiguity is not uncommon in the poems.

HEROIC OR
HISTORICAL POEMS

The Germanic tribes—Angles, Saxons, and Jutes—who migrated to Britain in the fifth and sixth centuries brought with them a storied code of heroic values, including a profound loyalty to kin and countrymen, a devotion to duty, and a mutual sense of obligation between lord and thanes, including protection and generosity on the part of the lord and service on the part of the thanes. It also incorporated a sharing of war-booty for both economic and symbolic reasons, a desire for honor and glory, and a love of oral poetry, especially that dealing with the history of their people. The Latin historian Tacitus describes the early tradition of loyalty and battlefield courage of the early Germanic tribes:

> On the field of battle it is a disgrace to a chief to be surpassed in courage by his followers, and to the followers not to equal the courage of their chief. And to leave a battle alive after their chief has fallen means lifelong infamy and shame. To defend and protect him, and to let him get the credit for their own acts of heroism, are the most solemn obligations of their allegiance. The chiefs fight for victory, the followers for their chief. (113)

Tacitus may have had his own agenda in such overarching praise, but Alexander notes that "although there is a propaganda element in the account of the Germani, the number of correspondences between the warlike code described there and the code observed in Old English (and other northern) heroic poetry and saga is too great to allow one to dismiss Tacitus as a fictionalist" (55). These heroic values were certainly modified by time and place and the powerful influence of Christianity in Anglo-Saxon England, but they are nostalgically evident in much of Old English heroic poetry, from the vows of battlefield loyalty in "The Battle of Maldon" to the importance of gift-giving in *Beowulf*. (For more on the warrior ethic, see Hill 2000.)

THE BATTLE OF MALDON

"The Battle of Maldon" is a heroic poem that gives poetic treatment to a battle that took place in 991 between Anglo-Saxons and Vikings; it was probably written in the decades after the battle. As the poet relates, the Anglo-Saxons are outmatched from the beginning, even though they hold a strategic advantage on the field. Unfortunately they give up this advantage, either out of over-eagerness or in the name of fair play. The battle is engaged and eventually most of them stand strong in the face of overwhelming odds, even as they die avenging their lord and defending their land.

Though "The Battle of Maldon" recounts an actual battle, the treatment is heroic poetry, not realistic reporting. Donoghue notes that "although it draws on the specifics of the local geography and personal names, the poem clothes the action with literary conventions that create a general tone of nostalgia for a timeless heroic past" (15). Grand speeches are offered in the middle of violent battle-clashes. Arrows are suspended to give time for the making of moral judgments. Vikings blend into a horde of tormenting demons, and Byrhtnoth prays that his spirit will be "carried in peace / To the place of angels."

A little geography is necessary to explain the nature of Byrhtnoth's controversial decision to allow the Vikings access to the mainland battlefield. Near the town of Maldon in the tidal flats is Northey Island; the river Pante (now Blackwater) flows to the north of it and Southey Creek to the south. The rivers flow into the sea. At high tide, the island is entirely cut off from the mainland to the west. At low tide, there is a causeway of stones about eight feet wide and eighty yards long that allows passage of limited numbers at a time between the island and the mainland.

The Vikings have anchored their ships and set up camp on the island. They stand at the western shore waiting for the tide to go out so they can come west across the causeway or "bridge" to engage the Anglo-Saxon troops who are gathered on the mainland. At the beginning of the poem, the two sides call out their challenges and responses across the water while the tide is in and passage is blocked. When the tide goes out, the Vikings start to come across the causeway in small numbers at a time and are easily ambushed by the Anglo-Saxon archers. Obviously the war-savvy Vikings will not march endlessly to their doom in this fashion. They call out to Byrhtnoth to allow them to come across for a "fair fight." The implication is probably that if Byrhtnoth does not allow them this passage, they will return to their ships, sail off to some unprotected town, and sack it without much resistance. The Viking messenger uses guile, asking for fair play, snidely questioning the Anglo-Saxons' courage, offering to take tribute instead of lives, mocking the English with devious and dark humor.

Unfortunately, Byrhtnoth allows the Vikings to come across the causeway because of his *ofermōd*, literally his "overweening pride," or "too much heart or temper." It is a heroic quality, *mōd*, meaning "spirit, mind, courage," which has gone too far. Its occurrences in Old English nearly all carry negative connotations of some sort. Tolkien wrote a trenchant analysis of "The Battle of Maldon" that includes an essay on *ofermōd* and a dramatic dialogue written in a modern version of Old English alliterative verse. His major point is that Byrhtnoth's *ofermōd*, his "desire for honor and glory, in life and after death, tends to grow, to become a chief motive, driving a man beyond the bleak heroic necessity to excess" (1953, 14). Other critics argue that Byrhtnoth's *ofermōd* is like Greek hubris, a necessary self-confidence carried into battle, but here passing over into unbounded pride that leads to tragedy. What is never in doubt, however, is the courage shown by most of Byrhtnoth's battlefield retainers as they die avenging the death of their lord. As Leofsunu says so poignantly, "I promise not to flee one foot from this field—/ I will avenge my lord Byrhtnoth in battle."

The opening and closing lines of the poem are missing, probably a few lines from the beginning and a more substantial passage at the end (Scragg, 16). From the context it is also clear that something is missing after line 285, and I've supplied lines 286–88 in an attempt to recover the sense of the lost passage. For more on the poem from a variety of contexts (heroic tradition, military tactics, geography of the causeway, etc.), see Scragg's collection of essays, *The Battle of Maldon AD 991*.

The Battle of Maldon

           . . . and that was broken.
Then Byrhtnoth commanded his courageous warriors
To dismount quickly and drive off their horses,
Move forward on foot, trusting hands and hearts.
That's when Offa's kinsman first found   5
That the earl would never endure slackers,
Keep cowards in his company. The leader let fly
From his hand his beloved, brave hawk
Which took to the woods while he stepped up
To meet the battle, a man of his word.   10
Then warriors knew that he would not weaken
In war-play but wield his battle-weapon.
Eadric also intended to serve his lord;
He lifted his shield and broad sword,
Embracing battle. He fulfilled his boast   15
On the mead-bench that he would drink danger
And fight fiercely to defend his lord.
Then Byrhtnoth began to rally his troops,
Advising his men. He rode to each group,
Giving instructions, teaching and telling them   20
How they should stand and hold their lines,
Grasping their shields hard in their hands,
Forgetting fear, refusing to yield.
When his troops were ready, he gave up his horse,
Walking among them where he longed to be,   25
Where his hearth-companions kept courage.
Then a Viking messenger, the marauders' mouthpiece,
Stood up on the shore, announcing from the island
On the opposite bank, a boast to the earl
From bold seafarers, baiting Byrhtnoth: 30
"Brave sea-warriors sent me here to simply say
That you might want to give us gold rings
As a defense, rich gifts and offerings
To ease your peril, protect your people.
A tribute of treasure is always better   35
Than receiving a rush of battle-spears

When we exchange both blade and blood.
If you Byrhtnoth, lord and leader,
Mightiest of men, would redeem your people,
Then give us what we ask, the price of peace—   40
Then seafarers can go home with your gold,
Offering a promise of protection and peace,
And you can be whole in heart and home."

Byrhtnoth responded, raising his shield,
Brandished his ash-spear, angry and resolute—   45
Calling on courage, threw back this answer:
"Can you hear, seafarer, you hated pirate,
What my people say? They will give you spears
As a take-home treasure, bitter blades
And savage swords. Trust this tribute—   50
A booty that will not help you much in battle.
Messenger of the Vikings, mouthpiece of evil,
Bear back to your men this hard, grim vow:
Here on this shore stands an earl with his troop
Who will defend his homeland, kith and kin,   55
The land of Æthelred, my own dear lord.
You heathens shall be hewed down in battle.
It would be a shame to have come so far
To retreat to your ships with our tribute,
Embarking in boats instead of in battle.   60
Seamen cannot so easily steal our gold.
Let's resolve this argument with the edge of iron,
In the battle-play of blades not devious words."

Then Byrhtnoth ordered his men to bear shields
To the stream's bank by the causeway-bridge.   65
The tide was in, so neither band could safely cross;
The ebb-tide flowed across the bridge.
It seemed too long to wait to lift their spears.
On both sides of the River Pante, the warriors waited,
East-Saxons on the shore, seamen on the island,   70
An army of ash-spears. They couldn't kill
Each other except by death-arching arrows.

The tide turned, the flood went out,
The causeway cleared. Vikings stood ready,
Ravenous for war. Byrhtnoth ordered   75
The battle-hard Wulfstan, son of Ceola,
To hold the bridge. He speared the first seaman
Bold enough to step across the stones.
Two fearless fighters, Ælfhere and Maccus,
Guarded the ford against the fiends' crossing,   80
Letting no one pass while they might wield weapons.
When the Vikings knew that the narrow bridge
Would be blocked by fierce fighting Saxons,
Those alien guests began to offer guile,
To bait their trap with warped words,   85
Asked out of courtesy the chance to come
Across the causeway for a fair fight.
Then with a brash heart, Byrhtnoth began
To yield the bridge to the savage seamen—
Offered too eagerly an untouched crossing.   90
Byrhthelm's bold son called across the stream,
Where the Viking warriors laughed and listened:
"The causeway is opened to you. Come quickly to us.
Let's greet each other as equals in battle.
Only God knows who will wield power   95
And be standing after strife in the slaughter-field."

The ravenous wolves crossed the bridge
Without worry over the shallow water.
Over the river came the Viking hordes,
Bearing linden-shields over bright water.   100
Byrhtnoth and his men were brave guardians
Against the grim wolves' fierce crossing.
He ordered the shield-wall raised high
Against the surge of seafarers. It was battle-time—
The hour for heroes to gather glory,   105
For hard, fated men to fall in fight.
Screams were raised in the clash of swords—
Ravens circled, screeching for corpses—
The eagle was ravenous for a feast of flesh—

All earth was in endless uproar.   110
Warriors thrust file-hardened spears
From their hands, grim shafts at guts—
Bows were busy, shields shot with arrows—
Bitter was the battle-rush. Warriors fell
On both sides—youngbloods lay dead.   115
Wulfmær was wounded, nephew of Byrhtnoth—
He chose a slaughter-bed, savaged by swords.
Cruel death was common, repaid in kind.
I heard that Eadweard slew one with his sword—
The doomed Dane fell dead at his feet.   120
His lord gave him thanks for that later.
The Saxons stood strong-hearted in battle,
Each man looking for a life to take,
To catch the heart of a warrior with his weapon.
Slaughter fell on earth like bloody snow.   125
The Saxon defenders were all steadfast.
Byrhtnoth directed them, urged them on,
Bade each warrior to brood upon battle,
To win great glory against the Danes,
Fame in fighting and a warrior's doom.   130
A battle-hard Dane came after Byrhtnoth,
Who lifted his shield to defend his body.
Each warrior was resolute, earl against churl—
Each plotted murder against his aggressor.
The churl was quicker—the seaman thrust   135
His southern spear into the earl.
Byrhtnoth broke that shaft with his shield
With such force that it shivered and shook out.
That battle-lord sprang up in bold rage,
Stabbed the proud Viking who had speared his breast—   140
The wise warrior shoved his Saxon spear
Through the Viking's neck, guiding with his grip
So that he reached the life of the fierce raider.
Then he speared another venomous Viking
Whose chain-mail burst. He was breast-dead,   145
Killed through his corselet, pierced through his heart.
This pleased Byrhtnoth more—he lit up with laughter—

Thanked God for a good day's work with the Danes.
Then a pirate speared him, threw his shaft
Through Byrhtnoth's chest with his hard hands, 150
Draining the life of Æthelred's noble thane.
By the earl's side stood a boy in battle,
A brave young Saxon who plucked the spear,
The bloody shaft out of Byrhtnoth's body.
The youngster was Wulfmær, Wulfstan's son. 155
He sent the spear back to its Viking owner,
Point-first so the fierce one fell to the ground,
Killing the one who had wounded his lord.
Then an armed Viking approached the earl
To plunder his body, seize armor and rings, 160
Take home the treasure of his decorated sword.
Then Byrhtnoth drew his sword from its sheath,
Broad and gleaming, and cut through the mail-coat
Of the Viking marauder. Like lightning
Another seaman slashed through his arm 165
So his gold-hilted sword fell to the ground.
Byrhtnoth could no longer hold up his spear,
Wield his weapon. Yet the grizzled warrior
Encouraged his troops to go boldly forward,
Never forgetting camaraderie and kin, 170
Never foregoing their commitment and courage.
He couldn't stand any longer on his feet—
He looked up at Heaven and spoke these words:
"I offer you thanks, Lord of my people,
For all of the joys I've experienced in this world. 175
Now I have need, gentle protector,
For the gift of grace, so my spirit can soar
Away from this slaughter into the arms
Of my Father's embrace, carried in peace
To the place of angels. I beg this boon: 180
Let me be freed from the savage hell-fiends."
Then the heathens hewed him down
With two warriors who stood beside him,
Ælfnoth and Wulfmær, loyal Saxons
Who gave up their lives, fighting for their lord. 185

Then three warriors bolted from battle,
The sons of Odda, cowardly brothers,
Deserting their lord to save their lives.
Godric was the first to flee in shame,
Leaving his lord who had given him horses.   190
He leapt in the saddle of Byrhtnoth's steed
And galloped off. That was not right.
Godwine and Godwig followed behind;
They shunned their duty and sought safety
In the nearby woods. Many warriors followed   195
Who should have remembered their lord's favors
And kept their trust. So Offa had once said
To his lord Byrhtnoth in a meadhall meeting
That many who spoke boldly there in the hall
Would never make good on the field of battle.   200

So Byrhtnoth fell, Æthelred's earl,
The protector of his people. His hearth-companions
Knew in their hearts that their lord lay dead.
Then the proud thanes went forward
Eager and undaunted, hungry for battle.   205
They wanted one of two outcomes:
To leave life or avenge their lord.
So the noble Ælfwine, Ælfric's son,
Young in his years, urged them on,
Exhorted the warriors with bold words: 210
"Remember the speeches we bravely shared
At the meadhall tables—we boasted from the benches
That we would be heroes, hard-fighting in battle.
Now we'll see who's worthy of his vow,
Who'll back up his boast in the rush of battle.   215
I will make known my lineage to all of you:
I come from a mighty family of Mercians;
My grandfather was Ealhelm, a wise nobleman,
A lord and landowner. My people at home
Will have no reason to reproach me for flight   220
From the battlefield, for seeking safety
And skulking home, now that Byrhtnoth

Lies broken in battle. This is my greatest grief—
That he was both my kinsman and lord."
Then he went forth, his mind on vengeance,   225
Reaching a seafarer's heart with his spear,
Piercing that pirate's loathsome life.
He urged the troops on, his friends and comrades.
Then Offa shook his spear and spoke:
"So Ælfwine, you've encouraged us all   230
In our time of need. Our lord lies dead,
Slain by a spear, an earl on the earth.
Each of us needs to encourage the other
To battle these heathens with hand and heart,
Spear-thrust and blade-bite,   235
While we can still wield weapons.
Godric the cowardly son of Odda
Has betrayed us all. Too many believed,
When they saw him mounted on that fine horse
And fleeing to the wood, that it was our lord.   240
Many broke ranks—the shield-wall was breeched.
Curse him and his memory for his lack of courage
Which has caused too many men to flee."
Leofsunu lifted his strong linden shield
In defense and defiance, speaking these words: 245
"I promise not to flee one foot from this field.
I will avenge my lord Byrhtnoth in battle.
The steadfast warriors in my hometown Sturmere
Will have no reason to reproach me with words,
Saying that once my leader lay dead on the ground,   250
I left the battlefield lordless to come home safe.
I will seize sword and spear, wield my weapons."
He went like a warrior full of righteous wrath,
Fighting boldly in battle and scorning flight.
Then Dunnere spoke, shaking his spear,   255
A simple churl with short words,
Urging each warrior to avenge Byrhtnoth:
"A man who means to avenge his lord
Cannot flee. He must keep courage,
Fight keenly, and have no care for his life."   260

Then the men surged forward—feared nothing
For their lives. The troops and retainers,
The grim spear-bearers, fought fiercely,
Praying for God's help in avenging their lord
By fighting the fiends, bringing death to the foe.   265
Then even a hostage began to help—
Æscferth, son of Ecglaf, a hard Northumbrian.
He shot all his arrows without flinching,
Threw every spear without wavering once
From the war-play. Sometimes he hit a shield;   270
Sometimes he pierced through a man's skin.
As long as he stood, he slew someone,
Handing out wounds while he wielded weapons.
Eadweard the Tall held his place in the battle-line,
Ready and eager to meet the enemy.   275
He vowed he'd never flee from the Vikings,
Give one foot of land to the foreign fiends
Or turn back now that his better lord lay dead.
He broke through the shield-wall, fighting the foe,
Until he avenged the death of his dear lord,   280
His treasure-giver, on the deadly Danes,
Before he lay down in the bed of slaughter.
So did Ætheric, brother of Sibyrht—
Wading eagerly into battle, with many others
Defending their homeland keenly with courage.   285
[Then one of the slaughter-wolves attacked Offa,
The second-in-command of Byrhtnoth's Saxons—
The seafarer shoved a spear at his chest.]
His shield-rim broke and his mail-shirt sang
A song of horror. Offa slew his attacker,   290
Then fell to the ground, the kinsman of Gadd.
He was quickly cut down in that cruel fray.
He had kept both his courage and his vow
To his lord in the hall, his good ring-giver,
That they should ride home whole together   295
Or fall side by side, wasted by wounds,
Comrades together in the field of corpses.
Then shields were shattered and seamen came through

In a rage of battle. The ravenous spear
Often thrust through a man's bone-house.   300
Wistan went forward, Thurstan's son,
Fought against seamen, the slayer of three
In a battle-throng, before he lay down,
In a heap of slaughter, the son of Wigelm.
That was a murderous meeting, a savage struggle.   305
Warriors clashed, fought without yielding,
Killed without wavering. The field filled with corpses.
All through the battle, Oswold and Eadwold,
Brothers fighting together, encouraged the troops
With strong battle-words, telling them all   310
To stand firm against savage seafarers,
Wield their weapons without weakening.
Then Byrhtwold spoke, raising his shield—
Byrhtnoth's old retainer urged on the others,
Boldly instructing the last of the troop: 315
"The spirit must be stronger, the heart fiercer,
The courage keener, as our strength slips away.
Here lies our lord, savagely slain,
A great leader on the ground. Ever may a man mourn
Who thinks to flee from this fierce war-play.   320
I am old in winters, weary with years,
But I will not leave this field. I mean to lie down
Beside my dear lord, the leader I love."
So also Godric, Æthelgar's son,
Urged them all, battle-comrades together   325
To keep their courage, continue fighting.
Often he let his slaughter-spear fly
Against the Vikings; he was first in the front,
Striking and slaying till he fell in battle.
That was not the Godric who fled . . .   330

DEOR

"Deor" is rare among Old English poems in that it is written in stanzas and includes a refrain. It has been interpreted in many ways—among them a dramatic monologue, a charm for good fortune, a begging poem, an elegy, and a poem of consolation (Muir, vol. ii, 597–98). In the Exeter Book, it follows a series of homiletic or religious poems and precedes "The Wife's Lament," "Wulf and Eadwacer," and the first group of riddles. "Deor" is a poem that bridges the homiletic and the enigmatic. Both the form of the poem and its murky historical details are much debated.

"Deor" weaves stories out of Germanic history and legend and shapes a moral reflection from them. Each stanza details a particular story of misfortune and suffering and ends with a refrain intended to generalize sorrow and to hold some hope for its passing away with time. The refrain, *Þæs ofereode; þisses swā mæg*, means "That passed over—so can this." The central paradox here is that while misfortunes may "pass over" in time, they remain fragmented in the mind of the singer, and the poem ironically conveys a deep sense of loss even as it claims to ameliorate it.

The opening stanza of the poem deals with a famous smith named Weland, who is mentioned in *Beowulf* as the maker of Beowulf's mail-coat. In Germanic legend Weland had his hamstrings cut by King Nithhad in order to enslave the smith and force him to make beautiful objects for the king. Nithhad sent his daughter Beadohild to Weland each day with his meals. In retaliation against the king or out of lust (or both), Weland seduced or raped Beadohild, leaving her pregnant. He also killed the king's sons, shaping drinking bowls from their skulls to present as gifts to the king. Weland was rescued by his brother, who wove a coat of feathers for him to use in his escape, but this rescue is missing from the account here.

In the second stanza, Deor notes that the death of Beadohild's brother was less painful to her than her own suffering once she discovered that she was pregnant. He says that "she tried not to think how it all happened." This is partly a grim litotes: she knows all too well how she became pregnant. It is also a recognition of her repression of these terrible events, the result of a feud begun by her father that destroys her family. Legend tells us that eventually Weland and Beadohild were reconciled, and their son Widia became a great hero, but again, this happier resolution is missing from "Deor."

In the third stanza, the story of Mæthhild and Geat is cryptically mentioned. There is much critical debate about this story, which has no known medieval origin. The stanza tells us little more than that the two lovers shared a "bottomless love" that caused Mæthhild sleepless nights.

In the fourth stanza, Deor mentions a ruler, Theodric, who ruled the Mærings for thirty winters (years were often marked by winters in Anglo-Saxon England). This probably refers to Theodoric the Ostrogoth who was exiled among the Huns for thirty years. In some Old English literature he is portrayed as a tyrant; in others he's a victim.

In the fifth stanza, Deor mentions the tyrant Eormanric, a fourth-century king of the Goths. His "wolfish ways" lead to such suffering that his subjects hope that some foe might attack him and take over his kingdom. An unknown conqueror might prove kinder than their cruel king.

After his cryptic catalogue of the misfortunes of other legendary people in the first half of the poem, the narrator tells us that his name is Deor, and that he once served as the *scop* or singer in the court of the Heodenings until he was unceremoniously displaced by another singer, Heorrenda. Heorrenda is mentioned in one of the sagas, but there is no record of a singer named Deor. His name may be a poetic fiction. "Dēor" can mean "brave, bold" but also "grievous, ferocious." As a noun it means "wild beast." A similar word, *dēore*, means "dear, precious, beloved," and a word-play seems possible here, as Deor moves from a beloved place in the Heodenings' court to a life of loneliness and wild exile, "apart from joy." Deor's loss is finally twofold. He misses the life he once had as a prized singer in the court, but beyond that he can no longer remember the details of his old life or the stories he once sang. He can only recall these in bits and pieces. For all his hope in their passing over, they remain like barbs in the mind.

Deor

Weland the smith made a trial of exile.
The strong-minded man suffered hardship
All winter long—his only companions
Were cold and sorrow. He longed to escape
The bonds of Nithhad who slit his hamstrings,   5
Tied him down with severed sinews,
Making a slave of this better man.
That passed over—so can this.

To Beadohild her brother's death
Was not so sad as her own suffering   10
When the princess saw she was pregnant.
She tried not to think how it all happened.
That passed over—so can this.

Many have heard of the cares of Mæthhild—
She and Geat shared a bottomless love. 15
Her sad passion deprived her of sleep.
That passed over—so can this.

Theodric ruled for thirty winters
The city of the Mærings—that's known to many.
That passed over—so can this. 20

We all know the wolfish ways of Eormanric—
That grim king ruled the land of the Goths.
Many a man sat bound in sorrow,
Twisted in the turns of expected woe,
Hoping a foe might free his kingdom. 25
That passed over—so can this.

A man sits alone in the clutch of sorrow,
Separated from joy, thinking to himself
That his share of suffering is endless.
The man knows that all through middle-earth, 30
Wise God goes, handing out fortunes,
Giving grace to many—power, prosperity,
Wisdom, wealth—but to some a share of woe.

Let me tell this story about myself:
I was singer and shaper for the Heodenings, 35
Dear to my lord. My name was Deor.
For many years I was harper in the hall,
Honored by the king, until Heorrenda now,
A song-skilled shaper, has taken my place,
Reaping the rewards, the titled lands, 40
That the guardian of men once gave me.
That passed over—so can this.

ELEGIES

The Old English elegies are notoriously difficult to define. Traditional elegies lament the death of a particular person and celebrate the accomplishments of that person's life. The Old English elegies are usually dramatic monologues in which the speaker expresses some sense of separation and suffering and attempts to move from a *cri de cœur* to some form of consolation. The term "elegy" was not applied to these poems until the nineteenth century, and there is some debate about its usefulness as a generic marker. Nonetheless, the term serves to characterize a group of Old English poems which share some or all of the following elements:

1. An isolated or exiled speaker who laments a loss
2. Longing for earlier days of joy with loved ones
3. Bad weather reflecting the wintry storms of mental life
4. Fluctuating mental states (memory, dream, hallucination)
5. The use of reason to try to understand life's misfortunes
6. Recognition that life is *lǣne*, "transient, fleeting"
7. Use of occasional proverbial wisdom to generalize one's lot
8. Searching for consolation, sometimes finding it in religious belief

Most elegies move from a personal lament to at least an attempt at consolation. This movement may derive in part from the influence of *The Consolation of Philosophy* by Boethius, a sixth-century Latin work that was translated into Old English and probably widely known (see, for example, Lumiansky, 104 ff.). If we look at the relationship between lament and consolation in the four elegies included here, we find some telling differences, particularly with respect to their endings:

A. The speaker in "The Wanderer" tries to use reflection and generalization to come to a sense of consolation and a belief in providential order, but the religious argument seems finally less compelling than the articulation of personal sorrow. The power of the poem lies more in its images of loss than in its crafted consolation.

B. The speaker in "The Seafarer" seems wise and controlled right from the beginning. He is probably meant to be a pilgrim who chooses exile, unlike the wanderer who is forced into exile by fate. He wanders for the purpose of understanding the instability of this world and believing in the permanence and order of the next. The philosophical argument and the consolation are more powerful than the sense of isolation and loss.

C. The speaker in "The Wife's Lament" is more isolated than the other two. She doesn't know why her husband has left her. She wants to generalize her suffering and sorrow to include everyone, most especially her absent husband, and in this her consolation seems to mask a complaint or curse.

D. The speaker in "Wulf and Eadwacer," like her sister in sorrow in "The Wife's Lament," seems to have less access to the tools of philosophical reflection than the male elegiac speakers. Her poem ends not with a sense of resolution or consolation but with an apparently unsolvable riddle.

THE WANDERER

"The Wanderer" is a powerful and puzzling poem. It has intrigued critics and inspired poets like Auden and Tolkien to echo its elements in their own works. It is a poem of complex consciousness. The wanderer, who is the narrator of the poem, reflects upon his past, lamenting his loss of king and kin. Mitchell and Robinson point out his vulnerability as a lordless exile in Anglo-Saxon society:

The wanderer who speaks the monologue is in the worst possible cir-
cumstances for an Anglo-Saxon warrior in the heroic age: he is a re-
tainer who has lost his lord and comrades and who therefore finds
himself with no place in society, no identity in a hostile world. He is a
man *in extremis*, alone with his memories and naked to his enemies.
This plight moves him to strenuous and painful reflection. (2007, 280)

The speaker's task is to move through both physical and mental wandering
to arrive at a sense of resolution and recovery—to find his wiser self and to
locate a new philosophical or religious "homeland."

The narrator moves back and forth between personal sorrow and gnomic
generalizations about the nature of life. By shifting from first-person lament
to third-person description or reflection, he both generalizes his own condi-
tion and establishes some distance between the suffering man and the re-
flective man. As his mind moves back through remembered adversity, he
reexperiences the loss of his lord, whom he seems to have buried in an earth-
cave. He wanders in exile, and his only companion is sorrow. He battles
both bad weather and his own stormy mind. Beginning at line 40, he moves
through a variety of mental states from memory to dream to hallucination.
He dreams of laying his head in his lord's lap and communicating with
hearth-companions but wakes suddenly to find not friends in the hall but
sea-birds bathing and screaming. He says he can't think why his mind
doesn't "sink into shadow" when he contemplates the death and destruction
of the world. The heart of his difficulty here is that he must use his mind
to cure his mind.

The wanderer generalizes that "the wise man who ponders this ruin of a
life" will remember his earlier hall-joys and cry out: "Where has the horse
gone? Where is the rider? Where is the giver of gifts?" This *ubi sunt* ("where
are they?") motif is derived from a Latin tradition, and it expresses both a
lament over loss and a recognition of transience. Life is on loan. Everything
is fleeting—goods, friends, kith and kin—"all this earthly foundation."
Here philosophical speculation competes with apocalyptic images.

The poet breaks in at the end to remind us that this is the wise man's
reflection upon his wandering past. The interruption suspends the storm
and produces a moment of providential quiet. We hear that the now wise
wanderer sits by himself in contemplation, keeping his faith, moving be-
yond pain and passion, to "perform a cure on his own heart." He sees that
he must seek mercy from his Father in heaven, which is the only place

where the transience of the world is transcended, where "security stands," and where he can find a permanent place "beyond perishing." Perhaps he has moved beyond the plaintive laments into a philosophical understanding of the unseen stability of the ways of Providence in this world. Perhaps the consolation is undercut by the power of the images of instability and suffering right up to the end of the poem.

The Wanderer

Often the wanderer walks alone,
Waits for mercy, longs for grace,
Stirs the ice-cold sea with hands and oars—
Heart-sick, endures an exile's road—
A hard traveler. His fate is fixed.   5

So said the wanderer, old earth-walker,
His mind choked with the memory of strife,
Fierce slaughter and the fall of kinsmen:

Often alone at the edge of dawn,
I must wake to the sound of my own sorrow,   10
The mute song of a muffled heart,
Sung to no listener, no lord alive.
I know the custom. A noble man
Must seal up his heart's thoughts,
Drag the doors of his mind shut,   15
Bind sorrow with silence and be still.

A weary mind cannot fight fate—
A savage soul cannot find solace,
Help or healing. Who wants fame,
A home in the tribe's long memory,   20
Must seal off sadness, bind up woe.

So often I've locked up my heart-sorrow
In a breast-hoard, a cage of bone,
Cut off from kinsmen after I covered
My gold-lord in the dark hold of ground.   25

I went winter-sad with the weight of years
Over the winding waves, seeking some lord
Who might heal my history, hold my heart,
Welcome me home with gifts or grace.

A man without country, without kin,   30
Knows how cruel it is to have sorrow
As a sole companion. No one waits
To welcome the wanderer except the road
Of exile itself. His reward is night-cold,
Not a lord's rich gift of twisted gold   35
Or a warm hearth and a harvest of wealth.
He remembers hall-thanes, shared treasures,
His place at the table, his lord's trust.
His dreams are done—they taste like dust.

A man knows who has lost his lord's counsel   40
How sorrow and sleep can bind the mind.
A man may wander his own headland,
Discover his lord unburied, undead—
He kisses and clutches his dream lord,
Lays in his lord's lap his head and hands,   45
As he once did in those generous days
When he knew the joys of hall and throne.
Then the wanderer wakes without friends,
Alone except for sea-birds bathing
In the dusky sea, spreading wide wings—   50
As snow falls, frost feathers the land,
And hard hail harrows the living.

Then the wounds of the heart are heavier,
Aching so long for his lost lord.
Sorrow is renewed with the memory of kinsmen   55
Wandering his mind, each guest a ghost
Who gathers and greets him with signs of joy,
Eagerly searching for old companions.
They all drift away—the unknown floaters
Bring no known sayings or songs to him.   60

Care is renewed for a man who must send
His brooding heart over the bond of waves.

So I can't think why in this uneasy world,
My mind shouldn't darken, sink into shadow,
When I think through the lives of men—   65
How warriors and retainers have suddenly slipped
From the hall-floor, brave ones gone.
So the days of middle-earth fail and fade.
No man's wise till he's walked through winters,
Suffered a world of unshared grief.   70
A wise man must be patient, not hot-hearted,
Not quick-tongued, not weak-willed at war,
Not reckless or unwitting, not eager to boast
Before he has thought things through.
A warrior must wait when he makes a vow   75
Until his mind is sure and his heart strong,
And he can read the road his traveling takes.

The wise warrior knows how ghostly it will be
When all the world's wealth is a wasteland,
As middle-earth is now in many places—   80
Wall fragments stand, blasted by winds,
Covered by frost—ruined hallways in snow.
Wine-halls decay, lords lie dead,
Deprived of joys—the proud troop
Has fallen by the wall. War took some   85
On a long death-road; a bird bore one
Over the deep sea; the gray wolf shared
One with death; a sad-faced earl
Hid one in an earth-hole, a bleak barrow.
So the Maker of men laid waste to the world,   90
Until the old works of giants stood idle
And empty of the hall-joys of men.

The wise man who ponders this ruin of a life—
The hall that crumbles into a broken wall,
The hall-guest now only memory's ghost—   95

Remembers slaughter and strife, crying out:
Where has the horse gone? Where is the rider?
       Where is the giver of gifts?
Where is the seat of feasting? Where is the hall-joy?
Gone is the bright cup. Gone is the mailed warrior.   100
Gone is the glory of the prince. How the time has slipped
Down under the night-helmet as if it never was.
The only thing left is traces of the tribe,
A strange, high wall with serpentine shapes,
Worm-like strokes, what's left of runes.   105
The strength of spears has borne off earls,
Weapons greedy for slaughter. Some glorious fate!

Raging storms crash against stone-cliffs;
Swirling snow blankets and binds the earth.
Winter howls as the pale night-shadow darkens,   110
Sending rough hail-storms from the north,
Bringing savagery and strife to the children of men.
Hardship and suffering descend on the land;
The shape of fate is twisted under heaven.
Life is on loan: Here goods are fleeting,   115
Here friends are fleeting, here man is fleeting,
Here kith and kin are fleeting. Everything passes—
All this earthly foundation stands empty and idle.

So a man wise in mind spoke to himself as he sat:
Good is the man who holds trust, keeps faith,   120
Never speaks too quickly about the storm
Of his pain or passion unless he knows
How to perform a cure on his own heart.
It is well for a man to seek mercy for himself
From his Father in heaven where security stands,   125
And where we can still find beyond perishing
A permanent place, an eternal home.

THE SEAFARER

This poem, like "The Wanderer," has puzzled scholars with its strange combination of voices and attitudes. In the first half of the dramatic monologue, the seafarer comments on his experience at sea, contrasting it with the apparent joys which land-inhabitants experience. His soul is stirred not by harp-songs or the sharing of mead in the hall but by the tumult of waves on the high seas and the testing of his strength and spirit. In the middle of the poem, the speaker shifts into a philosophical and religious mode, never mentioning the sea or land again as the poem shifts into what Gordon calls "an act symbolic of the renunciation of worldly life generally and the ready acceptance of the struggles and sufferings involved in the quest for eternal bliss" (7).

Kennedy notes in similar fashion that "the use of sea imagery in an allegorical contrast of earthly existence and the Christian vision of life after death is not without parallel in Old English poetry" (112). He points to a passage from Cynewulf's *Christ II (The Ascension)*, which may have drawn its inspiration and imagery from Gregory's homily on the Ascension. In this passage the turmoil of life is compared to a rough sea journey, and the salvation of Christ to a safe harbor:

Life is a hard and harrowing voyage,
Sailing our ships across cold waters,
Riding our sea-steeds over the deep,
Alone on the ocean in a seafaring wood.
The current is dangerous, the sea savage,
The waves driven by wind, as we struggle
In this weak world, this unstable life—
Till at last we sail over roiling seas
Into a safe harbor, guided by God's grace,
His Spirit-Son, our help and haven,
Our safety and salvation, so that we may know
While riding high, where to heel and hove
Our sea-steeds, moor our crafts,
Lock on land, and leave hard traveling.
Let's anchor hope in that harbor,
Leave transience for trust, where the Lord and Savior
Has opened a way, prepared a port,

A haven for us, ascending into heaven. (*Christ II*, 850–66; my
    translation)

Here the seafarer travels through the rough seas of worldly life, aiming at a
safe harbor with God's Son in heaven.

    Where the Old English wanderer was thrust into a life of exile, a long
road of suffering, the seafarer deliberately chooses his lonely and difficult
life. He rides his ship of sorrow, eschewing the joyful life on land because
only in suffering and contemplation can he discover the transience of this
worldly life and the stability of the afterlife in heaven. As the poem moves
from seafaring to sermonizing, it seems only appropriate that it should end
with "Amen."

The Seafarer

I can sing this truth-song about myself—
Of harrowing times and hard traveling,
Of days of terrible toil. Often I endured
Bitter heartache on my ship of sorrow,
In my hall of care, on the heaving waves.   5
The narrow night-watch often held me,
Anxious and troubled at the ship's prow,
As we sailed, tossing close to sea-cliffs.
My feet were pinched by cold, bound by frost.
Hunger and longing tortured and tore   10
My sea-weary mind. No man knows
Who lives on the land in comfort and joy
How I endured suffering and sorrow
On the ice-cold sea through endless winters
On the exile's road, cut off from kin,   15
Surrounded by icicles. Hail flew in showers.
There I heard nothing but the roaring sea,
The ice-cold waves, the frozen surf.
Sometimes I listened to the swan's song,
The curlew's cry, the gannet's call—   20
A seagull singing instead of men laughing,
A mew's music instead of meadhall drinking.
Storms battered sea-cliffs—the tern answered,

Icy-feathered. Often the eagle screeched back—
Dew on its wings. No kinsman was close   25
To guard the heart, comfort the wretched spirit.
The man who lives a joyful life on land,
Secure in the city, proud and passionate
In the company of friends, drinking wine,
Can never fathom how I wandered weary,   30
Sad and suffering, on the long sea-road.
Night-shadows darkened, snow fell from the north,
Frost bound the land, hail fell on earth,
The coldest of grains.
                          Still my heart is stirred
To seek the sea-streams, the tumult of waves,   35
By my wandering thoughts. The mind always urges
The soul to set out, seeking some foreign soil,
A land of strangers. No man is so proud,
Or so endowed with gifts, so bold in his youth,
Or so brave in his deeds, so safe and secure   40
In his lord's grace, that he harbors no worries,
No sorrows or cares, in his seafaring days,
Over what his lord might ultimately offer him.
He never dreams of the delight of the harp,
Or receiving gold rings, or the joys of a woman,   45
Or any other earthly pleasure. His dreams
Are driven by the sea—the longing of his heart
Lingers on the thrashing tumult of the waves.
The groves burst into bloom, adorning the towns,
Meadows grow beautiful—the world hastens on: 50
All this urges the restless heart to travel,
The eager mind of the sailor to seek the sea.
The voice of the cuckoo, summer's harbinger,
Sings of sorrow, bodes mourning,
The heart's keen, sad song. A man of comfort,   55
Proud and prosperous, never knows
What seafarers endure on the exile-road.
So my thoughts sail out of my unstill mind,
My heart heaves from my breast-hoard,
Seeking the sea—my spirit soars   60

Over the whale's home, twists and turns
Over the earth's surfaces, rolls and returns,
Greedy and ravenous. The solitary flier screams,
Rousing the quickened heart on the whale-road
Over the stretch of sea.

For me the joys of the Lord   65
Are keener than the dead life loaned to us on land—
I can never believe that all this worldly wealth
Will last forever. One of three things
Always threatens a man with uncertainty
Before he travels on his final road—   70
Illness or old age or the sword's grim edge.
Therefore each man must earn the honor
And respect of the living, the praise of posterity,
Secure his reputation with speech-bearers
Before his death by striving to accomplish   75
Great deeds against fiends, against the devil.
Then the children of men will honor him,
And his glory will live forever with the angels,
An eternity of joy with the heavenly host.

The days of greatness are now gone,   80
The wealth and power of earthly kingdoms.
There are no kings or emperors left alive,
No gold-givers as there once were,
When the greatest warriors won glory.
The troops have perished, the joys passed on.   85
Weaker men remain and rule the world
In toil and turmoil. Glory is laid low.
Earthly nobility is aging, fading away,
As every man withers on middle-earth.
Old age sneaks up on him, his face pales—   90
The gray-haired man mourns, misses his friends,
The children of men who have left the earth.
When life leaves a man, he cannot taste joy
Or feel pain any longer in his flesh-house;
His hand cannot stir, his head cannot think.   95
He may strew his brother's grave with gold,

Enrich that body-barrow with great treasure,
But gold cannot travel on the spirit-road,
Cannot help the soul weighed down with sin,
Cannot hide that heaviness from God's wrath.   100

Great is the terrible power of God—
All earth turns aside before it.
God created the wide world, the broad plains,
The surfaces of land and sea, the high heavens.
Foolish is the man who does not fear God—   105
Death sneaks up on him like an unexpected guest.
Blessed is the man who lives humbly in the Lord—
Mercy comes down to greet him from the heavens.
God strengthens and supports that soul
Because the believer trusts in His power.   110
A man must keep control of a strong spirit,
A willful heart—keep it steady and constant,
Pure in its promises, holding to its vows.
Each man must be measured and moderate
In affection to friends and enmity to foes,   115
Even though one may often wish another
In the embracing fire of a funeral pyre—
Enemy or friend. Fate is stronger,
The Lord mightier, than any human desire.
Let us consider where our true home lies   120
And plan how we might come to that place.
Let us aspire to arrive in eternal bliss,
Where life is attained in the love of the Lord,
Where hope and joy reside in the heavens.
Thanks be to Holy God, the Lord of Glory,   125
Who honored us and made us worthy,
Our glorious Creator, eternal through all time.

Amen.

THE WIFE'S LAMENT

"The Wife's Lament" has been read as a riddle, an allegory of the Church's longing for Christ, a retainer's lament for his lost lord, a speaking sword, and even the cry of a lost soul speaking out from beyond the grave. Scholars today mostly agree that it is a poem of love and lament, spoken by a woman who has lost her husband, who is also her lord. Like other Old English elegies, this poem begins as a heartfelt cry, moves through a struggle for consolation, and ends as a generalized piece of gnomic wisdom. The speaker recalls that her husband has left her for unknown reasons. Some plotting involving kinsmen has taken place, and he has fled. She has discovered that he was feuding with unknown people or possibly against her and plotting murder. She desperately remembers their love, but this memory increases her sense of loss and pain. In the end she tries to generalize her suffering to include all people, especially her husband. She assumes or she hopes that he is suffering lost love, loneliness, and torment, just as she is. He should have his share of suffering if indeed his leaving was the result of some family or tribal feud, and if he still loves her. The speaker, however, doesn't know why her husband has left, why he began to hide his thoughts from her, why he was plotting murder, or even whom he planned to kill. Because of this uncertainty, she doesn't know whether to pity him or to curse him. The generalizations at the end of the poem allow her to do both. If he is faultless and suffering, he joins her in grief and deserves pity and consolation. If he has been plotting against her or has simply left her out of lack of love, he deserves the curse she is uttering under her breath.

Finally, of course, the wife cannot know why the husband has left her in such dire straits. Her only recourse is the consolation of language itself as she turns an insufferable longing into the sharp consolation of her own lament. There's no surety here in knowing the other, the husband, whose intentions and actions are hidden from her. The only surety she has is in her song. Tormented by a twisted fate, dark memories, and a grim landscape, she expresses her pain and suffering through the song she sings. In so doing, she transforms the elegiac mode into something deeper and darker, where longing and anger are inexorably mixed.

The Wife's Lament

I tell this story from my grasp of sorrow—
I tear this song from a clutch of grief.
My stretch of misery from birth to bedrest
Has been unending, no more than now.
My mind wanders—my heart hurts.   5

My husband, my lord, left hearth and home,
Crossing the sea-road, the clash of waves.
My heart heaved each dawn, not knowing
Where in the world my lord had gone.

I followed, wandering a wretched road,   10
Seeking some service, knowing my need
For a sheltering home. I fled from woe.

His cruel kinsmen began to plot,
Scheming in secret to split us apart.
They forced us to live like exiles   15
Wretched, distant lives. Now I lie with longing.

My lord commanded me to live here
Where I have few friends, little love,
And no sense of home. Now my heart mourns.

I had found the best man for me,   20
My husband and companion, hiding his mind,
Closing his heart, bound in torment,
Brooding on murder beneath a gentle bearing.

How often we promised each other at night
That nothing would part us except death.   25
But fate is twisted—everything's turned.
Our love is undone, our closeness uncoupled.
The web of our wedding is unwoven.

Something now seems as if it never was—
Our friendship together. Far and near,   30
I must suffer the feud of my dear lord's brooding.

I was forced to live in a cold earth-cave,
Under an oak tree in an unhappy wood.
My earth-house is old. I lie with longing.

Here are steep hills and gloomy valleys,   35
Dark hideouts under twisted briars,
Bitter homes without joy. My lord's leaving
Seizes my mind, harrows my heart.

Somewhere friends share a lover's bed,
Couples clinging to their closeness at dawn,   40
While I sing each morning's sorrow
Outside my earth-cave, under my oak tree,
Where I spend the summer-long day,
Mourning my exile, the cares of my heart,
The wandering of my tormented mind.   45
My spirit cannot rest, my heart be healed,
My mind be free from this life's longing.

A young man must surely wake at dawn
With hard-edged sadness in his lonely heart.
He must brook misery beneath a gentle bearing   50
While he suffers his own stretch of sorrow,
Endless and undoing. May he look for joy
In an empty bed, exiled also in an alien land—
So that my friend sits under stone cliffs,
Pelted by storms, stranded by waves,   55
Chilled to the bone in his cruel hall.
In the comfort of cold, the embrace of anguish,
He may remember a kinder hearth and home.
Woe waits for the lover who lies longing.

WULF AND EADWACER

"Wulf and Eadwacer" is a poem that tugs at the heart and baffles the brain. It moves readers deeply, but no one can quite figure it out. At first people thought it was a riddle, largely because of the deliberate obscurity of its language and the enigma of its last lines. It has also been "identified as a charm, a complaint that a passage of verse has been misplaced, an account of romance among dogs (facetiously), and of an anthropomorphic pack of wolves" (Fulk and Cain, 191). Now most critics consider the poem a dramatic monologue spoken by a woman who is separated from her lover Wulf and unhappy in her marriage to Eadwacer. Her voice echoes the lonely voice in "The Wife's Lament." A woman alone is a woman at risk in the world of Anglo-Saxon poetry.

The whole poem is addressed to Wulf, who is probably the woman's lover. The speaker also seems to cry out to another man, Eadwacer, in line 19, but since *ēadwacer* means literally "guardian of wealth or fortune," this might simply be an epithet for Wulf or even for God. Is Wulf the speaker's husband or lover? Is Eadwacer a different person? We'll probably never know. What is clear is that the speaker laments her separation from Wulf and fears for his safety.

There is also a child in the poem, the whelp of line 20. We don't know whether the father of this child is Wulf or Eadwacer, or why Wulf may be bearing this child to the wood (or perhaps "wood" is a riddle for something like a cradle or even the grave). Maybe the woman is married to Eadwacer but in love with Wulf and wants to escape with him. Maybe she both longs for, and fears, the return of Wulf. We don't know whose embrace it is that is both lovely and loathsome to the woman. Is this the embrace of the unloved husband who has engendered the whelp? Is it the embrace of Wulf who seldom comes or who never comes (a grim litotes) after engendering the child? Another theory is that the speaker's child is actually Wulf and that the poem is a mother's lament for her lost or separated son.

The half-line refrain which is rare in Old English poetry, *ungelīc(e) is ūs*, means literally, "It's different (unlike) for us (between us)." But who is this "us"? Does the refrain mean that the speaker is different from Wulf or from Eadwacer? Or does it mean that she and Wulf are different from her own people or even from the rest of the cruel world? We're never sure, but we feel keenly the sense of separation and suffering.

At the end of the poem, the narrator closes with a kind of riddle, which reads literally: "That can easily be torn apart that was never attached—our song (story, riddle) of two together." These lines (discussed at length in the essay on translation at the beginning of this book) point to the paradox of the apparently deep connection between the speaker and her husband or lover or child which can so easily be broken. "Wulf and Eadwacer" may be a celebration of impossible love or a poignant lament over loss or both. Perhaps the poem is a form of delicate, ambiguous play between the poles of passion and peril, love and loss. We'll probably never know exactly what the poem means, but when the woman sings in lament and longing, "Wulf, my Wulf," it moves us beyond understanding.

Wulf and Eadwacer

If he comes home here to my people, it will seem
A strange gift. Will they take him into the tribe
And let him thrive or think him a threat?
It's different with us.

Wulf is on an island; I am on another.   5
Fast is that island, surrounded by fens.
There are bloodthirsty men on that island.
If they find him, will they take him into the tribe
And let him thrive or think him a threat?
It's different with us.   10

I've endured my Wulf's wide wanderings
While I sat weeping in rainy weather—
When the bold warrior wrapped me in his arms—
That was a joy to me and also a loathing.

Wulf, my Wulf, my old longings,   15
My hopes and fears, have made me ill;
Your seldom coming and my worried heart
Have made me sick, not lack of food.
Do you hear, Eadwacer, guardian of goods?
Wulf will bear our sad whelp to the wood.   20

It's easy to rip an unsewn stitch
Or tear the thread of an untold tale—
The song of us two together.

SELECTED EXETER BOOK RIDDLES

There are over ninety Old English lyric riddles in the Exeter Book. Some, such as Riddle 81, "Fish and River," are based on medieval Latin riddles, but most appear to be original. They may have been written by a single author or by several. Cynewulf, whose runic signature appears in two of the Exeter Book poems, was once thought to be the author of the riddles, but on stylistic grounds this now seems unlikely. Aldhelm of Malmesbury, the seventh-century English churchman who wrote one hundred Latin riddles, may have written some of the Old English riddles. His love of vernacular poetry was legendary. He is said by William of Malmesbury to have charmed Anglo-Saxons into church by chanting Old English songs from a wayside bridge.

The use of riddles or of riddlic metaphors is an important rhetorical device in medieval dialogue poetry. It occurs in poems such as Alcuin's eighth-century Latin "Dialogue with Pippin," which poses riddlic questions and answers such as, "What is the moon?—the eye of night." "What are the lips?—the door of the mouth." "What is the wonder of a dead man walking?—an image in water" (noted in Turner, 3: 380 ff.). Riddlic dialogues also occur in the ninth- or tenth-century Old English poem, "Solomon and Saturn," and in early Germanic stories like the Old Norse *Vafthruthnismal*, in which Odin and the giant Vafthruthnir engage in a riddle-like contest of wits. They also occur in the Icelandic *Heidreks Saga*, where the god Odin in the disguise of an old man, Gestumblindi, matches riddlic wits with his proud persecutor, King Heidrek. Riddlic dialogues like Alcuin's almost certainly took place in the Anglo-Saxon monasteries and in the greater courts as part of the learning process. Whether the game was carried out in the vernacular, as "Solomon and Saturn" and the northern Germanic stories suggest, is not known, but it seems likely.

In formal poetic terms, there are two kinds of riddles. In third-person descriptive riddles, the human speaker describes a wondrous creature he has seen or heard about. These riddles often begin with a formula, "I saw (heard about) a creature," or "The creature is," and end with "Say what I mean." First-person persona riddles give voice to the non-human creature and often begin with "I am (was) a creature" and end with "Say who I am." The tension between these two different kinds of riddles raises a question about the implied relationship between perception and being, or hermeneutics (how we make meaning) and ontology (how we define being). How we perceive the world, how we make meaning with language, helps to shape who we are. Our recognition of the other in the riddles helps us to enlarge both our sense of human perception and our understanding of alternate ways of being in the world. I summarize this process elsewhere:

> The Old English riddlers have meaning to peddle and part of the meaning lies in the game. The riddlers taunt and cajole, they admit and deny, they peddle false hopes and paradoxes, they lead the reader down dark roads with glints of light. And in the end they never confess except to flatter, "Say what I mean." What they mean is the riddle-solver's meaning. What they mean is that reality exists and is at the same time a mosaic of man's perception. What they mean is that man's measure of the world is in words, that perceptual categories are built on verbal foundations, and that by withholding the key to the categorical house (the entitling solution) the riddlers may force the riddle-solver to restructure his own perceptual blocks in order to gain entry to a metaphorical truth. In short the solver must imagine himself a door and open in. (Williamson 1977, 25)

What's most important is the power of the guessing game to expand the limits of our perception, to move beyond the ordinary modes or categories of thought, and to appreciate more acutely the otherness of the world— especially the natural world—around us.

The riddles, however, also point to the limits of our ability to catch the real world by means of language. Barley, for example, argues that the riddle-game is "a complicated play on reality and appearance, linking the unlike, denying conventional similarities, and generally dissolving barriers between classes, to make us realize that the grid we impose upon the world is far from a perfect fit and not the only one available" (143–44). Tiffany points to the "inherently seductive quality of a riddle, which can be attributed in part to a manner of speaking that simultaneously illuminates and obscures its object" (80). He analyzes the process of deception and illumination in the case of Riddle 9 (whose solution is probably "Wine-cup") as follows:

> The thing becomes human and then performs a verbal striptease in the dark, before our eyes, divesting itself of its human attributes. The suggestive verbal gestures that constitute the striptease are, at the same time, the movement that obscures the thing and transforms it into what it is not. For that is what a riddle does: it withholds the name of a thing so that the thing may appear as what it is not, in order to be revealed for what it is. (79)

Another kind of striptease takes place in those riddles which are characterized as bawdy, double entendre riddles. These appear to have two solutions, one for the prim and one for the saucy. The onion masquerade hides a penis, the butter churn a vagina. The sword tells us he's the battlefield brawler, not that bedroom carouser. These riddles which were once termed "obscene" and considered "folk riddles" are now thought to be complex lyric explorations of human sexuality and of the way we use language to characterize it or play seductive games with it. In these riddles, the female character often begins with a sense of wonder over the male member, only to take agency and power in the sexual act itself. This pattern leads Williams to posit a female authorship for such riddles and to argue that from them "we get a picture of [the Anglo-Saxon woman] as a spirited individual, fully capable of physical and emotional gratification in this most important area of human life" (55).

In other formal terms, the Old English riddles are built upon the techniques of metaphor and metamorphosis. They are metaphoric because each riddlic creature takes on the guise of another: the bagpipe is a bird that sings through its foot; the rake scruffs like a dog along walls; the butter churn is engaged in a bawdy bit of bouncing to produce its baby butter; and the bookworm is a plundering beast that wolfs down a tribal heritage. Tolkien wisely points out that the power of riddles is their root connection to "the spirit of poetry which sees things, whether familiar or strange, in the light of resemblance to other things, and in the comparison illuminates both the thing and the thing observed—a cloud as a bird, smoke, a sail, cattle on a blue pasture" (from his notes on the riddles in the Bodleian Library at Oxford, cited by Lee and Solopova, 78). Riddles are also metamorphic because in the natural flow, all creatures shift shapes: the horn turns from twinned head-warrior of the wild aurochs to battle-singer or mead-belly; the hide of the cow is transformed into a man's shoe or the vellum pages of a holy book.

The riddles lend voice to, and encourage understanding of, a variety of nature's creatures—fish and river, moon and mead, iceberg and onion, fox and moth. In so doing, they may be both shaping and showing an Anglo-Saxon sense of ecological awareness. At the very least they imply that the keys to understanding both self and other are forged out of the interplay between the language of humanity and the wonder of nature. The riddles seem to reverberate this double truth: we are symbol-makers, and we are also one of nature's animal wonders.

The riddle numbers in the selection here follow those of my edition of *The Old English Riddles of the Exeter Book*, and my book of translations, *A Feast of Creatures: Anglo-Saxon Riddle-Songs*. In Appendix D, I include a brief discussion of possible solutions as modern scholars see them. The solutions may be correct or not; the debates go on. So the clever reader is encouraged to come up with a new solution—and as the riddler invites, "Say what I mean."

Riddles

3

I am the lone wood in the warp of battle,
Wounded by iron, broken by blade,
Weary of war. Often I see
Battle-rush, rage, fierce fight flaring—
I hold no hope for help to come   5
Before I fall finally with warriors
Or feel the flame. The hard hammer-leavings
Strike me; the bright-edged, battle-sharp
Handiwork of smiths bites in battle.
Always I must await the harder encounter,   10
For I could never find in the world any

Of the race of healers who heal hard wounds
With roots and herbs. So I suffer
Sword-slash and death-wound day and night.

5

My gown is silent as I thread the seas,
Haunt old buildings or tread the land.
Sometimes my song-coat and the supple wind
Cradle me high over the homes of men,
And the power of clouds carries me   5
Windward over cities. Then my bright silks
Start to sing, whistle, roar,
Resound and ring, while I
Sail on untouched by earth and sea,
A spirit, ghost and guest, on wing.   10

7

I was an orphan before I was born.
Cast without breath by both parents
Into a world of brittle death, I found
The comfort of kin in a mother not mine.
She wrapped and robed my subtle skin,   5
Brooding warm in her guardian gown,
Cherished a changeling as if close kin
In a nest of strange siblings. This
Mother-care quickened my spirit, my natural
Fate to feed, fatten, and grow great,   10
Gorged on love. Bating a fledgling
Brood, I cast off mother-kin, lifting
Windward wings for the wide road.

9

My dress is silver, shimmering gray,
Spun with a blaze of garnets. I craze
Most men: rash fools I run on a road
Of rage, and cage quiet determined men.
Why they love me—lured from mind,   5
Stripped of strength—remains a riddle.

If they still praise my sinuous power
When they raise high the dearest treasure,
They will find through reckless habit
Dark woe in the dregs of pleasure.   10

10

Foot-furrowing, I walk and wound—
Living I ravage the raw land;
Lifeless I bind lord and servant.
Sometimes out of my belly I bring
The rush of drink to the fierce-hearted   5
War-man. Sometimes the arch-wild,
Fierce-footed woman treads my back.
Sometimes the dark-haired, drunken slave
Lifts me up near the night fire
With hot hands—turns, teases,   10
Presses, thrusts, warm and wet,
Down dark ways. Say what I am,
Who living plunder the down land
And after death serve man.

12

Once I was a plain warrior's weapon—
Now a stripling prince wraps my body
With bright twists of silver and gold.
Sometimes men kiss me, or carry me to battle
Where I call my lord's companions to wage war.   5
Bright with jewels, I am borne by a horse
Over hard plains, sometimes by the sea-stallion
Over storm-waves. Sometimes a woman,
Ring-adorned, fills my breast for the table—
Later I lie stripped of sweet treasure,   10
Hard and headless on the long boards.
Clothed in gold, I may grace the wall
Where men sit drinking, a soldier's gem.
Wound with silver, I sometimes ride
A warrior's horse, swallowing soldier's breath,   15
Blasting battle-song. Sometimes I bring

Bold men to wine; sometimes I sing caution
Or rescue thieves' catch or scatter foes
For my lord. Say what I am called.

13

I am a warrior with a white throat.
My head and sides are tawny. Two ears
Tower above my eyes. My back and cheeks
Are furred. I bear battle-weapons.
My gait is swift. I lope through green   5
Grass on battle-toes. My song is sorrow
If the slaughter-hound scents the narrow
Hall where I lie hidden with a brood
Of children, and we wait nestled in the curve
Of love while death snuffs at the door.   10
The dog drags doom—so quick with terror,
I seize my children for a secret flight.
If he bellies down, stalking in my chamber,
I cannot choose to fight—that is fools'
Counsel—I must tunnel a quick road   15
Through a steep hill, paw for the light,
Rush mothered babes through the burrow
Safely on secret streets out the hill-hole.
Brood-free I do not fear the hound's rush.
If the death-foe tracks the fierce mother   20
Through side streets, he will find
A narrow road through Grimsgate and a hard
Meeting on hilltop as I turn battle-tooth
And war-claw on the foe I once fled.

18

I am a strange creature shaped for battle,
Coated in colors, dear to my lord.
Bright thread lurks and swings in my mail,
Cradles the death-gem, gift of a lord
Who grips and guides my body forward   5
Through the wide rush of war. In the clear
Court of day, I bear the glint of gold,

Bright song of smiths. Often I slay
Soul-bearers with thrust and slash.
Sometimes the hall-king decks me in silver   10
Or garnet praise, raises my power
Where men drink mead, reins my killing
Or cuts me loose, heart-keen, swing-tired,
Through the broad room of war. Sometimes I sing
Through the throat of a friend—the curse   15
Of weapons. No son will seek vengeance
On my slayer when battle-foes ring death.
My tribe will not count children of mine
Unless I lordless leave the guardian
Who gave me rings. My fate is strange: 20
If I follow my lord and wage war,
Sure thrust of a prince's pleasure,
Then I must stroke in brideless play
Without the hope of child-treasure.
I am bound by an ancient craft to lose   25
That joy—so in sheer celibacy I enjoy
The hoard of heroes. Wrapped with wire
Like a bright fool, I frustrate a woman,
Steal her joy, slake desire. She rants,
Rails, curses, claps hands, chants   30
Unholy incantations—bladed words
In a bloodless battle I cannot enjoy . . .

19

Head down, nosing—I belly the ground.
Hard snuffle and grub, I bite and furrow—
Drawn by the dark enemy of forests,
Driven by a bent lord who hounds my trail,
Who lifts and lowers me, rams me down,   5
Pushes on plain, and sows seed.
I am a ground-skulker, born of wood,
Bound by wizards, brought on wheel.
My ways are weird: as I walk, one flank
Of my trail is gathering green; the other   10
Is bright black. Through my back and belly

A sharp sword thrusts; through my head
A dagger is stuck like a tooth: what I slash
Falls in a curve of slaughter to one side
If my driving lord slaves well.   15

21

Wob is my name twisted about—
I'm a strange creature shaped for battle.
When I bend and the battle-sting snakes
Through my belly, I am primed to drive off
The death-stroke. When my lord and tormentor   5
Releases my limbs, I am long again,
As laced with slaughter, I spit out
The death-blend I swallowed before.
What whistles from my belly does not easily pass,
And the man who seizes this sudden cup   10
Pays with his life for the long, last drink.
Unwound I will not obey any man;
Bound tight, I serve. Say what I am.

23

I am a wonderful help to women,
The hope of something to come. I harm
No citizen except my slayer.
Rooted I stand on a high bed.
I am shaggy below. Sometimes the beautiful   5
Peasant's daughter, an eager-armed,
Proud woman grabs my body,
Rushes my red skin, holds me hard,
Claims my head. The curly-haired
Woman who catches me fast will feel   10
Our meeting. Her eye will be wet.

24

A life-thief stole my world-strength,
Ripped off flesh and left me skin,
Dipped me in water and drew me out,
Stretched me bare in the tight sun;

The hard blade, clean steel, cut,   5
Scraped—fingers folded, shaped me.
Now the bird's once wind-stiff joy
Darts often to the horn's dark rim,
Sucks wood-stain, steps back again—
With a quick scratch of power, tracks   10
Black on my body, points trails.
Shield-boards clothe me and stretched hide,
A skin laced with gold. The bright song
Of smiths glistens on me in filigree tones.
Now decorative gold and crimson dye,   15
A clasp of wire and a coat of glory,
Proclaim the world's protector far and wide—
Let no fool fault these treasured claims.
If the children of men make use of me,
They will be safer and surer of heaven,   20
Bolder in heart, more blessed in mind,
Wiser in soul: they will find friends,
Companions and kinsmen, more loyal and true,
Nobler and better, brought to a new faith—
So men shall know grace, honor, glory,   25
Fortune, and the kind clasp of friends.
Say who I am—glorious, useful to men,
Holy and helpful from beginning to end.

25

I am man's treasure, taken from the woods,
Cliff-sides, hill-slopes, valleys, downs;
By day wings bear me in the buzzing air,
Slip me under a sheltering roof—sweet craft.
Soon a man bears me to a tub. Bathed,   5
I am binder and scourge of men, bring down
The young, ravage the old, sap strength.
Soon he discovers who wrestles with me
My fierce body-rush—I roll fools
Flush on the ground. Robbed of strength,   10
Reckless of speech, a man knows no power
Over hands, feet, mind. Who am I who bind

Men on middle-earth, blinding with rage
And such savage blows that dazed
Fools know my dark power by daylight?   15

27

I saw a wonderful creature carrying
Light plunder between its horns.
Curved lamp of the air, cunningly formed,
It fetched home its booty from the day's raid
And plotted to build in its castle if it could   5
A night-chamber brightly adorned.
Then over the east wall came another creature
Well known to earth-dwellers. Wonderful as well,
It seized back its booty and sent the plunderer home
Like an unwilling wanderer. The wretch went west,   10
Moved morosely and murderously on.
Dust rose to the heavens, dew fell on earth—
Night moved on. Afterwards no one
In the world knew where the wanderer had gone.

29

Middle-earth is made lovely in unmatched ways
Rich and rare. Across the hall
I saw a creature singing—nothing wilder
In the haunts of men. Her shape is strange.
Her beak hung down, her hands and feet   5
Slung up like a shouldered bird—she waits
Song-hungry in the hall of earls her hour
Of craft. She cannot feast or fly about,
Drink man's delight (she dreams of skill,
A task, her art), but begins to dance   10
On a road of hands—brash mute lies dumb,
Gathering glory while a beautiful haunting
Song sails through her strange foot—
A gift of sound. How her long dangling
Legs chant is a wonderful riddle.   15
Jeweled, naked, proud of rings—
She sings like a mighty sister,

Guardian of air, bearing bass brothers
Droned on her neck. Let the song-lifter,
Truth-shaper, name this creature.   20

30

Middle-earth is made lovely in unmatched ways
Rich and rare. I saw a strange creature
Riding the road, weird craft and power
From the workshops of men. She came sliding
Up on the shore, shrieking without sight,   5
Eyes, arms, shoulders, hands—
Sailed on one foot over smooth plains—
Treasure and haul. Her mouth in the middle
Of a hoard of ribs, she carries corn-
Gold, grain-treasure, wine-wealth.   10
The feast-floater brings in her belly food
For rich and poor. Let the wise who catch
The drift of this riddle say what I mean.

31

An awesome beauty angled the wave;
The deep-throated creature called to land,
Laughed loud-lingering, struck terror
Home to men. Her blades honed sharp,
She was slow to battle but battle-grim,   5
Savage wound-worker. The slaughterer
Struck ship-walls, carried a curse.
The cunning creature said of herself:
"My mother, who comes from the kind of women
Dearest and best, is my daughter grown   10
Great and pregnant; so is it known to men
On earth that she shall come and stand
Gracefully on the ground in every land."

32

I saw close to the houses of men
A strange creature that feeds cattle.
By tooth-hoard and nose-haul

(A useful slave), it scruffs the ground,
Scratches at plants, dogs walls   5
Or drags fields for plunder—seeks
A crop-catch and carries it home.
Its prey is bent stalk and weak root;
Its gift is firm grain and full flower
On a glittering plain—growing, blooming.

37

Writings reveal this creature's plain
Presence on middle-earth, marked by man
For many years. Its magic, shaping power
Passes knowing. It seeks the living
One by one, winds an exile's road,   5
Wanders homeless without blame, never there
Another night. It has no hands or feet
To touch the ground, no mouth to speak
With men or mind to know the books
Which claim it is the least of creatures   10
Shaped by nature. It has no soul, no life,
Yet it moves everywhere in the wide world.
It has no blood or bone, yet carries comfort
To the children of men on middle-earth.
It has never reached heaven and cannot reach   15
Hell—but must live long through the word
And will of the king of creation's glory.
It would take too long to tell its fate
Through the world's web: that would be
A wonder of speaking. Each man's way   20
Of catching the creature with words is true.
It has no limbs, yet it lives!
If you can solve a riddle quickly,
Say what this creature is called.

43

I heard of something rising in a corner,
Swelling and standing up, lifting its cover.
The proud-hearted bride grabbed at that boneless

Wonder with her hands; the prince's daughter
Covered that swelling thing with a swirl of cloth.   5

45

A moth ate songs—wolfed words!
That seemed a weird dish—that a worm
Should swallow, dumb thief in the dark,
The songs of a man, his chants of glory,
Their place of strength. That thief-guest   5
Was no wiser for having swallowed words.

52

The young man came over to the corner
Where he knew she stood. He stepped up,
Eager and agile, lifted his tunic
With hard hands, thrust through her girdle
Something stiff, worked on the standing   5
One his will. Both swayed and shook.
The young man hurried, was sometimes useful,
Served well, but always tired
Sooner than she, weary of the work.
Under her girdle began to grow   10
A hero's reward for laying on dough.

57

I saw heart-strong, mind-sharp men
Gazing in a hall at a golden ring.
Who turned the ring prayed to God
For abiding peace, the hall guests'
Grace. The bright circle of gold   5
Spoke the name of the Savior of good
Men to the gathering, proclaimed to the eye
And mind of man the most glorious token,
Spoke though dumb of the suffering king
To all who could see in its bodied wounds   10
The hard carving of Christ. An unfulfilled
Prayer has no power in heaven; the dark
Soul will not find the city of saints,

The throne of power, the camp of God.
Let the man who knows how the wounds   15
Of the strange ring spoke as it passed round
The hall—twisting, turning in the hands
Of proud men—explain the riddle.

71

I grew in the ground, nourished by earth
And cloud—until grim enemies came
To take me, rip me living from the land,
Strip my years—shear, split, shape me
So that I ride homeless in a slayer's hand,   5
Bent to his will. A busy sting,
I serve my lord if strength and strife
On the field endure and his hold is good.
We gather glory together in the troop,
Striker and death-step, lord and dark lunge.   10
My neck is slim, my sides are dun;
My head is bright when the battle-sun
Glints and my grim loving lord bears me
Bound for war. Bold soldiers know
That I break in like a brash marauder,   15
Burst the brain-house, plunder halls
Held whole before. From the bone-house
One breaks ready for the road home.
Now the warrior who feels the thrust
Of my meaning should say what I'm called.   20

74

Suckled by the sea, sheltered near shore,
Cradled in the cold catch of waves,
Footless and fixed—often I offered
To the sea-stream a stretch of mouth.
Now a man will strip my bonelike skin   5
From the sides of my body with a bright blade
And bolt my flesh, relish me raw:
A quick cuisine—crack to jaw.

76

I am a prince's property and joy,
Sometimes his shoulder-companion,
Close comrade in arms, king's servant,
Lord's treasure. Sometimes my lady,
A bright-haired beauty, lays serving   5
Hands on my body, though she is noble
And the daughter of an earl. I bear
In my belly what blooms in the wood,
The bee's delight. Sometimes I ride
A proud horse in the rush of battle—   10
Harsh is my voice, hard is my tongue.
I bear the scop's meed when his song is done.
My gift is good, my way winning,
My color dark. Say what I'm called.

77

I am puff-breasted, proud-crested,
Swollen-necked. I strut on one foot.
I sport a fine head, high tail,
Eyes, ears, back, beak, two sides.
I ride a stiff nail, my perch above men.   5
I twist in torment when the forest-shaker
Whips and shoves; where I stand the storm-
Wind-waters roll, hail stones,
Sleet shrouds, frost slips freezing,
Snow drifts down. One-foot, hole-belly,   10
I mark the seasons with a twist of fate
I cannot change. My stake is grim.

79

My race is old, my seasons many,
My sorrows deep. I have dwelt in cities
Since the fire-guardian wrought with flame
My clean beginning in the world of men,
Purged my body with a circling fire.   5
Now a fierce earth-brother stands guard,
The first to shape my sorrow—I remember

Who ripped our race, hard from its homeland,
Stripped us from the ground. I cannot bind
Or blast him, yet I cause the clench of slavery   10
Round the world. Though my wounds are many
On middle-earth, my strength is great.
My craft and course, power and rich passage,
I must hide from men. Say who I am.

81

Shunning silence, my house is loud
While I am quiet: we are movement bound
By the Shaper's will. I am swifter,
Sometimes stronger—he is longer lasting,
Harder running. Sometimes I rest,   5
While he rolls on. He is the house
That holds me living—alone I die.

91

I am noble, known to rest in the quiet
Keeping of many men, humble and high born.
The plunderers' joy, hauled far from friends,
Rides richly on me, shines signifying power,
Whether I proclaim the grandeur of halls,   5
The wealth of cities, or the glory of God.
Now wise men love most my strange way
Of offering wisdom to many without voice.
Though the children of earth eagerly seek
To trace my trail, sometimes my tracks are dim.   10

GNOMIC OR WISDOM POEMS

U nder this heading, scholars normally include a diversity of genres such as charms, proverbs, gnomes or maxims, advice poems, and homiletic poems. Gnomic poems tend to be didactic and moralistic. The writers of these poems want to give us advice about life, to cure illness, and to tell us how to act or where to be in the social or natural matrix. But they are full of artful mystery, tangled ambiguity, surreal gaps in meaning. So they are also telling us how difficult it is to know the truth, to pass on proverbial advice, to guide the listener in the proper way of living. Hansen recognizes this when she describes the complex mystery of these poems:

> Wisdom literature . . . is literature written in a non-realistic, non-narrative mode that hopes for and encodes the active involvement of its audience in both the self-conscious construction of meaning in the text and the application of that meaning outside of the text. It defines this double activity, which we might call both playful and serious, as essentially linguistic and quintessentially human. It often reminds its audience that such activity is necessary not because truth is absolute and context-free, but because all human understanding is contingent and context-bound. It celebrates human systems that organize experience while it recognizes their frailty. (10–11)

This is the paradox of gnomic poems: they pass on received wisdom even as they call that wisdom into question. They postulate fixed truths even as they suggest that all such truths are contextually bound. They begin with didactic solutions, but in the end they call into question the whole tenor of giving uncontested advice.

Whether the maxim applies or the charm works or the catalogue of fortunes encourages us in the direction of the craftsman or king and away from the drunkard or outlaw may depend upon our perception of the poems, our reading of the contexts of proverbial advice, and our reaction to the gnomes and the nascent stories. Gnomes move from known truths to ambiguous meanings. In this they are the opposite of riddles, which move from an ambiguous unknowing to the security of a solution (even though the solution may be difficult to discover and ultimately debated by solvers and critics). Finally though, gnomes raise the same sorts of questions about perception and meaning that the riddles raise—namely, what is the relation between what we observe, how we use language to characterize it, and who we are as human beings.

MAXIMS II (COTTON MAXIMS)

The poem "Maxims II (Cotton Maxims)" consists of a list of short, pithy statements about various creatures, human and non-human, and their appropriate, typical, or desired context, action, or condition. These poems derive from a medieval and classical tradition of catalogic and encyclopedic works, but they have a tone and structure uniquely Anglo-Saxon. Each maxim is a mini-definition usually built on the verb *byð* ("is," "is always," "will be") or *sceal* ("shall be," "should be," "must be," "ought to be," "is typically"). These simple verbs are notoriously difficult to translate. Greenfield and Evert list the following possibilities for the opening half-line, *Cyning sceal rīce healdan*:

> "A king ought to rule (or preserve) a kingdom" (i.e., a king ought to rule it rather than abuse or neglect it), or "A king shall rule a kingdom" (i.e., it is the nature of a king to rule a kingdom), or "A king must rule a kingdom" (i.e., each kingdom must be ruled by some king). (342)

Beneath the apparently straightforward gnomic half-line, the poem points to a wide variety of possible kingly behaviors. What is slides into what should be or might be. The possibility of "might not" lurks beneath the surface. The ideal is haunted by the shadow of real-world kingly faults and failures. Nearly every gnome is like this, hiding beneath its supposedly simple statement a provocative mixture of possibilities.

The ambiguity of meaning within each individual maxim is matched by the often inexplicable relation between maxims. Lines 4–5 of "Maxims II," for example, read: "Thunder (is) the loudest at times. The glories of Christ are great. / Fate is the firmest, winter the coldest." What are the connections between thunder, Christ's glories, fate, and winter? Do seasons (winter) and natural phenomena (thunder) come under the rubric of Christ's glories? Does the power and providence of Christ's working in the world overthrow or redefine an older notion of inexorable *Wyrd* or Fate? Has fate been reduced to a worldly season or a bit of bright thunder? We could assume that the Anglo-Saxon poet had a haphazard pattern of construction or embraced an ordered world view that we no longer comprehend. Or we might strain to make modern order out of the catalogue only to erase some significant points of disjuncture in the poem. Alternatively, we can assume that the gaps between maxims serve some purpose, some intended ambiguity, some moment of surprise intended to challenge our ordinary way of perceiving and ordering the world.

Each creature in "Maxims II" has its context, a proper place or action. The dragon dwells in the cave; the boar in the wood. A good man seeks homeland glory; a king gives gold rings in the hall. But the abutting of maxims often leads to an unexpected and tantalizing comparison. To take one example, the poet says:

> The dragon shall dwell in a barrow,
> Old and treasure-proud. The fish must spawn
> Its kin in water. The king must give out
> Rings in the hall. (26b–29a)

A good and wise king should give out rings in the hall to his loyal retainers. In poems like *Beowulf*, this is done to cement the bonds between the king and his thanes and to signify loyalty and protection on both sides. What has this to do with the fish spawning in water or the dragon hoarding in his barrow? Perhaps a generous king is like the fish spawning peace in the hall, while the greedy king is like a dragon, hoarding his treasure (as Heremod does in *Beowulf*) so that he has no loyal thanes and spawns only strife. This begins to look like the ghost of a riddle hiding out in the gaps between the conventional maxims (for more on this, see Williamson 1982, 30–33).

The placement of maxims against one another—colluding, colliding—raises the question of perception. It defamiliarizes and deepens reality. It sparks surreal possibilities so that the wooden gnomes are set alight with a provocative fire. Early in the poem, the poet says *sōð byð swicolost,* which means "truth is the trickiest." Often scholars emend this passage to read *sōð byð switolost* (or *swutolost*) to mean "truth is the clearest," which is more understandable. But in support of the manuscript reading, Robinson points to the context of the following maxim, *sinc byð dēorost,* "treasure (gold) is dearest (most precious)," arguing that "it may be then that 'truth is most tricky' because man's inordinate love of money is constantly inducing him to make falsehoods look like truth and truth like falsehoods" (1982, 10–11). Probably not all of the "mismatched" maxims can be elucidated in this way, but the invitation to explore not only the obvious connections in the universe but also the less obvious and even the inexplicable ones seems clear. At the very least, we should recognize in the maxims and their gaps what Howe calls a "strangeness of taxonomy," whose apparent disjunctions force us to see beyond our ordinary categories of perception, and whose apparent absurdity "is also deeply disconcerting, for it challenges our fundamental ways of ordering experience" (10).

Maxims II (Cotton Maxims)

A king shall rule a kingdom. Cities are seen from afar,
The cunning work of giants, wonderful wall-stones,
The works left on earth. Wind is the swiftest creature in air,
Thunder the loudest at times. The glories of Christ are great.
Fate is the firmest, winter the coldest,   5
Spring the frostiest, its chill the longest.
Summer is sun-brightest, the sky then hottest,
Autumn most glorious, harvest-heavy,
Bringing the year's fruit given by God.
Truth is the trickiest, treasure the dearest,   10
Gold made for men, the old one wisest,
Rich in experience, enduring for years.
Woe is wondrously clinging. Clouds drift off.
Good companions should encourage a prince

To be a battle-warrior and ring-giver.   15
A man must have courage, the sword a helmet
To bite in battle. The wild hawk must find
A home on the glove; the wolf haunts the wood,
The eagle soars alone. The boar in the forest
Shall be tusk-strong. A good man seeks glory   20
In his homeland. A spear dwells in the hand,
Stained with gold. A gem stands on the ring,
High and prominent. The stream will be wave-bound
To mix with the flood. The mast must stand on a boat,
Lifting the sail-yard. The sword shall be on the lap,   25
A noble iron. The dragon shall dwell in a barrow,
Old and treasure-proud. The fish must spawn
Its kin in water. The king must give out
Rings in the hall. The bear shall be on the heath,
Old and awesome. The river flows from the hill   30
To the flood-gray sea. The army shall fight together,
Fixed on glory. Faith and trust must be in a lord,
Wisdom in a man. The wood shall be on the earth
With fruit and bloom—the hills of the world
Stand green and gleaming. Only God in heaven   35
Shall be judge of deeds. The door of a building
Is its broad hall-mouth. The boss must be on the shield,
Finger-fast protection. The bird must sail and soar,
Sporting with the wind, the salmon dart through water
Like a quick shot. Showers shall start in the heavens,   40
Churning with wind, then fall on the land.
A thief must hide out in gloomy weather.
A demon must live alone in the fen.
A woman must seek her secret lover
With craft and cunning if she has no wish   45
To be bound in marriage, bought with rings,
Thriving as a proud wife among her people.
Water-flow shall be salt-surge, cloud-cover,
Sky-mist, and mountain stream. Cattle on earth
Shall teem and thrive. Stars in heaven   50
Shall shine brightly as the Creator commanded.

Good shall oppose evil, youth oppose age,
Life oppose death, light oppose darkness,
Army oppose army, one enemy against another.
Foe against foe shall fight over land,   55
Engage in feud, accuse each other of crimes.
Ever must a wise man think about struggle
And strife in this world. An outlaw must hang,
Pay for the terrible crime he committed
Against mankind. The Creator alone knows   60
Where the soul will turn after the death-day
When all spirits journey to the judgment of God
In their Father's embrace. The shape of the future
Is secret and hidden. Only God knows that—
Our saving Father. No one returns here   65
Under our earthly roofs to tell us the truth—
What the Lord's shaping creation holds forth
Or what heaven's hall with its victory-people
Looks like in that place where the Lord lives.

CHARMS

Old English charms are part of both magical and medical traditions. They
are often accompanied by medicinal directions such as "boil feverfew and
plantain and the red nettle that grows in grain," by practical advice such as
"throw earth over [swarming bees]," and by magical incantations such as
"get out little spear, don't stay in here." The magical element of charms
often involves some form of comparison or substitution corresponding to
the poetic devices of simile and metaphor. In the first charm below, the
charmist uses simile in exhorting the tumor to "shrivel like coal in the catch
of fire" or "disappear like dirt on the wall." In the other charms, the char-
mist uses metaphor in comparing swarming bees to a band of "victory
women" or rheumatic pain to an "iron stitch . . . the work of witches." The
use of such poetic and incantatory language may be a means of preserving
and passing down effective practices. It may lend concrete visual imagery to
a practical cure at hand. It may also function as a way of verbal healing
since we know from both anthropological studies of primitive cures and
modern medical experiments that a patient's response to positive feedback

from a physician is sometimes as effective as any prescribed potion. The charms are thus both poetical and practical, and they serve the twin purposes of cure and care.

The sympathetic function of magic assumes a metaphoric equation between objects or actions ("things alike are equivalent"). Thus, the knives of elves and the pains of a "sudden stitch," which might be anything from a muscle cramp to rheumatism or an angina pain (Cameron, 141), may be poetically and magically linked since they both attack the body. The contagious function of ritual magic assumes a metonymic equation between objects or actions ("things contiguous are equivalent"), so that by controlling dirt, which is a part of the bees' world, the charmist can magically control the bees as well. Throwing the dirt or dust might also help to settle the bees in a purely practical way. In addition, the charm for the swarm of bees may be sent forth in a veiled metaphoric fashion against other angry or harmful bee-like creatures such as the "slanderous tongues of man." The beekeeper and charmist need the bees to form a properly sustaining community, just as they need a supportive human community free from slander and threat. The human and natural stingers must be sheathed and a sustaining honey produced.

Charm for Wens (or Tumors)

Wen, wen, chicken-wen,
Build no house to enter in,
No town to hold. Go north, wretch,
To the neighboring hill where your brother waits
With a leaf for your head. Under wolf's paw,   5
Under eagle's wing, under eagle's claw,
May you shrivel like coal in the catch of fire,
Disappear like dirt on the wall, water in a bucket,
Tiny as linseed, smaller than a hand-worm's
Hip-bone, smaller than something that is not!   10

Charm for a Swarm of Bees

Take earth and throw it down with your right hand
under your right foot, saying:

I catch it under foot—under foot I find it.
Look! Earth has power over all creatures,
Over grudges, over malice, over evil rites,   5
Over even the mighty, slanderous tongue of man.

Afterwards as they swarm, throw earth over them
saying:

Settle down, little victory-women, down on earth—
Stay home, never fly wild to the woods.   10
Be wise and mindful of my benefit,
As every man remembers his hearth and home,
His life and land, his meat and drink.

Charm for a Sudden Stitch

Boil feverfew and plantain and the red nettle
that grows in the grain—boil in butter, saying:

Loud, they were loud, riding over the mound,
Fierce and resolute, riding over the land.
Find a shield for their evil and save yourself.   5
Get out, little spear, if you are in here.
I stood under linden, under a light-shield,
When the mighty women stole strength
And sent screaming spears against my skin.
I will send them back an answering spear,   10
An arrow flying back at their savage front.
Get out, little spear, if you are in here.
A smith sat shaping a little knife,
Forging a blade, a wounding iron.
Get out, little spear, if you are in here.   15
Six smiths sat, shaping slaughter-spears.
Get out, little spear. Don't stay in here.
If there is any iron stitch in here,
The work of witches, let it melt in here.
If you were shot in skin or shot in flesh,   20
Or shot in blood or shot in bone,

Or shot in limb, may your life be unscathed.
If you were shot by Æsir or shot by elves,
Or shot by hags, I will help you now.
Take this for Æsir-shot, this for elf-shot,   25
This for hag-shot—this will help and heal.
Fly out, fly away, to the woods or hills.
Be whole, be healthy. May the Lord help you.
Take this knife now and wash it in water.

THE FORTUNES OF MEN

"The Fortunes of Men" is another kind of catalogue poem. It begins with a
family setting where loving parents nurture and teach their son. But the boy
must eventually "walk out of youth" into the adult world where only God
knows what his fate will be. The poet begins his list of possible fortunes
with a catalogue of dire fates: a wolf eats one, the sword slays one, a storm
drowns one. One goes blind, another lame. In a riddlic passage, one falls
from a tree like a wingless bird, lands on the ground to rot like fruit, and
discovers that "root-sick, his bloom is done." The catalogue finally turns at
line 56 to positive fortunes, emphasizing various human crafts, implying
that the answer to an inhospitable world might be hard work and a tradi-
tional place in the social fabric. One man is an archer, another a chess
player. One is a goldsmith rewarded with a gift of land. A *scop* or poet-
singer sits at his lord's feet, entertaining hall-thanes with stories and songs.
A falconer tames and teaches his wild hawk, perhaps as God humbles us
and "creates our crafts" and "shapes our endings."

The poet concludes by saying that every man should give thanks to God
for fixing his fate and measuring out mercy to mankind, but the presence
of mercy in the catalogue is muted. Shippey points out that the poem begins
with the human concern of parents for their children, but that "right at the
start, humanity is brought into opposition with, and under subjection to,
time," so that we are left with a sense of mourning in the face of what seems
to be an impersonal universe (1976, 10). The catalogue form itself may
reflect the human desire for order, even as it undermines this in its some-
times arbitrary choice of fates and its inexplicable sense of connection be-
tween them. Hansen argues that such poems "address a puzzling and
inexplicable aspect of human experience, in this case, the inequity and un-
predictability of the lots that befall individual persons; they argue that this

apparent enigma can in fact be read, if we organize our observations rightly, as a sign of the self-revealing activity of a powerful and concerned deity," and she goes on to argue that "in supporting this claim with the catalogue itself, poets in fact presume to imitate that deity as they organize another set of allegedly meaningful signs (that is, their own words) in order to control the significance of experience" (98). In "The Fortunes of Men," the poet's attempt at human ordering only partly succeeds. The tension remains between the human desire to believe in providential order and the doubt that the worldly evidence of arbitrary fortunes can sustain this belief.

The Fortunes of Men

Often it happens through the glory of God
That a man and woman bring into the world
A child by birth, give him colorful clothes,
Cuddle and coax him, teach and train him,
Till the time comes when his young limbs   5
Are strong, lithe, and fully grown.
His father and mother first carry him,
Then lead him, and finally walk beside him.
They feed and clothe him, but God alone knows
What the years will bring the growing boy.   10
One walks out of youth to a woeful end,
A misery to mankind. Out on the moor
A gray wolf will eat him and his mother mourn—
His fierce fate is beyond man's wielding.
Hunger haunts one, the sword slays one,   15
The storm drowns one, the spear guts one—
War is his stalker, battle his bane.
Blind-eye gropes with his hands through life,
Lame-foot crawls sinew-sick through pain,
Bird-man flies wingless from the tree,   20
Doing wind-tricks as he soars down.
On the ground he rots like dead fruit—
Root-sick, his bloom is done.
One shall walk on a far-winding road,
Bear his food and home on his back   25
Into foreign lands, leaving a damp track

On dangerous ground. He has few friends
To offer him greeting as they gather round.
A friendless man finds no welcome—
Men fear his long trail of misfortune.   30
One man rides the high gallows-tree,
Dangling in death till the raven swoops
Down on his bone-house, his bloody flesh,
Scoops out his eyeballs, pecks at his head,
Tears at his corpse. He can't keep at bay   35
That dark-coated bird, ward off the black flier
With his useless hands. His life has fled.
He feels nothing on the gallows-tree—
His face is pale, his fate is fixed.
He swings in death's shrouded mist—   40
Outlaw and alien, his name is cursed.
Another sleeps on a funeral pyre—
The fierce flame, the red fire
Will devour the doomed. He leaves life quickly.
The woman will wail who loses her son   45
To the flames' embrace, his last kiss.
Sometimes the sword's edge steals the life
Of an ale-drinker or a wine-weary man
At the mead-bench. His words are too quick.
Another drinks beer from the cup-bearer's hand,   50
Grows drunk as a mead-fool, forgets to check
His mouth with his mind, seeks suffering,
Finds fate, life's joyless end.
Men call him a mead-wild self-slayer,
Give him an unholy name in words.   55
One will be lucky with God's help,
Leave the wrack and ruin of youth,
The spilling of fortune, the heft of hardship,
Find days of joy and the treasure of gems,
Mead-cups and crafted gifts in old age,   60
The camaraderie of kin—all worth keeping.

So mighty God gives out destinies,
Deals out fortunes to all men on earth.

One finds wealth, another finds woe,
One finds gladness, another finds glory,   65
One shoots arrows, another throws dice,
One is crafty at the gaming table,
One chooses chess, another wise words.
One has skill as a great goldsmith—
He hardens rings, adorns kings,   70
Who reward his craft with gifts of land.
One shall gladden hearts in the hall,
Delight the drinkers, delivering joy.
One sits with his harp at his lord's feet,
Takes his treasure, a reward of rings,   75
Plucks with his harp-nail, sweeps over strings,
Shapes song: hall-thanes long for his melody.
One will tame the proud, fierce bird,
Hold hawk in hand, till that sword-swallow
Gentles down to the arm's delight—   80
He gives the bird food and foot-rings
Until that savage slayer in its hooded grace
Humbles himself to his trainer's hand.
So God gives out varied fortunes,
Fixes fates, shapes our endings,   85
Creates our crafts, decides the destiny
Of every man throughout middle-earth.
So every man should give thanks to him
For the mercy he measures out to mankind.

RELIGIOUS POEMS

The power of the Christian message for the early Anglo-Saxons is told in legendary form by Bede when he recounts the story of the conversion of King Edwin of Northumbria in his *History of the English Church and People*. When Edwin asks his counselors for their opinion about this new faith, his chief priest Coifi admits that the old religion seems powerless and without value. An unnamed advisor then says:

> Your Majesty, when we compare the present life of man on earth with that time of which we have no knowledge, it seems to me like the swift flight of a single sparrow through the banqueting-hall where you are sitting at dinner on a winter's day with your thanes and counselors. In the midst there is a comforting fire to warm the hall; outside, the storms of winter rain or snow are raging. This sparrow flies swiftly in through one door of the hall, and out through another. While he is inside, he is safe from the winter storms; but after a few moments of comfort, he vanishes from sight into the wintry world from which he came. Even so, man appears on earth for a little while; but of what went before this life or of what follows, we know nothing. Therefore, if this new teaching has brought any more certain knowledge, it seems only right that we should follow it. (Bede, 127)

The eighth-century Bede surely colored this story of the seventh-century King Edwin with his own religious convictions, but Edwin did convert to Christianity, and in time England became one of the centers of religious learning and power in early medieval Europe. There is a wide variety of Christian religious poetry in Old English, including narrative treatments of Old Testament stories, depictions of Christ as hero, stories of saints' lives, homiletic poems, and "The Dream of the Rood." The Christian literature in Old English is extensive and represents a varied and compelling testament to the strength of the Anglo-Saxons' faith and the poetic power of their religious vision.

CÆDMON'S HYMN

"Cædmon's Hymn" comes down to us from a story in Bede's *Ecclesiastical History of the English People* and exists in 21 manuscripts, whereas most Old English poems exist in only a single manuscript. The poem is an important cornerstone in Anglo-Saxon history and legend. It purports to be the first poem in which the new Christian teachings were set down in the alliterative, strong-stress poetic traditions of the Germanic peoples who had migrated to England.

Bede's eighth-century description of the seventh-century Cædmon's miracle begins with the setting of the monastery at Whitby. The monastery was a double monastery with separate houses for men and women, which was not uncommon at the time. Cædmon worked in a secular capacity at the monastery. After dinner the harp would sometimes be passed around the table for each person to sing something, but on such occasions Cædmon would excuse himself and leave the festivities because he didn't know how to sing. On one such occasion, he left the harp-passing party, went to the livestock shed where he was assigned night-duty, and lay down to sleep. Then an awe-inspiring figure came to him in a vision or dream and called to him, *Cædmon, sing mē hwæthwugu*, "Cædmon, sing me something." Cædmon answered humbly, "I don't know how to sing—that's why I always leave the table." The voice answered, "Yet you will sing for me." "What shall I sing?" Cædmon asked. The voice answered, *Sing mē frumsceaft*, "Sing me Creation, the beginning of all things." And Cædmon, who had never sung anything before, began miraculously to sing the song now known as "Cædmon's Hymn."

The next morning, Cædmon remembered the song and told his steward and then the abbess who directed the monastery. The abbess, knowing this to be a divine inspiration and miracle, invited Cædmon to join the monastery, study the religious traditions and teachings, and spend the rest of his life writing about Christian subjects in the vernacular Anglo-Saxon poetical mode—which he did. Bede says that Cædmon devoured the teachings and ruminated on them like a cow chewing on a cud, and then converted them to the sweetest songs, transforming his teachers into an audience of rapt students (250 ff.).

Cædmon thus becomes the nexus of the meeting of two cultures, Christian and Germanic, which would be the heart of English culture for centuries to come. Lerer points to the significance of this cultural connection:

> His departure from the feast, inspiration in the cow-shed, and entry into the monastery chart a progressive synthesis of two contrasting cultures. He himself comes to embody the traditions of both sacred and secular, social and monastic. Read more specifically in Dumézil's terms, Cædmon straddles the worlds of those who represent fecundity and prosperity (i.e., the cowherds, farmers, or other providers who participate in the feast) and those who represent sovereignty and force (i.e., the Church and its members, and the monastic community that owns the land on which Cædmon and his peers had worked). . . . In its verbal transformation of religious history into heroic diction, the poem, as it were, "makes peace" with two opposing ideologies, and it is at this moment that the poet is himself "created." (1991, 43)

For "Cædmon's Hymn," I offer the poem first in an Old English version (based on texts by Krapp and Dobbie, Pope, and others), then in a literal line-by-line translation, and finally in my poetic translation.

Cædmon's Hymn (Old English)

Nū sculon heriġean heofonrīċes Weard,
Meotodes meahte, ond his mōdġeþanc,
weorc Wuldorfæder, swā hē wundra ġehwæs,
ēċe Drihten, ōr onstealde.
Hē ærest sceōp ielda bearnum   5
heofon tō hrōfe, hāliġ Scyppend.
Þā middanġeard monncynnes Weard,
ēċe Drihten, æfter tēode
fīrum foldan, Frēa ælmihtiġ.

Cædmon's Hymn (literal translation)

Now let us praise the Guardian of heaven's kingdom,
The Creator's might, and his mindful purpose,
The work of the Glory-father, as he, of each of wonders,
The eternal Lord, established the beginning.
He first created for the children of men   5
Heaven as a roof, the holy Shaper.
Then middle-earth, the Guardian of mankind,
Eternal Lord, afterwards created,
As a land for man, God almighty.

Cædmon's Hymn (poetic translation)

Now let us praise the Creator and Guardian
Of the heavenly kingdom, his power and purpose,
His mind and might, his wondrous works.
He shaped each miraculous beginning,
Each living creature, each earthly kind.   5
He first made for the children of men
Heaven as a roof. Then our Holy Shaper
Crafted middle-earth, a home for mankind,
Our God and Guardian watching over us—
Eternal, almighty—our Lord and King.   10

PHYSIOLOGUS:
PANTHER AND WHALE

The Old English "Physiologus" is a poem that contains separate but related
allegorical poems, "The Panther" and "The Whale." A third poem, a frag-
ment of one and one-half lines, is about a bird of some sort. Marckwardt
and Rosier note that "the medieval Latin versions of the Greek *Physiologus*
(or *Bestiary*, as it was sometimes later called) contained between twenty-six
and forty-nine chapters, each devoted to a real or legendary creature to-
gether with its interpreted moral or theological significance" (236). The
panther in this Old English "Physiologus" is associated with Christ, proba-
bly because of a mistranslation of the word for "lion" in a rare reference to
the Lord in Hosea, where the Septuagint has "panther" instead of "lion."

The description of the panther here is both allegorical and legendary; the Anglo-Saxons obviously had little knowledge of panthers. "The Whale" also involves a mistranslation from earlier versions, as the creature is called *Fastitocalon*, probably derived from an Irish-Latin form of the Greek word for "shield-turtle" (237). The name lost its meaning to the Anglo-Saxons and was used as a name for the Satanic whale in this poem. The description of the whale seems more realistic than that of the panther, probably because the Anglo-Saxons knew something about whales, as is indicated by their use of *hwæl*, "whale," both as a single word and in compounds such as *hwælhunta*, "whale-hunter," and *hwælweg*, "whale-road" (a kenning for "sea").

The Christlike panther in the opening poem is a handsome and exotic beast, friendly to all creatures except the serpent or dragon who represents his arch-enemy Satan in this particular allegory. The panther has a magical coat of many colors like that of Joseph, its "luminous hues" an indication of its compelling beauty. The panther eats its fill, then sleeps in a cave for three nights, increasing its power. This corresponds to the period of Christ's entombment after the crucifixion, during which time he harrowed hell and left the Devil enchained. At the end of this period, the panther emerges from the cave and emits an alluring music and scent from its mouth which symbolizes the redemptive grace of the resurrection. The musical scent (or the perfumed melody) draws the faithful to him. The implicit connection between Christ and the panther is made explicit in the concluding half of the poem.

In the second poem, Satan is represented by the dangerous and deceptive whale who floats like an island, drawing unwary sailors to his thick-skinned shore. The sailors, relieved to find a respite in the middle of the sea-strife, build a fire, share a feast, and lie down in trusting sleep. The whale then dives down with the men into the ocean's depths to drown and devour them. The poet tells us that this is the way devils and demons lure unwitting men into evil ways, drawing them away from the righteous and tempting them to rely upon the judgment of wicked people. Once the Devil has them mired in sin, he bolts into hell, dragging them behind him, just like the whale.

The poet makes clear that mankind must be wary of the Devil's deceptions. This is especially true in terms of the allegorical details, since both panther and whale give off a pleasing scent. How exactly the unwary traveler is to discern the difference between the scents is not made clear. Perhaps this is a warning that the proper perception of the difference between good and evil is not always so easily attained. One is reminded here of the line in "Maxims II" that "truth is the trickiest."

In "The Whale," I have restored the sense of lines 89–91b where a brief passage is missing.

Physiologus: Panther and Whale

I. The Panther

There are many creatures on middle-earth
Whose nature and origin we cannot know,
Whose numbers we cannot easily count—
Birds and beasts on air and land
Who wander to the water at earth's edge,   5
Where the rolling waves, the roiling seas,
Surround the shores, embracing earth.
We've heard about one curious kind
Of wild creature, an exotic animal,
Who inhabits the hills in distant lands,   10
Living in caves. It's called the panther—
As the wise sons of men say in writings
About this wild wanderer, this beautiful beast.
He's a friend to all except the serpent,
The devilish dragon, whom he hates and harrows,   15
Fighting that fierce fiend at every opportunity.
The panther has a coat of many colors.
Just as holy men say that Joseph's coat,
A delight of dyes, a catch of colors,
Was brighter, more beautiful and varied   20
Than any worn by the children of men—
So the panther's coat has luminous hues,
A rainbow range, a shimmering skin,
Each color brighter, more beautiful than the next—
The fairest of furs, the sleekest of skins.   25
This panther is unique, one of a kind—
Mild and meek, gentle and loving.
He will harm no creature except his foe,
His ancient enemy, the poisonous serpent,

The dangerous demon, whom I've mentioned before.   30
When the panther is full, pleased with his feast,
He seeks out his secret resting place,
His cave in the hills where he sleeps soundly
For three nights, slumber-fast, storing strength.
Then on the third day when mind and muscle   35
Have grown great, there comes quickly
From the mighty beast's mouth, strange music,
A sonorous mewing, a miraculous song.
After that melody a strange smell rises
And plays like perfume in that same place,   40
Sweeter and stronger than any scent,
Than the blooms and blossoms of any plant,
Any flower in the wood, any fairness on earth.
Then from all the cities and kingdoms,
From the houses and halls, multitudes of men   45
Take to the roads, throng the earth-ways,
Hasten along with all the animals to the hills—
A company of creatures to the scent and song.

Likewise the Lord God, our ruler and redeemer,
Our judge and joy, giver of all gifts,   50
Earthly and eternal, is gentle to all creatures
Except the serpent, the bitter enemy,
The devious dragon, the source of all poison,
Who is God's enemy, his fiendish foe,
Whom he bound hard in hell's torments,   55
Wrapped in chains of fire, blazing fetters,
Sheathed in misery. Then on the third day
The Lord rose from the grave, from a strange and secret
Sleep where he suffered death for us all,
The prince of angels, the giver of glory,   60
Who died for our sake. That was a sweet smell,
Beautiful as a song that blessed the world.
Righteous men came from all over creation
Seeking that scent. So St. Paul said,
There are many good things on middle-earth   65
Granted by God, the giver of gifts,

Ruler of rewards, our Savior and Redeemer,
The only hope of all earth's creatures
Above and below. What draws us to God
Is the finest fragrance, the sweetest scent. 70

II. The Whale

Now I will draw words from the well
Of memory, shaping with song-craft
The tale of a fish, the great whale
Who's discovered unwittingly, unwillingly,
By seafarers and wave-travelers. 5
He's deadly and dangerous, cruel and savage,
To every man. He is life-grim.
The name of this ancient sea-floater
Is Fastitocalon. His form is like rough stone,
Like sea-weed floating near sand-banks, 10
Drifting up and down at the water's edge.
Sailors think him a lovely island
When they see him, so they can safely fasten
Their high-prowed ships to that un-land
With anchor-ropes, moor their sea-steeds 15
At the dark edge of this dissembling strand.
Then the sea-weary men disembark
On the devious shore, leaving their ships
Bound fast to the rim, surrounded by sea.
The sailors make camp, expecting no evil, 20
Fearing no fight. They kindle a flame,
Build a fire on that floating island,
Mind-weary men thankful for a rest,
Glad for the gift of a safe harbor.
When the fiendish fish, cruel and crafty, 25
Senses that the seafarers are finally settled down
On his sandlike skin, enjoying the weather,
Then suddenly the demon dives down,
Rides the salt-roads into sea-depths,
Settles on the bottom where he drowns them all 30
In a dark death-hall, both ships and men.

This is also the way of demons and devils
Who snare life's travelers through secret power
And devious plots; they seduce and ruin
The good will and works of men,   35
Tricking them into turning to their foes,
Depending on their enemies, finding cruel
Companionship in the comfort of fiends,
So they settle down in the Devil's home.
When he knows through his cruel craft   40
And perverse purpose that some people
From the race of men are in his power,
Bound by his chains, then the soul-slayer
Takes their lives through his savage skill,
The high and the humble, the proud and perishing,   45
Who do his dark will, mired in sin,
Here in this human land. Suddenly he bolts into hell,
Hiding under the dark helmet of night.
Deprived of good, he seeks the bottomless surge
Of terrible torment in the opaque gloom,   50
Just like the great whale who sinks ships,
Dragging sailors to the death-hall of doom.

The sea-charger, the proud whale
Has another strange trait. Out in the ocean
When hunger harrows the awesome beast   55
And he's desperate for food, the sea's guardian
Opens his mouth, stretching his lips.
A beautiful scent rises up from inside him
Which snares all kinds of smaller fish.
They dart on the waves to that sweet smell   60
Streaming out. They all crowd into that cave
Without thinking, wary of nothing,
Until the monster's maw is overflowing.
Then quickly he claps his grim jaws shut,
Snaring his battle-prey in his savage mouth.   65

So it is with each unwary man
Who wastes his days, his fleeting years,

His tenuous life—who loses his will
And is deceived by the sweet scent—
So that stained with sin, drunk with desire,   70
He is marked with guilt before God,
The King of Glory. The cursed one
Opens for him the gates of hell
At the end of life's great journey
And offers his dark gift to those   75
Who have falsely and foolishly followed
The joys of the flesh, delighting in the body
Against the wise guidance of the soul.
When the deceiver has dragged them down
Into that fierce prison with craft and cunning,   80
Into the ravening fire, that raging flame,
Then he attacks those who have listened to him in life
And taken his teachings eagerly to heart.
After the life-slaughter, he snaps shut
His grim jaws, the gates of hell.   85
No one inside can ever escape—
No exit, no return. Just like small fish,
Such seafarers cannot escape from the whale's maw.

Therefore [we must always be wary of the whale's trap,
The Devil's trickery, any unholy deceit,   90
And put our trust] in the Lord of lords,
Strive against all devils, whether fish or fiend,
With words and deeds, so that we can fix our eyes
On the King of Glory. Let us look to him
For peace and salvation in this fleeting life,   95
So that we may dwell in glory with the dear one,
Near and far, both now and forever.

VAINGLORY

"Vainglory" is a poem of advice, a passing on of wisdom from a teacher to a pupil. It is part sermon, part homily, part religious reflection. In its substance and tone, it shares many characteristics with Hrothgar's advice or sermon to Beowulf. The poem includes both example and admonition, as well as a brief narrative of the rebellion in heaven by Satan and his minions, recounted so powerfully in the Old English poem, *Genesis*, and by Milton centuries later in *Paradise Lost.*

The speaker of the poem draws upon a variety of modes—personal experience, contrasting exempla, and religious narrative—to pass on advice and wisdom to his student listener, as he says his own teacher has done with him. The speaker repeats the advice of a prophet at line 58, then gradually segues into a melding of his voice with that of the prophet. Most editors mark the prophet's passage in quotations, but there is disagreement about where the prophet's voice ends and the speaker's begins again. Shippey wisely recognizes that the shift of voices is a complex one, noting that in these lines, "the voices of the poet and prophet are hardly to be distinguished" (1976, 129). The pupil learns from the teacher and becomes the teacher himself, passing on wisdom to yet another pupil. One voice flows naturally into the other. In that spirit, I have refrained from marking off the prophet's speech with quotation marks; the reader should pass gradually from one voice to another. This passing of voice from the wise man to the student (or from the poet to the reader) is a crucial part of the learning process described in the poem.

While the central dichotomy of good and evil or pride and humility seems carefully constructed in the poem, and while the religious exhortations are clear and forceful, what is unexpected and even a bit odd is the conditional clause in line 94, "If the wise prophet has not deceived us." This clause calls into doubt man's ability to discern the truth and to recognize the difference between good and evil. It seems more appropriate to the perceptual and mental fragility of elegies like "The Wanderer" and "The Wife's Lament" than it does to a religious homily and exhortation. The point may well be that we must rely upon a careful perception of truth and of the nature of good and evil in order to choose the right way and follow God. Satan, of course, in his rebellious and proud reasoning in the war of heaven, is a prime example of misguided perception and wrong reason.

Vainglory

Listen! A wise man once told me long ago
Of many wonders—a teacher and truth-sayer.
He unlocked his word-hoard, his wise lore,
His mind schooled in the sayings of prophets,

So I could listen and truly perceive,   5
By holy song and enchanted story,
God's own son, a welcome guest
In our human home, and also that other
Weaker one, mankind unshielded,
Different and distinct, separated by sin.   10
A man who reflects may easily see
How in this loaned life a wanton pride
May mar his mind, how savage drinking
Can destroy his spirit over many dark days.
Many loud speakers who love boasting,   15
Warriors trading insults with tall tales,
Inhabit our cities, feast at our tables,
Talking together, drinking in delight,
Sharpening strife in the family hall,
Making of home a haven of spears.   20
When wine drives the soul, excites the heart,
Then outcry and uproar arise in the company,
Shouting and screaming, clamor and crash.
But men's hearts and minds are made differently—
Not all are alike. One is arrogant,   25
Swollen with pride, pushy and violent.
Many men suffer vainglory like that—
Sometimes it swells unchecked into insolence,
Sometimes it shifts into anger or insult,
Filling the heart with fiendish arrows,   30
Cunning and deceit. Then a man begins
To lie and cheat, curse and cry out,
Belch and boast more than a better man might.
He thinks his behavior is honorable and good,
But he may see otherwise at his evil end.   35
He spins his web of dark intrigue,
Devious plots, dangerous lies—
He's a back-stabber, a wily devil.
He shoots forth his mind-barbs in showers,
While he shields himself from his stabbing sin.   40
He hates his betters out of envy and malice,
Lets arrows of spite shoot through the walls

Of the soul's fortress shaped by the Creator
To shield us from sin. He sits at the table,
Proud of his place, swollen with food,   45
Flush with wine. He draws his mind
Like a dangerous bow, shoots his words,
Feathered with anger, aimed with envy,
Poisoned by pride. Now you can recognize
His devious craft, his dangerous talk   50
When you meet him conniving in the court.
Know from these signs he's the devil's child
Enveloped in flesh. He's proud and perverse,
Grounded in hell, empty of honor,
Deprived of God, the King of glory.   55
The prophet said, the word-ready man,
The ancient shaper, singing these words:
Whoever exalts himself in evil days,
Haughty in heart, proud in mind,
Swollen in spirit, shall be heeled and humbled   60
After his final journey on the corpse-road;
He shall dwell in hell, beset by serpents,
Twisted by torment in the woe of worms.
It was long ago in God's kingdom
That pride was born—arrogance arose   65
In the conflict of angels. They raised a raucous,
Hard war against heaven with seditious strife.
They renounced their King, embraced rebellion,
Plotted treason to steal the throne
Of their rightful God, the King of glory.   70
They planned to rule high heaven,
To secure their power and stifle joy.
The Father of Creation, the world-shaper
Withstood that strife, won that war—
That fight was too fierce for arrogant angels!   75
All this is different with another kind of man
Who lives humbly on earth, meek and mild,
At peace with people, dear to his friends,
Loving even his enemies who would offer harm.
He works to spread good will in this world;   80

He hopes to rise into heaven, the angels' home,
Know the joy of saints, the music of his Maker,
The gift of glory, the breath of bliss.
It's different for those who dwell in evil,
Settled in sin, comfortable in crime,   85
Perishing in pride. Their rewards are not so rich,
A grim gift from the God of glory.
So know this from the prophet's story—
That if you find one humble of heart,
Meek of mind, sharing in spirit,   90
You will see, linked and living with him,
A loving guest, God's own Son,
The desire of the world, the joy of mankind,
If the wise prophet has not deceived us.
Therefore we should always think of salvation,   95
The gift of God, remembering at all times
Our great Creator, the Lord of victories.

Amen.

TWO ADVENT LYRICS

"The Advent Lyrics" are part of a long triptych poem, *Christ,* now divided
into three parts: "Advent Lyrics," "Ascension," and "Doomsday." Alexander
points out that the lyrics are "based on twelve antiphons used by the Church
in the liturgy of Advent, expressing the longing of the faithful for the com-
ing of the savior" (208). The lyrics include petitions to Christ, Mary, and
the Trinity and often bring spiritual matters into the realm of the mundane
world, as when a skeptical Joseph in "Advent Lyric VII" questions Mary
about her unexpected pregnancy and possible adultery in an Anglo-Saxon
forerunner of the Annunciation play in the later medieval mystery cycles.

The antiphons for the two lyrics in this collection are given here in a
translation from the Latin:

For Lyric IV: O Virgin of virgins, how shall this come about? For one
like you has never been seen before, nor will there be a successor. O
daughters of Jerusalem, why are you amazed by my situation? The
mystery which you perceive is divine in nature.

For Lyric VII: O Joseph, why did you believe what before you feared?
Why indeed? The One whom Gabriel announced would be coming,
Christ, is begotten in her by the Holy Spirit. (Muir, vol. i, 47, 51)

The speakers and speech boundaries of "Advent Lyric VII" are not indicated
in the manuscript and are thus much debated. I have followed the demarca-
tions of Krapp and Dobbie and also of Campbell and Muir. The poems are
extraordinary in their combination of spiritual vision and poetic beauty.
Muir says, "Though they are seldom, if ever, anthologized, *The Advent Lyr-
ics* are some of the finest poems to have survived from Anglo-Saxon England
. . . rich in imagery and word-play and thoroughly infused with Christian
soteriology" (vol. ii, 384).

The speakers in "Advent Lyric IV" are a melding of medieval Christians
and the people of Jerusalem who are contemporaries of Mary and Joseph.
They question Mary about the miracle of her virginal pregnancy. Mary
responds, explaining the wonder of how she "kept [her] virtue, pregnant
and pure," becoming the "exalted mother of the Son of God." "Advent
Lyric VII" is constructed in dramatic dialogue form as Joseph and Mary
debate her pregnancy and Joseph voices his fear and anxiety about Mary's
possible adultery. Here, as Campbell observes, "the poet not only accom-
plishes his exposition but reveals something of Mary's character, her love
for Joseph, and her questioning, bewildered feeling at this moment in the
face of his announcement" (1959, 22–23). These poems are a wonderful
combination of Christian doctrine, spiritual vision, and the details of every-
day life.

Two Advent Lyrics

IV

O joy of all women, expectant, unending,
Bountiful blessing beyond glory,
Fairest of maidens over all the earth
Encircled by waves: unveil that mystery,
Tell us how delight descended from heaven,   5
Bearing God's gift in an untouched womb.
We can't understand how this miracle was made.
No such story was told in the past,
Nor is any expected in the days to come.

Yours is a gift that sets you apart, 10
A grace unsurpassed—a promise, a privilege.
The favor and faith abiding in you,
Both truth and trust, were steadfast and strong,
Worthy of worship, since you alone among women
Bore the glory of heaven, its might and majesty, 15
In your blessed womb—and your maidenhood
Remained unbroken, your virtue unblemished.
Yet as the children of men must sow in sorrow,
Conceive in care, so shall they reap,
Bearing pain in passion, braving death in delivery. 20

Then the Blessed Virgin, victorious mother,
Holy Mary began to speak:
"What is this mystery that moves beyond knowing,
This unsolved riddle that leaves you lamenting?
Why should you sorrow, O sons and daughters, 25
Children of Jerusalem? You cannot conceive
How I kept my virtue, pregnant and pure,
Exalted mother of the Son of God.
This riddle remains a mystery to mankind,
But Christ revealed his truth embodied 30
In the dear kinswoman of David—
That the guilt of Eve is gathered back,
The sin absolved, the curse cast off,
And the humbler sex, gifted and glorified.
Hope is conceived that this endless blessing 35
Will be shared by men and women together,
Now and forever in the harmony of heaven
With the exaltation of angels, under the eyes
Of our Truth-father to whom all eternally turn."

VII

[Mary:]
"O my husband Joseph, son of Jacob,
Descendant of David, kinsman and king,
Do you mean to cast off our love,
Unravel our vows, untie our oaths?"

[Joseph:]
"I'm deeply grieved—our trust is torn.   5
Without warning, my honor has fled,
My reputation is spoiled, my dignity undone.
Because of you, I hear harsh words,
Insult and sorrow, accusation and scorn.
Everyone bears me the gift of abuse.   10
Care is my constant companion. I cannot
Escape my shame or flee from my tears.
Only God may heal my heart's deep sorrow,
Bring comfort to my wounds, my woe—
O Mary, my maiden, my young virgin."   15

[Mary:]
"Why are you mourning, wounded with sorrow,
Crying this lament? I've never found any fault
In you, any crime or cause for blame.
You've done nothing wrong, yet you suffer
This wretched state, twisting words as if   20
Your life were tormented by some strange sin."

[Joseph:]
"This wicked conception is the source of my shame.
This pregnancy has been nothing but trouble.
How can I battle slander, struggle with woe?
How can I answer my endless enemies?   25
Their hateful words are like daggers in my heart.
Everyone knows that I gladly received
From the temple of God a clean maiden,
Pure and unstained. Yet now this is undone,
Your virtue unmade in some unknown way.   30
It does me no good to speak or keep silent.
If I speak the truth, then the daughter of David
Must suffer the law—death by stoning.
If I keep silent, concealing the crime,
Then I am bound to bear the burden   35

Of whispered perjury and malicious scorn,
Loathed by everyone, accused by all."

Then the maiden unraveled the riddle,
Unwound the mystery, revealing the wonder:
[Mary:]
"By the Son of God, the Savior of souls,   40
I speak the truth when I say to you
That I have never known a man's embrace
Or accepted any loving arms on this earth—
But a visitor from heaven appeared to me
In my own home where I was pure and innocent.   45
The archangel Gabriel came to greet me,
Granted this privilege, saying that heaven's spirit
Would illuminate my body so that I should bear
Life's lasting glory, God's bright son,
The power and prince illustrious, unending.   50
Now I am God's immaculate temple,
Free from sin. The spirit of comfort,
The heart's healer has lived in me.
Cast off your cares, set down your sorrows,
Give thanks to the Lord's magnificent Son   55
That I have become the wonder of women,
Maiden and mother, virgin victorious,
And you, his father in the eyes of the world,
So that in him the prophecy is at last fulfilled."

THE DREAM OF THE ROOD

"The Dream of the Rood" is the first dream vision poem in a vernacular language in Western Europe. It transforms Christ into an unconventional, self-sacrificing warrior and endows the cross with human consciousness and feeling. As both stand-in for Christ and witness to the crucifixion, the cross suffers and laments to the dreamer, while Christ remains stoically silent. As persecutor, the cross represents the human torturers. The poem translates the distance between God and man into the nearness and shared suffering of Christ and cross and mediates the gap between nature and humankind.

It shows us the power of the resurrection: the greatest warrior can embrace death and then rise up to slay it. A tree in the forest can be cut down and carried into consciousness as it moves from slayer to celebrant, from gallows to glory.

The poem draws upon the complex history of the cross and its symbolism. After the crucifixion, the cross was abhorred by the faithful. Then in 312, the Roman Emperor Constantine I had a vision of the cross before his battle with the rebel Maxentius. He ordered the Christian Chi-Rho symbol (the superimposed initial Greek letters in the word for "Christ") placed on the troops' shields, declaring, "Conquer by means of this symbol." He subsequently won the battle, adopted Christianity as the state religion, and encouraged the use of the cross as a Christian symbol. Questions about the nature of the cross and its role in the crucifixion were debated for many years, and these in turn were influenced by questions about the nature of the suffering Christ as a human and/or divine being on the cross. Portions of the poem are found carved in runes on a stone cross in Ruthwell, Dumfriesshire, Scotland, and two lines are also found on a reliquary of the True Cross in Brussels (for more on this, see Alexander, 217 ff.). The poem itself is in an Anglo-Saxon manuscript in the cathedral library in Vercelli, Italy, and must have been a gift presented by English churchmen traveling to Rome.

The formal heart of the poem is the device of endowing an inanimate object with consciousness and feeling and enabling the object to speak. This tradition is partly derived from the classical tradition of prosopopoeia, "discourse by inanimate objects" and partly from the medieval riddling tradition (see Schlauch, 23 ff. and Donoghue, 75 ff.). There are several medieval Latin cross riddles and some (with solution debated) in Old English. "The Dream of the Rood" makes use of both of the basic Old English riddle types: the third-person descriptive riddle ("I saw a creature") and the first-person persona riddle ("I am a creature"). It challenges us to say both who the cross is and what its identity and history mean. The dreamer begins by describing the cross as a wondrous creature whose nature shifts back and forth in the dream—sometimes drenched with blood, sometimes dressed in gold. When the cross begins to speak, it recounts its history from its homeland in the woods to its transformation into a gallows at the hands of man (compare, for example, the transformations of creatures such as "horn" and "mead" in the riddles). With these riddlic devices, the poet creates a rood that shifts shapes, recounts its history, and participates in the wonder of human perception and the enigmatic miracle of the crucifixion and resurrection.

In the middle of the poem, the cross suffers like a stand-in for Christ as nails are driven though his Lord's hands into its own sensitive wood. Like Christ it is mocked, tortured, and drenched in blood. Christ embraces the cross, his retainer and slayer, stretching out his arms to enfold the rood. At the darkest hour, the first-person riddle is in a sense "solved" as the rood names itself, accepts its role, and pays homage to its lord. The rood, once raised, raises up Christ. It bends its will to that of its lord.

At the death of Christ, the natural world weeps. Christ is said to be "limb-weary" and to "rest awhile." In heroic poetry this is usually a euphemism for death, since no warrior can really rest on the battlefield. Only here does the literal meaning miraculously seem to hold true: Christ is resting in death and will eventually "wake up" in the resurrection. Both Christ and the cross are entombed or buried; both are resurrected (the cross in a brief, obviously missing passage that I have restored here). Elsewhere in the Old English poem *Elene*, we learn how Constantine's mother Elene (or Helen) travels to the Holy Land to discover and dig up the true cross.

In the latter half of the poem, the cross tells the dreamer of his transformed life after the resurrection as he moves from "terrible torturer" to "tower of glory." It instructs the dreamer to tell his dream to other faithful followers and to warn them that Christ will return on the Day of Judgment to discover whether people have worn the cross on their breasts and in their hearts, willing to suffer for him as he did earlier for them. The cross stops speaking at line 128, and the dreamer details his own response to the dream. He explains his newfound zeal for the cross and Christ and his longing to be reunited with the company of Christ in heaven. There he will relive the dream and experience Christian camaraderie as he feasts forever at the Lord's table with saints and angels, dwelling in everlasting bliss in his "homeland in heaven."

The Dream of the Rood

Listen! I will speak of the best of dreams,
The sweetest vision that crossed my sleep
In the middle of the night when speech-bearers
Lay in silent rest. I seemed to see
A wondrous tree lifting up in the air,   5

Wound with light, the brightest of beams.
That radiant sign was wrapped in gold;
Gems stood gleaming at its feet,
Five stones shining from its shoulder-beam.
A host of angels beheld its beauty,   10
Fair through the ordained, ongoing creation.
That was not an outlaw's gallows, a criminal's cross.
Holy spirits, angels, men on earth—all creation
Stood watching that wondrous tree.
The victory-beam was beautiful, bright   15
And shining—but I was stained with sin.
I saw the tree of glory sheathed in gems,
Clothed in gold—jewels gleaming
On the Lord's tree; yet through that gold
I could see the ancient agony of the wretched—   20
The suffering and struggle—since it first began
To sweat blood from its right side.
I was seized with sorrow, tormented by the sight
Of that beautiful cross. I saw that creature
Changing its shape, its form and colors—   25
Sometimes it was stained with sweat,
Drenched with blood, sometimes finely
Dressed with gold. Lying there a long time,
Sadly gazing at the Savior's tree,
I heard the best of woods begin to speak: 30

"Many years ago—I still remember the day—
I was cut down at the edge of the forest,
Severed from my trunk, removed from my roots.
Strong enemies seized me, shaped me into a spectacle,
Ordered me to lift their outlaws, crucify their criminals.   35
Men bore me on their shoulders, set me on a hill,
Fastened their foes on me, enough of enemies.
Then I saw the Lord of mankind hasten to me,
Eager to climb up. I dared not bow down
Against God's word. I saw the earth tremble—   40
I might have slaughtered his foes, yet I stood fast.
The warrior, our young Savior, stripped himself

Before the battle with a keen heart and firm purpose,
Climbed up on the cross, the tree of shame,
Bold in the eyes of many, to redeem mankind.   45
I trembled when the Hero embraced me
But dared not bow down to earth—I had to stand fast.
A rood was I raised—I raised the mighty King,
Lord of the heavens. I dared not bend down.
Men drove their dark nails into me, piercing my skin—   50
You can still see my open malice-wounds—
But I dared not injure any of those enemies.
Men mocked us both—I was drenched with blood
From the side of the Man after he sent forth his spirit.
I endured much hostile fortune on that hill.   55
I saw the Lord of hosts stretch out his arms
In terrible suffering. Night-shadows slid down,
Covering in darkness the corpse of the Lord,
Which was bathed in radiance. The dark deepened
Under the clouds. All creation wept,   60
Lamenting the Lord's death: Christ was on the cross.
Yet eager ones came, believers from afar,
To be with the Lord. I beheld it all.
I was seized with sorrow, humbling myself
To men's hands, bowing down with bold courage.   65
They lifted up Almighty God, raising his body
From its burden of woe. Those brave warriors
Left me alone, covered with streams of blood—
I was wounded with arrows, pierced with pain.
They laid down the limb-weary Lord of heaven,   70
Gathering near his head, guarding his body.
He rested there awhile, weary after his struggle.
Men made him an earth-house, shaping a sepulcher
In the sight of the slayer, carved of bright stone.
Inside they laid the Lord of victories and started to sing   75
A long lament, a sorrow-song at evening,
As they began to depart, drained from the death
Of their glorious Prince. He rested in the tomb
With few friends, but we stood by weeping,
Unquiet crosses, when the cries of men   80

Had drifted off. The corpse grew cold,
The soul's fair house. Then men came along,
Cut us down to earth, carried us off.
That was a terrible fate. They buried us
Deep in a pit in the ground, a grave for crosses,   85
But servants of the Lord [learned of my tomb;
Friends hauled me out, offered me healing,]
Sheathed me in gems, in silver and gold.

Now you have heard, my dear dreamer,
How I have endured such sorrow and strife   90
From wicked men. The time is come
For all men on earth and throughout creation
To honor me and offer prayers to the sign of the cross.
The Son of God suffered on me for awhile—
Now I rise up high in heaven, a tower of glory,   95
And I can heal any man who holds me in awe.
Long ago I became hateful to man, hardest of woes,
A terrible torturer. Then I was transformed.
Now I offer the true way of life to speech-bearers,
A road for the righteous. The Lord of glory,   100
The Guardian of heaven has honored me
Above all trees, just as he also honored
His mother Mary above all women.
Now I command you, my dear friend,
To reveal this dream to other men,   105
Disclose to them that the tree of glory
Was Christ's cross where he suffered sorely
For the sins of man and the old deeds of Adam.
He tasted death, a bitter drink, yet rose again
In his strength and power to save mankind.   110
He ascended into heaven. Our almighty God
Will return to middle-earth on Judgment Day
With all of his angels to judge each man
In his wisdom and power according to how
Each man has lived his life on earth,   115
Spent the precious loan of his days.
No man can flee from the fear of God

Or the weight of his words. He will ask
Before the multitudes where the man is
Who would taste bitter death in his name,   120
Just as he did on the cross, the true tree.
Then they will fear and think a little
How they might answer Christ on that day.
No man needs to fear who wears on his breast
And bears in his heart the best of signs.   125
Each soul that longs to live with the Lord
Must make a journey from earth to heaven,
Seeking God's reward through the rood."

Then I prayed to the cross with an eager heart
And a zealous spirit where I was left alone   130
In such small company. My spirit was lifted,
Urged and inspired, to travel that long road.
I endured an endless time of longing.
Now my life's great hope is to see again
Christ's cross, that tree of victory,   135
And honor it more keenly than other men.
The cross is my hope and my protection.
I have few powerful friends left on earth—
They have passed on from the joys of the world,
Seeking the greater glory of God,   140
Longing to live with their Heavenly Father.
I live each day, longing for the time
When the Lord's cross that I saw before
In a wondrous dream will come back again
To carry me away from this loan of life   145
To the joys of heaven, to an everlasting bliss,
To the Lord's table where the company of Christ
Feasts together forever and ever, where I can dwell
In glory with the holy saints, sustained in joy.
I pray for God to be my friend, the Savior   150
Who suffered sorely on the gallows-tree
For the sins of men, who rose and redeemed us
With life everlasting and a heavenly home.
Hope was renewed with grace and glory

For those who before had suffered burning flames.   155
The Son and Savior was mighty and victorious
In his harrowing of hell when the Lord Almighty,
Came back home to the kingdom of heaven,
Leading a band of spirits to the saints and angels,
To their homeland in heaven where they dwell in bliss.   160

APPENDIX A

"Digressions": Battles, Feuds, and Family Strife in *Beowulf*

T his section contains brief summaries of the major feuds and battles in *Beowulf* and also of the major historical references which have sometimes been called "digressions." Some of these accounts are told in detailed fashion in the poem; others are only touched upon. The full story behind the historical references must sometimes be filled in from other sources. Often the details remain somewhat murky or they seem to be imaginatively reconceived in the poem. It seems likely that the Anglo-Saxon audience or readership knew something of these stories, so that even brief mentions or curtailed summaries reverberated for them in complex ways that are difficult for modern readers to experience.

DANISH FEUDS AND DIFFICULTIES

At the beginning of the poem, the Danish royal dynasty is traced back to the legendary Scyld Sceafing. The line comes down through Beow to Healfdene, Hrothgar's father. When Healfdene died, either Heorogar ruled for a very short time before dying, or perhaps the reign passed directly to Hrothgar for some reason. After Hrothgar became king, he solidified Danish power and built the great hall Heorot. Hrothgar's sister, possibly Yrse (we're not certain of the name), married Onela the Swede (see below), probably in a failed gesture of peace-weaving between the two warring peoples. Hrothgar married Wealhtheow; they had two sons, Hrethric and Hrothmund, and a daughter Freawaru. In the poem, Hrothgar intends to marry Freawaru off to Ingeld of the Heathobards in an attempt to weave a peace between their feuding peoples, but, as Beowulf predicts, this plan is almost certainly doomed to failure. Early on in the poem, we hear that Hrothgar's great hall is destined to fall in flames to this feud between father and son-in-law. Hrothgar's nephew, Hrothulf, is living in the court because he has lost his parents at an early age. He is being raised by Hrothgar and Wealhtheow, who treat him like one of their sons. Hrothulf seems to some critics to be plotting to seize the throne at some point, though there is great disagreement about this. The historical sources do tell us that he eventually came to power. Whether he exiled and/or killed Hrethric and Hrothmund remains unclear. Unferth may be part of this plot, especially since Beowulf says he's well known for his earlier murder of his brother, but this also is much debated. Wealhtheow at one point urges Beowulf to be the protector of her sons; she is probably wise to fear for their safety should Hrothgar die. Sources indicate that after Hrothgar died and Hrothulf took the throne, eventually Heoroweard, the son of Heorogar (Hrothgar's deceased older brother), may have killed Hrothulf and become king.

At some point in Hrothgar's reign, he took in Beowulf's father, who was fleeing from a feud. He protected him and later settled the feud for him. Beowulf's coming to Denmark to fight with Grendel is in part an act of repaying the family debt to Hrothgar for having saved his father's life.

THE STORY OF FINNSBURG

In the celebration in Heorot after Beowulf's battle with Grendel, the court *scop* or poet/singer chants the legendary story of the battle between the Half-Danes and the Finns at Finnsburg. There is also a fragmentary account of this battle in an Old English poem, "The Fight at Finnsburg." Hildeburh, daughter of King Hoc of the Half-Danes (a subgroup of the Danes), is married off to Finn, king of the Frisians, in another of those unlikely-to-succeed gestures of peace-weaving. She goes off to live with her husband's people, as is the common Germanic practice. Her brother Hnæf comes to visit with his chief thane Hengest and a retinue of retainers. The old feud between the Half-Danes and Frisians simmers, and one night a group of Frisians attacks the Half-Danes as the old feud breaks out between the two traditional enemies. Many warriors die on both sides. Hildeburh's brother Hnæf and her unnamed son are both killed. Finally the battle ends in a stalemate. Hengest, now leader of the Half-Danes, exchanges vows with Finn, and they both promise to live peacefully through the winter, although the Half-Danes remain in a untenable position with Finn as their overlord. A separate hall-space is established for the Danes (or perhaps a hall is built for them—this is not clear), and everybody appears to be working at keeping the peace, at least long enough to get through the winter.

When spring comes and the ice thaws, the feud returns with a vengeance. Two of the Half-Danes, Guthlaf and Oslaf, whose brother Hunlaf may have been killed in the earlier battle, lay a sword that has already tasted the blood of feud in the lap of Hengest as an invitation to revenge the death of Hnæf, and the slaughter begins again. Finn is killed, and the Half-Danes return home with Hildeburh and her treasures. The theme of this story hangs heavy over the entire poem: "The blood's revenge/Cannot be contained in a restless heart" (1153b–54). The feud seems to arise as relentlessly and predictably as spring itself.

FREAWARU AND THE HEATHOBARDS

When Beowulf returns home to Geatland and tells Hygelac and the court of his adventures in Denmark, he recalls that Hrothgar plans to marry off his daughter Freawaru to Ingeld of the Heathobards in another attempt to patch a peace with a traditional enemy. Beowulf has seen this gesture before and wisely predicts the failure of the plan. He argues that when the Danes visit the Heathobard court, old antagonisms will erupt again, and a warrior with a long memory will incite revenge. The marriage will be destroyed by the killing of Danish retainers and the resumption of feud. Then Beowulf suddenly shifts from the Heathobard feud to the story of Grendel's savagery, implying perhaps that monsters are somehow related to the monstrous passions of feud in his world. This is perhaps Beowulf at his wisest point in the story, or perhaps the poet's larger perceptions are blending in with his hero's at this point.

GEATISH-SWEDISH WARS
AND RELATED EVENTS

In the Geatish royal family, Hæthcyn kills his older brother Herebeald in a savage accident by missing his mark with his bow and killing him with an arrow. Given the circumstances, their father King Hrethel cannot seek revenge for the death of his favorite son, and he dies of grief. Hæthcyn becomes king, but the circumstances render him vulnerable, and the Swedes attack the Geats. The Swedes inflict damage on the Geats and return home. Hæthcyn later pursues a revenge expedition to Sweden and captures King Ongentheow's queen. Ongentheow retaliates, recaptures his queen, and kills Hæthcyn, driving the rest of the Geats into the woods, where they seem doomed. The next morning, however, Hygelac arrives with reinforcements and defeats the Swedes. Two Geats, the brothers Wulf and Eofor, kill Ongentheow. Hygelac becomes king, and he rewards the brothers for their valor. Eofor in particular is given Hygelac's daughter in marriage.

Flush with pride over his successes against the Swedes, Hygelac impulsively leads a war party against the Frisians and is killed. Beowulf fights valiantly and eventually escapes, making his way back to Geatland. He is offered the throne, but he humbly agrees only to be a caretaker king until Hygelac's son Heardred becomes old enough to rule.

After the death of Ongentheow, his son Ohthere presumably becomes king (though there is some debate about which son is the elder and which ascends the throne). He dies (whether naturally or not), and his brother Onela seizes the throne, causing great tension between him and the sons of Ohthere, Eanmund and Eadgils. The two brothers flee from Sweden and come to Geatland, where they are protected by Heardred, who has become king of the Geats. The Swedish King Onela brings an army to Geatland to attack his nephews and kills King Heardred. In this battle, Wiglaf's father Weohstan, who serves Onela, kills Eanmund with a sword he later gives to Wiglaf. Onela retreats to Sweden, leaving Beowulf in place as King of the Geats. Later Eadgils, with troops and supplies given to him by Beowulf, returns to Sweden and kills his uncle Onela and takes the throne. The feud between Eadgils and Weohstan, who killed his brother, remains in force, and Weohstan and Wiglaf flee to the Geats. Wiglaf serves Beowulf nobly in his fight against the dragon, but after Beowulf's death, it is predicted that the Swedes (and Frisians too!) will attack the Geats.

SIGEMUND AND HEREMOD

The morning after Beowulf's battle with Grendel, hall-thanes from Heorot follow Grendel's bloody tracks to the mere. On their way home, their scop begins to shape the story of Beowulf's battle and his glory, weaving his courage in a "weft of song." As part of his praise of Beowulf, the singer compares him to two legendary warriors, Sigemund and Heremod. The story of Sigemund is told in the Old Norse *Volsunga Saga*. Only a small part of the story is used in *Beowulf*. In the saga, Sigemund and Fitela (Sinfjotli in Old Norse) are part of a complicated revenge plot. Sigemund's sister is married against her will to an evil king who slays her father and all but one of her brothers, Sigemund, who escapes by killing a terrible wolf, tearing out its tongue. Sigemund's sister disguises herself and follows him into the woods, where she sleeps with him and bears his child Fitela, who later comes to join him. In the woods, the two of them lead the lives of outlaws and eventually don wolves' skins, which magically transform them into wolves. They barely escape this wolfish curse. Eventually they avenge the deaths of their family members with the help of Sigemund's sister.

The Danish scop also mentions Sigemund's fight with a dragon. This reference occurs only in *Beowulf*, and it may be borrowed from the Norse story of

Sigemund's son Sigurd, who fights the dragon Fafnir, in the *Volsunga Saga* (see Appendix C for details). The *Beowulf* poem's reference to Sigemund's fighting the dragon is probably meant to foreshadow Beowulf's own dragon fight. Sigemund is revered as a Germanic hero, though he does have his wolfish moments. One could, of course, argue that Beowulf himself has an occasional wolfish moment, such as his allowing Grendel to devour Hondscio before Grendel turns to him.

The Danish scop contrasts the example of Sigemund with that of Heremod, who is part of the Danish line in the legendary past. He was renowned as an arrogant tyrant who hoarded his gold and would not share his treasure with his retainers. Hrothgar warns Beowulf against Heremod's example, urging him to learn from his story and be both "manly and munificent."

FREMU AND OFFA

After Beowulf and the Geats have returned home and are marching toward the Geatish hall, they see King Hygelac and Queen Hygd, and there is a passage which describes Hygd as "wise and well-taught, courteous and accomplished," generous with gifts to the Geats, and not seductive and cruel like Fremu, "the queen of crime, / Who served up terror" (1927 ff.). The source and nature of the story of Fremu and Offa is still debated, as is the name of the queen, sometimes known as Thryth or Modthryth (see *Klaeber 4*, 222 ff. for details). The references are also debated, but in the poem at least, Fremu is cruel and manipulative, in sharp contrast to Hygd, who is generous and good. The young Fremu flirts with men, then accuses them of improper behavior. This often leads to a grim conclusion as she is responsible for their deaths. Once Fremu is married, however, to the good and strong-willed King Offa, she changes her ways and becomes generous and good, kind and loving, a model queen. As recent editors note, "Her story exemplifies the 'Taming of the Shrew' motif" (*Klaeber 4*, 222).

APPENDIX B

Genealogies in *Beowulf*

The major genealogies for Danes, Swedes, Geats, and Half-Danes and Frisians are given here. Men are in roman type; women in italics. I give some indication of the various feuds at work by indicating the following: eb = exiled by; k = killed (usually followed by the victim); kb = killed by (followed by the perpetrator); de = died early. A full description of the various feuds and wars is in the preceding section.

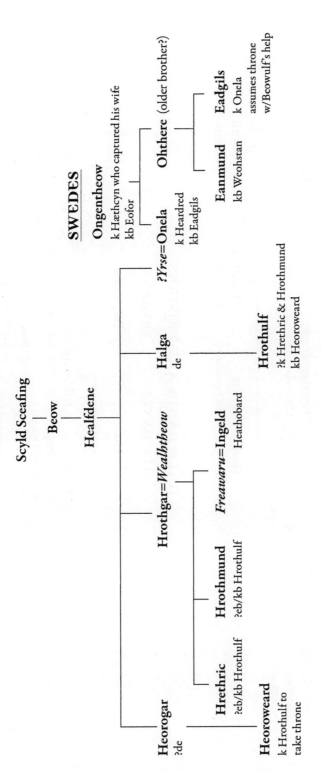

DANES

Scyld Sceafing

Beow

Healfdene

Heorogar
?de

Hrothgar=*Wealhtheow*

Hrethric
?eb/kb Hrothulf

Hrothmund
?eb/kb Hrothulf

Heoroweard
k Hrothulf to take throne

Freawaru=Ingeld
Heathobard

Halga
de

Hrothulf
?k Hrethric & Hrothmund
kb Heoroweard

?*Yrse*=Onela
k Heardred
kb Eadgils

SWEDES

Ongentheow
k Haethcyn who captured his wife
kb Eofor

Ohthere   (older brother?)

Eanmund
kb Weohstan

Eadgils
k Onela
assumes throne
w/Beowulf's help

GENEALOGICAL TABLE 1

THE DANES AND SWEDES

GEATS

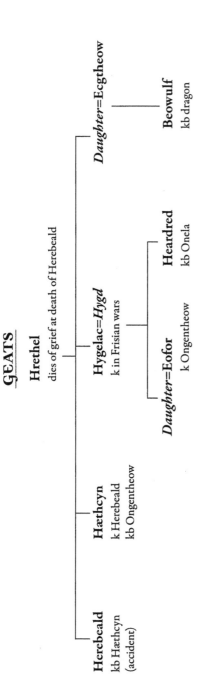

Hrethel
dies of grief at death of Herebeald

Herebeald
kb Hæthcyn
(accident)

Hæthcyn
k Herebeald
kb Ongentheow

Hygelac=Hygd
k in Frisian wars

Daughter=Eofor
k Ongentheow

Heardred
kb Onela

Daughter=Ecgtheow

Beowulf
kb dragon

HALF-DANES AND FRISIANS

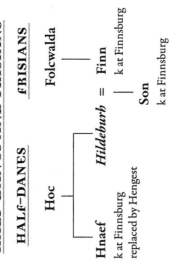

HALF-DANES

Hoc

Hnaef
k at Finnsburg
replaced by Hengest

Hildeburh = Finn

FRISIANS

Folcwalda

Finn
k at Finnsburg

Son
k at Finnsburg

GENEALOGICAL TABLE 2

THE GEATS, HALF-DANES, AND FRISIANS

APPENDIX C

Two Scandinavian Analogues of *Beowulf*

*B*eowulf has a number of possible sources and analogues for the historical references, religious allusions, and descriptions of monsters in the poem, but no direct source for the story of Beowulf and his battles with the Grendelkin and dragon. Some of the history in the poem is "poeticized" or slanted in ways to fit the story. Many of the relevant materials, especially the Nordic sagas, postdate *Beowulf*, though both may be based in part on earlier oral traditions. Readers interested in learning more about the historical or legendary materials should consult Andersson's "Sources and Analogues," in chapter 7 of *A Beowulf Handbook* (Bjork and Niles), Orchard's "Myth and Legend," in chapter 4 of his book, *A Critical Companion to Beowulf*, and Sections III and IV of the Introduction and Appendix A of *Klaeber 4*.

Limitation of space here makes it impossible to discuss all of the possible sources and analogues of *Beowulf*, but I want take up briefly portions of two important Nordic tales in relation to the poem—the battle between Grettir and the monsters in *Grettis Saga*, and the battle between Sigurd and the dragon Fafnir in *Fafnismal* and *Volsunga Saga*.

Klaeber 4 notes that "a genetic relation of some kind seems to exist between *Beowulf* and particular Scandinavian stories, including the one attached to Grettir the Strong" (xxxviii). Since the composition date of *Grettis Saga* is probably much later than that of *Beowulf*, it may have been influenced by the Old English poem. Another scenario is that both stories may owe something to a Nordic oral folktale, which was retold and reshaped as it moved westward into Iceland and Anglo-Saxon England. The story of Grettir's battles with *Beowulf*-like monsters is translated in Garmonsway and Simpson (all quotations below are taken from their text) and can be summarized as follows:

The owner of a haunted farmstead has trouble hiring shepherds because they are always savagely killed by a monster on Christmas Eve. They are discovered with their bones smashed up in landscapes that look as though there has been "some pretty violent wrestling there" (304). Grettir hears about this and decides to visit the farmstead, even though his uncle warns him of the danger. Grettir says, "Where there's trouble in my neighbor's house, there's trouble knocking at my door" (304). Grettir goes to the farmstead house and beds down there in his clothes, pretending to sleep, till the monster Glamr enters and grabs hold of him. Their savage battle nearly destroys the hall. Almost dead, Glamr puts a curse on Grettir, saying that he must live the life of an outlaw, his strength will never increase, and all his "deeds shall turn to ill-luck" (312). Then Grettir cuts off Glamr's head.

In a later story in the saga, Grettir comes to another farmstead called Sand-hauger, which is being similarly haunted on Christmas Eve. He comes in disguise because he has become an outlaw as Glamr predicted. Again he sleeps in his clothes, playing possum and waiting for his attacker. A she-troll comes into the hall with a trough in one hand and a knife in the other. They battle all night, and she drags him out of the hall, tearing down the hall-door and frame, and carries him down to a river gorge, where he cuts off her right arm. Dying, she escapes under a waterfall, and he returns to the hall, where he is nursed back to health.

After he recovers, Grettir and a priest return to the river gorge and the water-fall. There is a cave behind the waterfall that goes sixty feet down. Grettir anchors a rope for his return climb and tells the priest to guard it. He then dives down through the water into the cave, where he finds a great giant sitting by a fire. The two begin fighting ferociously. The giant takes down a sword hanging on the cave wall, but Grettir guts him so that his entrails fall into the river. The priest sees the guts in the water and flees, believing Grettir to be dead. Grettir explores the cave, finding human bones and some treasure. Because the priest has fled, Grettir is forced to climb hand over hand up the rope without help. He brings the bones to the church along with a wooden rune stick inscribed with a poetical account of his adventure. This account indicates that the giant was the "she-troll's ugly husband" (316). That's the end of troll troubles in the area.

There are interesting similarities and differences between these two stories and *Beowulf.* There is the tradition of the monster haunting the hall and the hero's hearing of it and coming to fight him or her. Both heroes play possum at night in order to grab the monster. Only Beowulf loses a thane to the monster, and the hero's famous hand-grip is not included in the saga. In the saga, it's the arm of the she-beast and the head of the male monster which are severed. Certain other themes are repeated, such as the destruction of the hall-door, the she-beast's home in an underwater cavern near a stream, the hero's diving down, the strange light of the hall, the cowardly fleeing of the watcher(s) above, and the treasure in the cave. All three monsters, however, are more easily defeated in the saga. The sword on the wall in the saga is wielded by the cave-giant and not by the hero. The she-troll lives in the cave with her husband the giant, not with a son. And the treasure plays only a minor role in the saga, whereas in *Beowulf* its place is moved to the dragon's lair where it plays a significant role. The runic stick brought back in the saga contains a kind of bragging poem ("The giant's breast and belly / I clove with my bright blade"—316), whereas the "gift" brought back from the Grendel-kin's cave by Beowulf is the sword hilt inscribed with runes or images which indicate the power of the Biblical flood over the monsters deriving from the race of Cain.

The *Beowulf* poet may be drawing upon the dragon story from the *Volsunga Saga* in the Danish court poet's recounting of the story of Sigemund, during his praise of Beowulf after the killing of Grendel. He associates the dragon battle with Sigemund instead of Sigurd his son, as is the case in the saga. The story of Sigurd and Fafnir is told in the *Volsunga Saga* or *The Saga of the Volsungs*, trans-lated by Byock (all quotations below are taken from Byock's text unless otherwise indicated). The story begins, not surprisingly, with a family feud:

Hreidmar has three sons—Otr, Regin, and Fafnir. Otr often takes the shape of an otter and fishes for food in this form. One day he is killed accidentally by three hungry gods who are then required by the family to give them a treasure as wergild for their loss. The gods take a treasure from a dwarf, who places a curse on it, and deliver it reluctantly to the family. Fafnir then kills his father to keep the treasure for himself while Regin flees. The curse is beginning to work: "Fafnir became so ill-natured that he set out for the wilds and allowed no one to enjoy the treasure but himself. He has since become the most evil serpent and lies now upon this hoard" (59).

Fafnir, like the dragonic Heremod in *Beowulf*, hoards his gold. In the saga, he actually becomes the dragon. Regin, who is a famous smith, fashions a sword for Sigurd, his foster-son, out of the broken pieces of the sword of Sigurd's father, Sigemund. Regin gives the sword to Sigurd in exchange for a promise to give Regin his brother Fafnir's heart once he has destroyed the dragon. First Sigurd goes off on an adventure to avenge his father's death. Then Sigurd and Regin go after the dragon. Regin tells Sigurd to dig a ditch outside the dragon's lair and lie in it, so that when Fafnir passes over he can stab him in the heart through his soft underside. Sigurd rides off to the dragon's lair, and Regin runs off in fear. Sigurd digs the ditch, hides in it, and strikes the dragon a deadly blow. The dying dragon wants to know who his killer is, and Sigurd hesitates to tell him but finally does.

The dragon and Sigurd trade talk, posing riddle-like questions and taunting each other. This part of the story is elaborated in the poetic edda *Fafnismal* or *The Lay of Fafnir* (Larrington, trans.). Fafnir advises Sigurd to ride away and forget the cursed treasure because the gold will be his death, but Sigurd says he will take the treasure.

Fafnir dies and Regin returns. Regin proclaims Sigurd a great hero and admits that he himself is not really blameless in his brother's killing. Sigurd chastises Regin for running off, saying, "When men come to battle, a fearless heart serves a man better than a sharp sword" (65). Sigurd cuts out Fafnir's heart and drinks his blood. Regin asks Sigurd to roast the dragon's heart and give it to him to eat. As Sigurd is roasting the heart, he gets some heart-juice on his finger and licks it off. When the blood from the dragon's heart touches his tongue, he can understand the speech of birds. The birds begin to sow discord between Sigurd and Regin. They tell Sigurd that eating the heart will bestow great wisdom on the devourer, and they claim that Regin desires this power because he intends to betray Sigurd. They advise Sigurd to kill Regin and claim all of the dragon's treasure. Sigurd then cuts off Regin's head and eats the serpent's heart. He goes to the dragon's cave and takes out a vast treasure of gold, gems, and armor.

There are significant similarities between this story and the story of Beowulf's killing the dragon. In each, a hero battles a dragon who is guarding a treasure hoard. Each dragon must be killed through a soft spot in the belly. There is a cowardly retainer or retainers fleeing the fight in each case. Each of the treasures carries a curse. Finally, each dragon battle is connected in some way with a human feud.

Of course, there are also many differences. The *Beowulf* dragon is not the transformation of a greedy king. The *Volsunga Saga* dragon speaks, poses questions like riddles, and sows distrust. The *Beowulf* dragon does not speak. Sigurd does not die fighting the dragon, as Beowulf does, though the curse of the treasure does seem to kill him eventually. Sigurd gets to use his gold for awhile; Beowulf's treasure is added to his pyre or barrow.

Tolkien says in several places that he prefers the cunning and sneaky Fafnir to the speechless dragon in *Beowulf*, but he argues that the *Beowulf* dragon is something quite different—not so much dragon as "dragon-ness" which he calls "a personification of malice, greed, destruction (the evil side of heroic life), and of the undiscriminating cruelty of fortune that distinguishes not good or bad (the evil aspect of all life)," noting that "for *Beowulf*, the poem, that is as it should be" (1936, 259). Tolkien implies that the *Volsunga Saga*'s Fafnir represents more overtly the devious and cunning voice of the feud, the impulse for revenge, and the sowing of distrust. The *Beowulf* dragon represents elements of the feud which we can only discern obliquely in the implied connection between the dragon and the history of Geatish feud and tragedy which surrounds it narratively. The *Beowulf* dragon points overtly to a theme which is covert in the *Volsunga Saga*, namely, the transience of the world, the dragging down of time, and the inescapability of death. Both dragons represent the greed for gold, though Beowulf seems less desperate for this than Sigurd and Regin. Sigurd wants the dragon's treasure for himself and kills his foster-father to get it. While some critics see greed in Beowulf's calling for the treasure on his deathbed, it's more likely that he wants the treasure to help his people after his death. He also views the treasure in a new light, as he understands more fully in the face of death that the value of treasure is not in the material wealth so much as it is in the giving of it to signify and solidify the bonds of the *sibb* or the love and loyalty that knits the comitatus together.

APPENDIX D
Possible Riddle Solutions

S olutions to the riddles are not given in the original manuscript, so scholars continue to debate them. Some solutions are now generally accepted; others are still hotly contested. Solutions often depend on different readings of ambiguous passages or on whether to take a particular description as literal or metaphoric. For a fuller discussion of possible solutions and scholarship on the riddles, see Williamson (1977, 1982), Muir (2000), Niles (2006), and Bitterli (2009).

Riddle 3

This fierce wooden warrior, difficult to slay, impossible to revive with ordinary herbal medicines, is a shield. Anglo-Saxon shields were made of wood, sometimes covered with leather, often adorned with metal fittings and ornamental mounts. The "hard hammer-leavings" and the "battle-sharp/Handiwork of smiths" are both kennings referring to the shield's enemy, the sword.

Riddle 5

This magical bird is a swan, whose feathers, according to an ancient tradition, were thought to make a musical sound when the bird was in flight. This capacity is mentioned in another Old English poem, "The Phoenix." It's possible that the bird mentioned here is a mute swan which makes a throbbing sound with its wings in flight, but the description is probably based on folklore and legend.

Riddle 7

The changeling who destroys its foster brothers and sisters is the cuckoo. Its bizarre craft and ungrateful behavior have made it a villain of the bird world. The mother cuckoo leaves her egg in the nest of another bird, and by an evolutionary adaptation known as egg mimicry, fools the host mother into adopting the egg as her own. The hatched cuckoo, often stronger than its siblings, is skilled in ejecting both eggs and fledglings from the nest.

Riddle 9

This lovely, dangerous lady, like Keats's Lamia, seems "some demon's mistress, or the demon's self." She has been identified as gold, night, wine, and night-debauch. Her gown of silver and garnet, her power to enfeeble or enrage men, and the reference to God's grim toast at the end of the riddle—all make "cup of wine or spirits" the probable solution. Like the lady "mead" of riddle 25 who is "binder and scourge of men," this seductress lures and lays out the strongest of warriors, stripping them of strength. There is a grim death-joke at the end of the riddle: As drunk fools continue to raise and praise the wine-cup which they take to be their "dearest treasure," grim God will raise, judge, and damn their souls (the real treasure) to an eternal drinking of hell's "dark woe in the dregs of pleasure." Tipplers may find this no happy wassail!

Riddle 10

This is one of several medieval ox riddles in Old English and Latin. The riddles are all fashioned about the central paradox: Living (ox), I break the land; lifeless (leather), I bind man. The ox of this riddle binds and braces lord and servant (shoe), brings wine to man (wineskin), arches up for the fierce-footed woman (boot), and thrusts against the lecherous slave-girl who comes to warm, wet, and work over her lord's or her own new "skin" (shirt or garment). At the end of the riddle the drunken, dark-haired, slave-woman works the leather in a way that leads to her own bawdy pleasure (on this topic, see Tanke, Rulon-Miller, and Higley).

Riddle 12

This creature is a horn, possibly from a rare aurochs (like the two discovered at Sutton Hoo) or a more common ox or cow. The animal's horn (already a weapon) is stripped by a hunter, adorned by a smith, borne to battle as a war-horn by a grim lord or to the table as a mead-vessel by a serving lady. Beautiful drinking horns were both a sign of wealth and an invitation to hard drinking because they would not stand upright on the table (once filled they had to be quaffed!). The horn is thus war-weapon and hall-joy: its song bodes wassail or slaughter—and sometimes at the banquet table of feuding families, a grim mixture of both.

Riddle 13

The savage protectress of this riddle is probably a female fox, or vixen, known to be a passionate mother and fierce defender of her young. Some solvers have suggested other animals such as badger, porcupine, hedgehog, and weasel, but the coloring and habits most closely fit the red fox. The fox's natural enemy is the dog, called a "slaughter-hound" in the riddle, probably a terrier of some sort. When the dog attacks, the vixen secures her young and then leads the stalker through tight burrow tunnels and lures him out her back door (Grimsgate) where she turns to offer him an unexpected feast of battle-tooth and war-claw.

Riddle 18

This deadly and beautiful creature is a sword. It celebrates its ominous splendor, the glint of death, then cuts through court-praise to its savage description of killing battle-foe and even bench-friend. The last half of the riddle plays upon an elaborate and bawdy conceit. The celibate weapon brings real death to men, not the little sexual death that women love. If the sword battles well, it begets no children; if it fails on the field, it is sent to the smithy to be melted down and reforged. In contrast, the phallic sword engenders life as it thrusts and parries. The battle-sword that serves well is a celibate killer; the phallic sword that serves well seeds life.

Riddle 19

The strange ground-skulker and dirt-biter is a wooden Anglo-Saxon plow; its dagger and sword are the metal coulter and share which turn over the earth. The plow is drawn by the "dark enemy of forests," the ox that has uprooted trees and turned woodlands to fields. It is driven by a "bent lord," the farmer who guides it. The farmer in Ælfric's *Colloquy* says: "When I've yoked the oxen and fastened the coulter and share to the plow, I must plow at least an acre a day." Paradoxically this driving lord of the plow must also slave over his fields.

Riddle 21

The twisted killer's name is Wob—Bow spelled backward. The riddlic bow is a wizard-warrior: when bent with the battle-sting in its belly, it is not dying (as a man might be) but priming to murder. It spits what it swallows—the whistling snake, the death-drink. The motif of the venomous cup hearkens back to the Devil's death-feast in the Garden of Eden. Man's fallen legacy seems symbolized by the bow. Bound, it serves its warlord properly but murderously in a world of vengeance.

Riddle 23

This is one of several Anglo-Saxon double-entendre riddles with a sexual solution for the bawdy and a plain solution for the prim. On the kitchen-counter carving-bed, the lady lays an onion—back in the bedroom, another bulb and skin. The onion begins its "song of myself" with a litany of power, but after the entrance of the warrior woman, eager-armed and proud, the "I" fractures into body, head, and skin—as the lady grabs, rushes, holds, and claims. The power struggle is resolved in the paradox of the fast catch, the mutual delight of "our meeting," the oblique conclusion, the enactment of "something to come." The phallic onion links the green world with the world of human sexuality. Nature is charged with human metaphor; passion is charted with natural myth.

Riddle 24

This creature is a book, probably a Bible or the Gospels. The riddle celebrates the parchment's life from beast-skin to book. The holy book suffers its own form of passion as it is ripped, stretched, scraped, cut, scratched by the quill ("the bird's once wind-stiff joy"), and tracked with ink; but as keeper and conveyor of the Word, it transcends its fate to bring grace, honor, and glory to men. Its inner treasure is reflected in its outer appearance—multicolored illuminations, gold leaf, and a jeweled cover. For recent work on the complexity of what constitutes a solution for this riddle, see Niles 2006, 117–19 and Holsinger, 621–22.

Riddle 25

This powerful creature is mead made from honey, a favorite Anglo-Saxon drink. The nectar is taken by bees and carried to the hive where honey is made. Man in turn takes the honey to make a powerful drink that can render him reckless or sap his strength. This is the central paradox of the riddle: Helpless to withstand man's plundering and processing, mead is transformed into a mighty agent that enters man's home (and head!) to render its conqueror helpless.

Riddle 27

This riddle describes an imaginary conflict between moon and sun. A few days before new moon, a waning sliver rises, stealing its strand of light from the sun. This "curved lamp of the air" fetches home to its night-chamber another booty of pale light between its tips or horns (sometimes called by sailors "the old moon in the arms of the new") which is actually earthlight—sunlight reflected from earth to moon. The crescent-moon marauder plots to keep this light-treasure in its sky-castle, but dawn appears and the pale treasure disappears, retaken by the sun. As the sun becomes visible, the moon itself pales, then disappears over the horizon. The next night (new moon), the plundering moon has disappeared, and groundlings wonder where the wandering thief has gone.

Riddle 29

This slung-up bird is a bagpipe, and this riddle is one of the earliest known descriptions of the instrument. Like a canny shaper or dream-singer, the bird plays mute—her beak (chanter) hung down and her hands and feet (drones and mouthpiece) slung up. Helpless but song-hungry, she is passed round the hall and pressed to sing. She drinks no mead but a bellyful of air—her hoard. Jeweled and naked, she sings through her dangling legs—makes melody with her chanter while the drones ride dangling from their glory-sister's neck. While her shape is strange, her song is sublime—she transforms the plain hall of earls into a dream-world of dance and song.

Riddle 30

This one-footed monster from the workshops of men that sails on the smooth plain is a merchant ship. Strangely misshapen, with a belly full of food for the disgorging, she slides onto the shore, carrying "corn-gold, grain-treasure, wine-wealth." Her hoard is not gold or jewels but the sustaining treasures of food and drink.

Riddle 31

This creature is an iceberg or ice-floe. Today these are not normally found in British waters, but occasional "erratics" from Greenland were probably sighted there in earlier times. The legendary creature may also derive from earlier Northern tales. The iceberg is depicted as a beautiful but dangerous woman-warrior armed with ice-blades and a ready curse. The riddle-within-a-riddle of the last five lines has as its solution, "water." Water is the mother of ice and also its daughter (pregnant again with potential ice). See Beechy for a recent exploration of the meaningful play in this riddle.

Riddle 32

This virtuous ground-dogger, plant-scratcher, crop-catcher is not some weird pooch but an Anglo-Saxon rake. It noses, scruffs, and plunders weeds, thins gardens and fields for a crop of fair flowers and good grain. It is both weed-warrior and farmyard slave. It feeds cattle with its catch of teeth. The tone here is a curious mixture of mock heroic and pastoral joy.

Riddle 37

There is no general agreement about the creature in this riddle, despite the riddler's insistence that writings reveal its plain presence among men. We should know it—it seeks each living person, moves everywhere in the wide world, and carries comfort to the children of middle-earth. Yet its power passes knowing. No wonder—it has no hands, feet, mouth, mind, or soul. Yet it lives. It is the poorest of creatures, yet it reaps glory. It is marvelously difficult to catch with words, yet everything said about it is true. Possible solutions include dream, language, speech, time, death, faith, moon, cloud, comet, and day. None of the proposed solutions wholly satisfies the descriptive details of the riddle. Paradoxically the creature closest to us remains to be discovered.

Riddle 43

For polite company the answer to this riddle is bread dough—though lustier spirits may find the phallic solution barely concealed. As in other bawdy, double entendre riddles, the poet is at pains to tease us with both solutions. In playful fashion the riddle is also an elaborate and punningly obscene etymological joke, since the Old English word for "lord," *hláford*, comes from *hláf-weard*, "guardian of the loaf," and the word for "lady," *hlǽfdige*, comes from *hláf-dige*, "kneader of the dough." The lady in question is presumably making more than bread.

Riddle 45

The thief who swallows songs is a bookworm. The moth lays its eggs in the spine of a manuscript made of cowhide. The larvae hatch and feed on the vellum leaves. To the worm, *Beowulf* or the Bible is just so much beef jerky. The riddler pokes mock-heroic fun at the worm, a midnight marauder who like a pedant devours the substance without the spirit. The word *wyrm* in Old English can mean "worm, moth, bug, dragon"—in short everything that treats man as a material body and wants to devour him. There is a wordplay in the riddle between *cwide*, "sayings," and *cwidu*, "cud" (see Robinson, 1975, on this and other examples of ambiguity and wordplay in the riddle). The worm treats our songs and sayings like so much lunch. But the riddler reverses this by turning the moth's munching into a rumination of song, and in so doing reclaiming what was lost in the original word-hoard of the mind and memory. In Anglo-Saxon England the oral tradition of the singer was being supplanted by the literary conjunction of poet, scribe, and reader. The old form of memory, the rhythmical word-hoard, was giving way to the material storehouse of the vellum page. What the mind of the singer guarded and passed on, the book made plain and perishable. The riddle reenacts the destruction of the written word and challenges the reader to not only solve the riddle but to reclaim the miracle of memory and the sustaining wonder of speech and song.

Riddle 52

Like the earlier sexual, double-entendre "bread" and "onion" riddles (23 and 43), this one also has ostensibly to do with food. The male servant thrusts his plunger into the female churn—together they make the baby, butter. The riddle opens with a burst of machismo, slightly surreal in its ravishing treatment of the passive woman in the corner. The man has the action—he steps, lifts, thrusts (his "something" is mock modesty), and works his will. Yet the paradox of sexuality here is that as man pumps, his power wanes. The dichotomy between active and passive, male and female, man and churn, disappears in a moment of lyric frenzy—"*Both* swayed and shook." The narrative voice swings over to the feminine: the man is a servant, only sometimes useful, and too often tired before the work's end. The woman's power is in the making: she bears the butter.

Riddle 57

This riddle celebrates the chalice. Here the sacred "ring" (an Old English *hring* can be a ring, chain-link, or something circular) is passed to the communicants who celebrate the deep mystery of the Mass. The circle of gold "speaks" of Christ in two ways: it offers the sacred blood-wine of the Savior, and its body like Christ's is scored with wounds, probably icons and inscriptions. Like the cross in "The Dream of the Rood," the chalice is both glorious token and wounded object. As it passes, "twisting, turning in the hands/Of proud men," its celebrants seem to reflect the torturers at the foot of the cross. Time collapses: Christ who was, is—and with the proper penetration of mystery, we become the celebrants-cum-crucifiers whom Christ has come to save. This is the larger riddle of God's grace.

Riddle 71

This creature which is hauled from its homeland, stripped and reshaped, forced to battle against its will for a grim lord, is a spear. Like the tree in "The Dream of the Rood," it is ripped from a natural innocence and made to murder in man's world. The riddle is a strange combination of heroic celebration and grotesque irony. Bright glory is a bit dimmed when warriors become marauders; and weapons, muggish tools for bashing brains. The unnamed one that "breaks ready for the road home" at the end of the riddle is the soul of an expiring recipient of the spear-man's quest for glory.

Riddle 74

The footless, fixed creature of the sea with its bone-skin and sweet flesh is an oyster. The sea-mouth is caught, cracked, and hauled to its own door of doom (man's mouth!). The paradox of the "eater eaten" can be found elsewhere in the riddles.

Riddle 76

Although this creature sounds like a cross between a musical battle-sword and a flowerpot, it is actually a horn which can be shaped into a war-horn or a drinking horn. In the battle-rush it can sing out with a clarion call. At the supper table it can bear wood-blooms and the bee's delight—mead made from honey. It can both sing and reward singers with the gift of brew. Tongue in cheek, it laments because the hands of the noble lady who serves its mead are a little too honeyed. Riddle 12 is a companion horn riddle.

Riddle 77

This suffering servant, bound to its perch, buffeted by winds, is a weathervane or weathercock. Because Peter denied Christ three times before cockcrow, iron cocks were placed on church towers as a sign of Christ's coming and as a call to vigilance and repentance. These apparently gave rise to the medieval weathercock. The riddler here has artfully created a Christlike cock perched on its nail, twisting in torment, bound to its fate, serving faithfully, a gift to men. Buffeted by storm, it marks the wind, and in that act of charting, rises above its fate. Its act of passion, like Christ's, is both literally and spiritually transcendent as it swings high above men.

Riddle 79

This riddle deals with the origin and outcome of some metal used in the making of artifacts and coins, probably gold. The ore is ripped from its homeland, smelted, wrought by a smith, and shaped to bear man's icons and inscriptions. Its wounds are many, yet paradoxically its power is great. Unable to defy miner, smelter, artisan—it reaps revenge on the collective shaper, man. Separated from its family in the ground, it separates and enthralls the family of man.

Riddle 81

This fish and river riddle is based on a fifth-century Latin riddle of Symphosius, translated here:

> This house echoes with a loud, clear sound,
> On earth, resounds while its guest is silent.
> Bound together, guest and home course and run.

The Old English riddle draws upon the Latin motif of the loud house with its quiet creature, then elaborates on a theme of common and contrastive movement. It concludes with a vital paradox: hauled from its house, the creature dies.

Riddle 91

This much debated riddle is the last one in the riddle collection in the Exeter Book manuscript. Its creature claims to be well known and often in the keeping of men, but it has yet to be identified to the satisfaction of all. Proposed solutions range from soul to wandering singer and include moon, quill pen, book, beech, prostitute, dream, and riddle. Is the "plunderers' joy" (an inset miniature riddle) the book's gold ornaments, the pen's ink, the moon's treasure of light, the singer's studded lyre, the prostitute's favors, the riddler's mystery, the spirit's quickness, or the splendors of dream? These questions continue to haunt the solvers. The creature seems so near—yet still strangely undiscovered. Guess what it is!

GLOSSARY
OF PROPER NAMES

I n the glossary below, all line references are to *Beowulf* unless otherwise indicated. Abbreviations for other poems are AL = "Advent Lyric"; D = "Deor"; DR = "The Dream of the Rood"; M = "The Battle of Maldon"; MII = "Maxims II"; PhP = "Physiologus: Panther"; PhW = "Physiologus: Whale"; R = "Riddle"; W/E = "Wulf and Eadwacer." The letter æ is alphabetized between ad and af. The abbreviation *mult* means that there are multiple occurrences of the term in that text. Wherever possible I have also tried to indicate the identity of the person or place in the translation itself.

A
Abel: Biblical son of Adam and Eve, killed by his brother Cain, 109
Adam: Biblical first man created by God, DR 108
Ælfhere: one of the ford guardians at Maldon, M 79
Ælfnoth: one of the loyal Anglo-Saxon warriors who falls with Byrhtnoth, M 184
Ælfric: father of Ælfwine, M 208
Ælfwine: kinsman of Byrhtnoth who is the son of Ælfric and grandson of Ealhelm, M 208, 230
Æschere: Hrothgar's retainer and counselor who is killed by Grendel's mother, 1324, 1419, 2122
Æscferth: Northumbrian hostage in Byrhtnoth's household, M 267
Æsir: gods in the Old Norse cosmology; probably a reference to pagan gods in "Charm for a Sudden Stitch," 23, 25
Æthelgar: father of Godric (the loyal Godric who did not flee from Maldon), M 324
Æthelred: King of England (978–1016), M 56, 151, 201
Ætheric: retainer of Byrhtnoth, brother of Sibyrht, M 283

B

Beadohild: daughter of Nithhad, mother of a son by Weland, D 9

Beanstan: father of Breca, 523

Beow: legendary early Danish king, son of Scyld, 19, 56

Beowulf: son of Ecgtheow and Hygelac's unnamed sister, *mult*

Breca: warrior of the Brondings, Beowulf's swimming opponent, 506, 515, 531, 540

Brondings: a Germanic people, the tribe of Breca and Beanstan, 520

Brosings: tribe that made or owned Hama's legendary necklace or collar, 1198

Byrhthelm: Byrhtnoth's father, M 91

Byrhtnoth: Earl of Essex who led the troops against the Vikings at Maldon and was killed, M *mult*

Byrhtwold: old retainer of Byrhtnoth, M 313

C

Cain: Biblical son of Adam and Eve, killer of his brother Abel, 107, 112, 1261, 1263

Ceola: father of Wulfstan who guarded the ford at Maldon with Ælfhere and Maccus, M 76

Christ: Biblical Son of God, R 57.11, MII 4, AL iv 30, DR 61, 107, 123, 135, 147

D

Dæghrefn: warrior of the Franks, killed by Beowulf, 2501

Danes: Danish people, *mult* (see also compounds such as Bright-Danes, Spear-Danes, South-Danes, etc.) in *Beowulf* and "Maldon"

David: Biblical King of Israel, slayer of Goliath, and ancestor of Christ, AL iv 31, AL vii 2, 32

Deor: singer or scop of the Heodenings, D 36

Dunnere: freeman who fought at Maldon, M 255

E

Eadgils: son of Ohthere the Swedish king and brother of Eanmund, 2380, 2392

Eadric: retainer of Byrhtnoth, M 13

Eadweard: (1) retainer of Byrhtnoth, M 119; (2) Edward the Tall, also a retainer of Byrhtnoth (possibly the same person), M 274

Eadwacer: husband of speaker of "Wulf and Eadwacer" (or possibly an epithet for Wulf meaning "guardian of property"), W/E 19

Eadwold: retainer of Byrhtnoth, brother of Oswold, M 308

Ealhelm: Mercian grandfather of Ælfwine, M 218

Eanmund: son of Ohthere the Swedish king and brother of Eadgils, killed by Weohstan, 2380, 2611, 2613, 2617

Earnaness: promontory on the Geatish coast, near where Beowulf fights the dragon, 3033

Ecglaf: (1) father of Unferth, *mult* (2) father of Æscferth, M 267

Ecgtheow: father of Beowulf, son-in-law of Hrethel *mult*

Ecgwela: Danish king whose sons were slain by Heremod, 1712

Eofor: Geatish warrior who slew the Swedish King Ongentheow and was rewarded with the hand of Hygelac's daughter in marriage, *mult*

Eomer: son of Offa, king of the Angles, 1962

Eormanric (Eormenric): fourth-century tyrannical ruler of the Goths, 1201, D 21

Eve: Biblical first woman created by God, AL iv 32

F

Fastitocalon: corrupted form in Latin of the Greek word for a kind of turtle that was the disappearing island in earlier forms of the story about the whale, PhW 9

Finn: king of the Frisians, husband of Hildeburh, killed by Hengest, *mult*

Finns: Finns or Lapps, 581

Fitela: son of Sigemund and Sigemund's sister; thus his father is also his uncle, 877, 887

Folcwalda: father of Finn, 1087

Franks: Germanic tribes, enemies of the Geats, *mult*

Freawaru: daughter of Hrothgar who will be married to Ingeld the Heathobard, 2021

Fremu: wife of Offa, king of the Angles, 1931 (there is extensive debate about the exact name of the queen in this passage; in earlier editions and translations, the queen is named Thryth or Modthryth, but *Klaeber 4* recommends Fremu)

Frisians: Germanic tribes, enemies of the Geats, *mult*

Froda: king of the Heathobards and father of Ingeld, 2026

G

Gabriel: Biblical archangel who announced to the Virgin Mary the forthcomng birth of Christ, AL vii 46

Gadd: kinsman of Offa, M 291

Garmund: grandfather of Eomer, father of Offa, king of the Angles, 1963

Geat: legendary lover or husband of Mæthhild, D 15

Geats: Scandinavian tribe, probably from southern Sweden and Gotland, Beowulf's people, *mult* (see also compounds such as Sea-Geats, Battle-Geats, etc.)

Godric: (1) son of Odda who fled from Maldon, M 189, 237, 330; (2) son of Æthelgar who stayed and fought at Maldon M 324

Godwig: son of Odda who fled with his brothers from Maldon, M 193

Godwine: son of Odda who fled with his brothers from Maldon, M 193

Grendel: the monster who attacks the Danes in Heorot and is slain by Beowulf, *mult*

Grimsgate: metaphoric description of a burrow opening, R 13.22

Guthlaf: Danish warrior at Finnsburg, 1149

H

Hæreth: father of Hygd who is Hygelac's queen, 1928, 1981

Hæthcyn: Geatish prince, the second son of Hrethel, killed by Ongentheow, *mult*

Halga: brother of Hrothgar, father of Hrothulf, 61

Half-Danes: tribe of the Danes to which Hnæf and Hildeburh belong, *mult*

Hama: legendary owner of the Brosning necklace or collar, 1197

Healfdene: king of the Danes, Hrothgar's father, *mult*

Heardred: son of Hygelac, later king of the Geats, *mult*

Heathobards: Germanic tribe to which Ingeld belongs, *mult*

Heatholaf: warrior of the Germanic Wylfing tribe, killed by Beowulf's father, 459

Heathoreams: tribe in southern Norway where Breca is washed up, 518

Hemming: kinsman of King Offa of the Angles and of his son Eomer, 1963

Helmings: family of the Danish queen Wealhtheow, 622

Hengest: at Finnsburg, leader of the Danes after Hnæf's death, *mult*

Heorogar: Hrothgar's older brother, possibly king for a short time before he died early, 60, 467, 2159

Heodenings: legendary Germanic people where Deor claims to have served as the court singer or scop, D 35

Heorot: the hall of Danish king Hrothgar, *mult*

Heoroweard: son of Heorogar, Hrothgar's elder brother, 2162

Heorrenda: *scop* or singer who Deor says displaced him in the court of the Heodeningas, D 38

Herebeald: prince of the Geats and eldest son of king Hrethel, killed accidentally by his brother Hæthcyn, 2434, 2435, 2464

Heremod: legendary Danish king before Scyld, 899, 915, 1711

Hereric: uncle of Heardred, possibly the brother of Hygd, 2205

Hildeburh: at Finnsburg, Half-Dane princess (sister of Hnæf), married to Finn, King of the Frisians, 1070, 1117, 1160

Hnæf: at Finnsburg, leader of the Half-Danes (brother of Hildeburh), killed in the first battle, *mult*

Hoc: father of Hildeburh and Hnæf, 1075

Hondscio: in Beowulf's party in Heorot, the Geatish warrior who is eaten by Grendel, 2077

Hrefnawudu: forest in Sweden, site of a battle between Swedes and Geats, 2925, 2935

Hreosnabeorh: hill in Geatland, site of a battle between Swedes and Geats, 2477

Hrethel: king of the Geats, father of Hygelac, grandfather of Beowulf (through his unnamed mother), *mult*

Hrethric: elder son of Hrothgar and Wealhtheow, 1189, 1835

Hronesness: headland on the Geatish coast where Beowulf fights the dragon, 2805, 3136

Hrothgar: king of the Danes, *mult*

Hrothmund: younger son of Hrothgar and Wealhtheow, 1189

Hrothulf: Hrothgar's nephew who aspires to power and is apparently a threat to Hrothgar's sons, 1017, 1168, 1183

Hrunting: Unferth's sword, which he lends to Beowulf for his fight with Grendel's mother (the sword proves useless), 1456, 1489, 1659, 1807

Hunlaf: in Finnsburg, Half-Dane probably killed in the first battle or a somewhat earlier one, 1149

Hunlafing: in Finnsburg, a warrior in Hengest's troop (probably son or descendant of Hunlaf) who urges him on to revenge, 1145

Hygd: queen of the Geats, wife of king Hygelac, *mult*

Hygelac: king of the Geats, son of Hrethel, uncle of Beowulf, *mult*

I

Ing: legendary early king of the Danes, 1044

Ingeld: prince of the Heathobards, to be married to Freawaru, Hrothgar's daughter, as a gesture of peace-weaving that fails, 2025, 2032, 2065

J

Jacob: Biblical father of Joseph (husband of Mary) in the New Testament, AL vii 1

Joseph: (1) Biblical son of Jacob in the Old Testament, famous for his coat of many colors and his ability to interpret dreams, PhP 18; (2) Biblical husband of Mary in the New Testament, AL vii 1

Judgment Day: in Christian belief, the Day of Judgment when souls are reunited with their bodies and come before the Lord to be judged, DR 112

L

Lapps: a tribe from northern Norway and Sweden, 581

Leofsunu: retainer of Byrhtnoth, M 244

M

Maccus: Anglo-Saxon warrior who defended the ford at Maldon, M 79

Mærings: tribe or people ruled by Theodoric, D 19

Mæthhild: legendary lover or wife of Geat in Old Norse and Icelandic tales, D 14

Mary: Biblical mother of Christ, AL iv 22, AL vii 15, DR 103

Mercians: people from the Anglo-Saxon area of the east midlands, M 217

N

Nægling: Beowulf's sword, 2683

Nithhad: legendary king in Germanic stories who persecutes Weland, D 5

Northumbria: Anglo-Saxon area in northeast England, M 267

O

Odda: father of the disloyal Godric, Godwig, and Godwine, who fled from Maldon, M 187, 237

Offa: (1) king of the continental Angles who married Fremu, 1944, 1949, 1952, 1959; (2) an officer in Byrhtnoth's troop who takes over the leadership after his death, M *mult*

Ohthere: son of Swedish king Ongentheow and brother of Onela, father of Eanmund and Eadgils, *mult*

Onela: son of Swedish king Ongentheow and brother of Ohthere; he takes the throne after the death of his father, *mult*

Ongentheow: king of the Swedes, father of Onela and Ohthere, killed by Wulf and Eofor, *mult*

Oslaf: Danish warrior, 1149

Oswold: retainer of Byrhtnoth, brother of Eadwold, M 308

P

Pante: river near Maldon, M 69

S

Scyld/Scyld Sceafing: legendary founder of the Danish kingdom, *mult*

Scyldings: name for the Danes from legendary founder Scyld Sceafing, *mult*

Sibyrht: brother of Æthelric, a retainer of Byrhtnoth, M 283

Sigemund: son of Wæls, legendary Norse hero, 873, 882, 895

St. Paul: leader of the early Christian church, converted on the road to Damascus, author of a number of New Testament epistles, PhP 64

Sturmere: village which Leofsunu comes from, M 248

Swedes: traditional enemy of the Geats, *mult*

Swerting: grandfather of Hygelac (or possibly his maternal uncle), 1204

T

Theodric: Theodoric, ruler of the Mærings, D 18

Thurstan: father of Wihstan, M 301

U

Unferth: retainer and advisor of Hrothgar, *mult*

W

Wægmundings: family or tribe to which Beowulf, Wiglaf, and Weohstan belong, 2605, 2814

Wæls: father of Sigemund, 873, 894

Wealhtheow: Hrothgar's wife and queen, *mult*

Weland: legendary Germanic smith, 455, D 1

Weohstan: father of Wiglaf, *mult*

Wigelm: father of Wistan, M 304; Thurstan is also called father of Wistan (the discrepancy is not easily resolved).

Wistan: son of Thurstan (or of Wigelm?), M 301

Withergyld: Heathobard warrior, 2052

Wonred: father of Wulf and Eofor, 2963, 2970

Wulf: (1) Geatish warrior, son of Wonred, brother of Eofor, *mult*; (2) lover (or husband? or child?) of the speaker of "Wulf and Eadwacer," W/E 5, 11, 15, 20

Wulfgar: retainer of Hrothgar, hall-guard at Heorot, *mult*

Wulfmær: (1) son of Byrhtnoth's sister, M 116; (2) Byrhtnoth's retainer, son of Wulfstan, M 155, 184

Wulfstan: defender of the ford at Maldon, M 76, 155

Wylfings: Germanic tribe of Heatholaf, who was killed by Beowulf's father, 460

Y

Yrmenlaf: Danish warrior, brother of Æschere, 1324

Yrse: Hrothgar's sister who is married to king Onela of the Swedes, 61

BIBLIOGRAPHY

This bibliography contains all the sources cited in this book as well as a selection of useful books and articles on Old English poetry.

Alexander, Michael. 2002. *A History of Old English Literature.* Peterborough, Ont.: Broadview Press.

Algeo, John, and Thomas Pyles. 2009. *The Origins and Development of the English Language.* 6th ed. Boston: Wadsworth.

Andersson, Theodore. 1997. "Sources and Analogues." In Bjork and Niles, 125–48.

Baker, Peter S., ed. 1995. *Beowulf: Basic Readings.* Basic Readings in Anglo-Saxon England 1. New York: Garland. Republished as *The Beowulf Reader.* New York: Garland, 2000.

———. 2007. *Introduction to Old English.* 2nd ed. Oxford: Blackwell.

Barley, Nigel. 1978. "Structural Aspects of the Anglo-Saxon Riddle." *Semiotica* 10: 143–75.

Bartlett, Adeline Courtney. 1935. *The Larger Rhetorical Patterns in Anglo-Saxon Poetry.* New York: Columbia University Press; reprint 1966, New York: AMS Press.

Bede. 1968. *A History of the English Church and People.* Trans. Leo Sherley-Price, rev. R. E. Latham. Harmondsworth: Penguin.

Beechy, Tiffany. 2010. "Bind and Loose: Aesthetics and the Word in Old English Law, Charm, and Riddle." In Hill 2010, 43–63.

Bennett, Helen T. 1994. "Exile and Semiosis of Gender in Old English Elegies." In Harwood and Overing. 43–58.

Bessinger, J. B., Jr., and Stanley J. Kahrl, eds. 1968. *Essential Articles for the Study of Old English Poetry.* Hamden, Conn.: Archon.

Bitterli, Dieter. 2009. *The Old English Riddles of the Exeter Book and the Anglo-Latin Riddle Tradition.* Toronto: University of Toronto Press.

Bjork, Robert E. and John D. Niles, eds. 1997. *A "Beowulf" Handbook.* Lincoln: University of Nebraska Press.

———. See also under Fulk, Bjork, and Niles 2008. *Klaeber 4.*

Blair, Peter Hunter. 1966. *An Introduction to Anglo-Saxon England.* Cambridge: Cambridge University Press; new ed. 2003, with introduction by Simon Keynes.

———. 1990. *The World of Bede (Studies in Anglo-Saxon England)*. New York: Cambridge University Press.

Bliss, Alan. 1962. *An Introduction to Old English Metre*. Oxford: Blackwell.

Boethius. 1962. *The Consolation of Philosophy*. Trans. Richard Green. Indianapolis: Bobbs-Merrill. See also Godden and Irvine for the Anglo-Saxon translation of this.

Bonjour, Adrien. 1950. *The Digressions in Beowulf*. Oxford: Blackwell; reprint 1970.

Bosworth, Joseph, and T. Northcote Toller. 1898. *An Anglo-Saxon Dictionary*. London: Oxford University Press; *Supplement by T. Northcote Toller*, 1921; *With Revised and Enlarged Addenda* by Alistair Campbell, 1972.

Brodeur, Arthur Gilchrist. 1959. *The Art of Beowulf*. Berkeley: University of California Press.

Bullough, Donald A. 1993. "What Has Ingeld to Do with Lindisfarne?" *Anglo-Saxon England*, 22: 93–125.

Burlin, Robert B. 1968. *The Old English Advent: A Typological Commentary*. New Haven, Conn.: Yale University Press.

Byock, Jesse, tr. 1999. *The Saga of the Volsungs*. London: Penguin.

Cameron, M. L. 1993. *Anglo-Saxon Medicine*. Cambridge: Cambridge University Press.

Campbell, Jackson J. 1959. *The Advent Lyrics of the Exeter Book*. Princeton, N.J.: Princeton University Press.

Campbell, James, ed. 1982. *The Anglo-Saxons*. Oxford: Phaidon; reprint 1991, Harmondsworth: Penguin.

Carnicelli, Thomas A. ed. 1969. *King Alfred's Version of St. Augustine's Soliloquies*. Cambridge, Mass.: Harvard University Press.

Carver, Martin. 2000. *Sutton Hoo: Burial Ground of Kings?* London: British Museum Press. Orig. British Museum Press and Philadelphia: University of Pennsylvania Press, 1998.

Chance, Jane. 1986. *Woman as Hero in Old English Literature*. Syracuse, N.Y.: Syracuse University Press.

———. 1990. "The Structural Unity of *Beowulf*: The Problem of Grendel's Mother." In Damico and Olsen, 248–61. Originally in *Texas Studies in Literature and Language* 22 (1980): 287–303 (published under the name Jane C. Nitzsche).

Chickering, Howell. D., Jr. 1977. *Beowulf: A Dual-Language Edition*. New York: Anchor; rev. 2006.

Clark Hall, John R. 1969. *A Concise Anglo-Saxon Dictionary*. 4th ed. with supplement by Herbert D. Meritt. Cambridge: Cambridge University Press.

Colgrave, Bertram, ed. and trans. 1956. *Felix's Life of Saint Guthlac*. Cambridge: Cambridge University Press.

Damico, Helen, and Alexandra Hennessey Olsen, eds. 1990. *New Readings on Women in Old English Literature*. Bloomington: Indiana University Press.

Deskis, Susan E. 1996. *Beowulf and the Medieval Proverb Tradition*. Medieval & Renaissance Texts & Studies 155. Tempe, Ariz.: Medieval & Renaissance Texts & Studies.

Dictionary of Old English. 1986–. Ed. Angus Cameron et al. Toronto: Centre for Medieval Studies, University of Toronto, Pontifical Institute of Mediaeval Studies.

Donaldson, E. Talbot, trans. 1966. *Beowulf*. New York: Norton.

Donoghue, Daniel. 2004. *Old English Literature: A Short Introduction*. Oxford: Blackwell.

Drout, Michael D. C., ed. 2002. *Beowulf and the Critics by J. R. R. Tolkien*. Medieval & Renaissance Texts & Studies 248. Tempe, Ariz.: Medieval & Renaissance Texts & Studies.

Dunning, Thomas Patrick and Alan Joseph Bliss, eds. 1969. *The Wanderer*. London: Methuen.

Earl, James W. 1994. *Thinking About Beowulf.* Stanford, Calif.: Stanford University Press.

Evans, Angela Care. 1995. *The Sutton Hoo Ship Burial.* Rev. ed. London: British Museum Press.

Fleming, Robin. 2010. *Britain After Rome: The Fall and Rise, 400 to 1070.* Penguin History of Britain, vol. 2. London: Allen Lane.

Foley, John Miles. 1988. *The Theory of Oral Composition: History and Methodology.* Bloomington: Indiana University Press.

Frank, Roberta. 2006. "The Incomparable Wryness of Old English Poetry." In Walmsley, 59–73.

Fulk, R. D., ed. 1991. *Interpretations of Beowulf: A Critical Anthology.* Bloomington: Indiana University Press.

———. 1992. *A History of Old English Meter.* Philadelphia: University of Pennsylvania Press.

———. See also under Pope; *Klaeber 4.*

Fulk, R. D., Robert E. Bjork, and John D. Niles, eds. 2008. *Klaeber's Beowulf and the Fight at Finnsburg.* 4th ed. Foreword by Helen Damico. Toronto: University of Toronto Press; based on 3rd ed. by Klaeber, Boston: D.C. Heath, 1950. Cited as *Klaeber 4.*

Fulk, R. D., and Christopher M. Cain. 2003. *A History of Old English Literature.* Oxford: Blackwell.

Garmonsway, G. N. and Jacqueline Simpson, trans. 1971. *Beowulf and Its Analogues,* including *Archaeology and Beowulf* by Hilda Ellis Davidson. New York: Dutton.

Garrison, Mary, Janet L. Nelson, and Dominic Tweddle. 2001. *Alcuin and Charlemagne: The Golden Age of York.* York: Maxiprint.

Gifford, Edwin, and Joyce Gifford. 2002. *Anglo-Saxon Sailing Ships.* 2nd ed. Woodbridge: Creekside Publishing for Sutton Hoo Society.

Godden, Malcolm, and Susan Irvine, eds. 2010. *The Old English Boethius: An Edition of the Old English Versions of Boethius's De Consolatione Philosophiae.* With chapter on the Metres by Mark Griffith and contributions by Rohini Jayatilaka. 2 vols. Oxford: Oxford University Press.

Godden, Malcolm, and Michael Lapidge. 1991. *The Cambridge Companion to Old English Literature.* Cambridge: Cambridge University Press.

Goldsmith, Margaret E. 1962. "The Christian Perspective in *Beowulf.*" *Comparative Literature* 14: 71–90.

———. 1970. *The Mode and Meaning of "Beowulf".* London: Athlone Press.

Gordon, Ida L. 1960. *The Seafarer.* London: Methuen; reprint 1990 with Bibliography by Mary Clayton, Exeter: University of Exeter Press.

Green, Charles. 1963. *Sutton Hoo: The Excavation of a Royal Ship-Burial.* London: Merlin Press.

Green, Martin, ed. 1983. *The Old English Elegies: New Essays in Criticism and Research.* Rutherford, N.J.: Fairleigh Dickinson University Press.

Greenfield, Stanley B. 1966. "The Old English Elegies." In Stanley, 142–75.

———. 1972. *The Interpretation of Old English Poems.* London: Routledge & Kegan Paul.

Greenfield, Stanley B., and Daniel C. Calder. 1986. *A New Critical History of Old English Literature.* New York: New York University Press.

Greenfield, Stanley B., and Richard Evert. 1975. "*Maxims II*: Gnome and Poem." In Nicholson and Frese, 337–54.

Hansen, Elaine Tuttle. 1988. *The Solomon Complex.* Toronto: University of Toronto Press.

Härke, Heinrich. 1998. "Archaeologists and Migrations: A Problem of Attitude?" *Current Anthropology* 39/1: 19–24.

————. 2002. "Kings and Warriors: Population and Landscape from Post-Roman to Norman Britain." In *The Peopling of Britain: The Shaping of a Human Landscape*, ed. Paul Slack and Ryk Ward. Oxford: Oxford University Press, 145–75.

Harris, Joseph. 1991. "*Beowulf* in Literary History." In Fulk 1991, 235–41.

Harwood, Britton J., and Gillian R. Overing, eds. 1994. *Class and Gender in Early English Literature: Intersections.* Bloomington: Indiana University Press.

Hieatt, Constance B. 1975. "Envelope Patterns and the Structure of *Beowulf.*" *English Studies in Canada* 1: 249–65.

Higley, Sarah L. 2003. "The Wanton Hand: Reading and Reaching into Grammars and Bodies in Old English Riddle 12." In Withers and Wilcox, 29–59.

Hill, John M. 1995. *The Cultural World in Beowulf.* Toronto: University of Toronto Press.

————. 2000. *The Anglo-Saxon Warrior Ethic.* Gainesville: University Press of Florida.

————. 2008. *The Narrative Pulse of Beowulf: Arrivals and Departures.* Toronto: University of Toronto Press.

————, ed. 2010. *On the Aesthetics of Beowulf and Other Old English Poems.* Toronto: University of Toronto Press.

Hill, Joyce, ed. 2009. *Old English Minor Heroic Poems.* 3rd ed. Durham: Centre for Medieval and Renaissance Studies, Durham University; Toronto: Pontifical Institute of Mediaeval Studies.

Hiltunen, Risto. 2006. "'*Eala, geferan and gode wyrhtan*': On Interjections in Old English." In Walmsley, 91–116.

Holsinger, Bruce. 2009. "Of Pigs and Parchment: Medieval Studies and the Coming of the Animal." *PMLA* 124: 616–23.

Howe, Nicholas. 1985. *The Old English Catalogue Poems.* Anglistica 23. Copenhagen: Rosenkilde and Bagger.

Hume, Kathryn. 1975. "The Theme and Structure of *Beowulf.*" *Studies in Philology* 72: 1–27.

Huppé, Bernard. 1968. "Caedmon's Hymn." In Stevens and Mandel, 117–38.

Irving, Edward B., Jr. 1961. "The Heroic Style in *The Battle of Maldon.*" *Studies in Philology* 58, 457–67.

————. 1968. *A Reading of Beowulf.* New Haven, Conn.: Yale University Press.

————. 1989. *Rereading Beowulf.* Philadelphia: University of Pennsylvania Press.

————. 1994. "Heroic Experience in the Old English Riddles." In O'Keeffe, 199–212.

————. 1997. "Christian and Pagan Elements." In Bjork and Niles, 175–92.

Isaacs, Neil D. 1968. *Structural Principles in Old English Poetry.* Knoxville: University of Tennessee Press.

Jackson, K. H. 1953. *Language and History in Early Britain: a Chronological Survey of the Brittonic Languages, 1st to 12th Century AD.* Edinburgh: Edinburgh University Press; reprint 2000, Dublin: Four Courts Press.

Jones, Chris. 2006. *Strange Likeness: The Use of Old English in Twentieth-Century Poetry.* New York: Oxford University Press.

Kaske, R. E. 1958. "*Sapientia et Fortitudo* as the Controlling Theme of *Beowulf.*" *Studies in Philology* 55: 423–56.

Kennedy, Charles. 1943. *The Earliest English Poetry.* New York: Oxford University Press.

Kiernan, Kevin S. 1990. "Reading Cædmon's 'Hymn' with Someone Else's Glosses." *Representations* 32: 157–74.

————. 1996. "*Beowulf*" and the "*Beowulf*" *Manuscript.* Rev. ed. Ann Arbor: University of Michigan Press.

Klaeber, Fr. *Beowulf and the Fight at Finnsburg.* 3rd ed. with supplements. Boston: D.C. Heath, 1950.

Klaeber 4. See Fulk, Bjork, and Niles. 2008.

Klink, Anne L. 1992. *The Old English Elegies: A Critical Edition and Genre Study.* Montreal: McGill-Queen's University Press.

Krapp, George Philip, and Elliott Van Kirk Dobbie, eds. 1931–53. *The Anglo-Saxon Poetic Records.* 6 vols. New York: Columbia University Press.

Lapidge, Michael. 2006. *The Anglo-Saxon Library.* Oxford: Oxford University Press.

Lapidge, Michael, and Simon Keynes. 1983. *Alfred the Great: Asser's "Life of King Alfred" and Other Contemporary Sources.* Harmondsworth: Penguin.

Larrington, Carolyne, trans. 1996. *The Poetic Edda.* Oxford: Oxford University Press.

Lawson, Graeme. 2001. "The Lyre Remains from Grave 32." In *Snape Anglo-Saxon Cemetery: Excavations and Surveys 1824–1992*, ed. William Filmer-Sankey and Tim Pestell. East Anglian Archaeology Report 95. Ipswich: Suffolk County Council Archaeological Service, 215–23.

Lee, Alvin A. 1998. *Gold-Hall & Earth-Dragon: Beowulf as Metaphor.* Toronto: University of Toronto Press.

Lee, Stuart D., and Elizabeth Solopova. 2005. *The Keys of Middle-Earth: Discovering Medieval Literature Through the Fiction of J. R. R. Tolkien.* New York: Palgrave Macmillan.

Lerer, Seth. 1991. *Literacy and Power in Anglo-Saxon Literature.* Lincoln: University of Nebraska Press.

———. 1997. "*Beowulf* and Contemporary Critical Theory." In Bjork and Niles, 325–39.

Leyerle, John. 1967. "The Interlace Structure of *Beowulf.*" *University of Toronto Quarterly* 37: 1–17; in Fulk 1991, 146–67.

Liuzza, R. M. ed. 2002. *Old English Literature: Critical Essays.* New Haven, Conn.: Yale University Press.

Lumiansky, Robert M. 1950. "The Dramatic Structure of the Old English *Wanderer.*" *Neophilologus* 34: 104–12.

Malone, Kemp. 1933. *Deor.* London: Methuen; rev. 1977, Exeter: University of Exeter Press.

———. 1948. "*Beowulf.*" In Nicholson, 137–54. Originally in *English Studies* 29: 161–72.

———. 1953. "Royal Names in Old English Poetry." *Names* 1: 153–62.

Marckwardt, Albert H., and James L. Rosier. 1972. *Old English Language and Literature.* New York: Norton.

McGeachy, Margaret Gillian. 2006. *Lonesome Words: The Vocal Poetics of the Old English Lament and the African-American Blues Song.* New York: Palgrave Macmillan.

Mitchell, Bruce. 1998. *On Old English: Selected Papers.* Oxford: Basil Blackwell.

Mitchell, Bruce, and Fred C. Robinson. 1998. *Beowulf: An Edition with Relevant Shorter Texts.* Oxford: Blackwell.

———. 2007. *A Guide to Old English.* Rev. 7th ed. Oxford: Blackwell.

Muir, Bernard J., ed. 2000. *The Exeter Anthology of Old English Poetry.* 2nd ed. rev. 2 vols. Exeter: University of Exeter Press.

Myres, J. N. L. 1986. *The English Settlements.* Oxford: Oxford University Press.

Nelson, Marie. 1974. "The Rhetoric of the Exeter Book Riddles." *Speculum* 49: 421–40.

Neville, Jennifer. 1999. *Representations of the Natural World in Old English Poetry.* Cambridge Studies in Anglo-Saxon England 27. Cambridge: Cambridge University Press.

Nicholson, Lewis E., ed. 1963. *An Anthology of Beowulf Criticism.* Notre Dame, Ind.: University of Notre Dame Press.

Nicholson, Lewis E., and Dolores Warwick Frese, eds. 1975. *Anglo-Saxon Poetry: Essays in Appreciation for John C. McGalliard*. Notre Dame, Ind.: University of Notre Dame Press.

Nielsen, Hans Frede. 2000. *The Early Runic Language of Scandinavia: Studies in Germanic Dialect Geography*. Heidelberg: Universitätsverlag C. Winter.

Niles, John D. 1980. *Old English Literature in Context: Ten Essays*. Cambridge: Brewer.

———. 1983. *Beowulf: The Poem and Its Tradition*. Cambridge, Mass.: Harvard University Press.

———. 2006. *Old English Enigmatic Poems and the Play of the Texts*. Turnhout: Brepols.

———. See also under Fulk, Bjork, and Niles 2008. *Klaeber's Beowulf*.

North, Richard. 2006. *The Origins of Beowulf: From Vergil to Wiglaf*. Oxford: Oxford University Press.

O'Keeffe, Katherine O'Brien, ed. 1994. *Old English Shorter Poems: Basic Readings*. Basic Readings in Anglo-Saxon England 3. New York: Garland.

Orchard, Andy. 2003. *A Critical Companion to Beowulf*. Cambridge: Brewer.

Osborn, Marijane. 1997. "Translations, Versions, Illustrations." In Bjork and Niles, 341–72.

Overing, Gilian R. 1990. *Language, Sign, and Gender in Beowulf*. Carbondale: Southern Illinois University Press.

Owen-Crocker, Gale R. 2000. *The Four Funerals in Beowulf*. Manchester: Manchester University Press.

Oxford English Dictionary (Online). 1989–. Oxford: Oxford University Press.

Page, R. I. 1970. *Life in Anglo-Saxon England*. London: Batsford.

Plotkin, Cary H. 1989. *The Tenth Muse: Victorian Philology and the Genesis of the Poetic Language of Gerard Manley Hopkins*. Carbondale: Southern Illinois University Press.

Pope, John C. ed. 2001. *Eight Old English Poems*. 3rd ed. rev. by R. D. Fulk. New York: Norton. [Note: Sometimes for this text I cite only Pope because the quote in question has not changed from earlier editions edited by Pope alone.]

Richards, Julian. 2003. "Pagans and Christians at a Frontier: Viking Burial in the Danelaw." In *The Cross Goes North: Processes of Conversion in Northern Europe, AD 300–1300*, ed. Martin Carver. York: York Medieval Press; reprint 2005, Woodbridge: Boydell, 383–95.

Robinson, Fred C. 1975. "Artful Ambiguities in the Old English 'Book-Moth' Riddle." In Nicholson and Frese, 355–62.

———. 1982. "Understanding an Old English Wisdom Verse: *Maxims II*, Lines 10 ff." In *The Wisdom of Poetry: Essays in Early English Literature in Honor of Morton W. Bloomfield*, ed. Larry D. Benson and Siegfried Wenzel. Kalamazoo, Mich.: Medieval Institute Publications. 1–11.

———. 1985. *Beowulf and the Appositive Style*. Knoxville: University of Tennessee Press.

———. 1994. "Did Grendel's Mother Sit on Beowulf?" In *From Anglo-Saxon to Early Middle English: Studies Presented to E. G. Stanley*, ed. Malcolm Godden, Douglas Gray, and Terry Hoad. Oxford: Clarendon Press, 1–7.

———. See also under Mitchell 1998, *Beowulf*; and 2007, *A Guide to Old English*.

Rosier, James L. 1964. "The Literal-Figurative Identity of *The Wanderer*." *PMLA* 79: 366–69.

Rulon-Miller, Nina. 2000. "Sexual Humor and Fettered Desire in Exeter Book Riddle 12." In Wilcox 2000, 99–126.

Schlauch, Margaret. 1940. "The *Dream of the Rood* as Prosopopoeia." In *Essays and Studies in Honor of Carleton Brown*. London: Oxford University Press; New York: New York University Press, 23–34. Also in Bessinger and Kahrl, 428–41.

Scragg, Donald, ed. 1991. *The Battle of Maldon AD 991*. Oxford: Blackwell.

Shippey, T. A. 1972. *Old English Verse.* London: Hutchinson University Library.
———. 1976. *Poems of Wisdom and Learning in Old English.* Cambridge: Brewer.
———. 1978. *Beowulf.* London: Edward Arnold.
———. 1997. "Structure and Unity." In Bjork and Niles, 149–74.
———. 2009. "Klaeber's *Beowulf* Eighty Years On: A Triumph for a Triumvirate." *Journal of English and Germanic Philology* 108, 3: 360–76.
Shippey, T. A., and Andreas Haarder, eds. 1998. *Beowulf: The Critical Heritage.* London: Routledge.
Sisam, Kenneth. 1965. *The Structure of Beowulf.* Oxford: Clarendon Press.
Smith, D. K. 2000. "Humor in Hiding: Laughter Between the Sheets in the Exeter Book Riddles." In Wilcox, 2000, 79–98.
Squires, Ann, ed. 1988. *The Old English Physiologus.* Durham Medieval Texts 5. Durham: University of Durham School of English.
Stanley, Eric, ed. 1966. *Continuations and Beginnings: Studies in Old English Literature.* London: Thomas Nelson.
Stenton, F. M. 1971. *Anglo-Saxon England.* 3rd ed. Oxford: Oxford University Press; reprint 2001.
Stevens, Martin, and Jerome Mandel, eds. 1968. *Old English Literature.* Lincoln: University of Nebraska Press.
Stewart, Ann Harleman. 1975. "Old English Riddle 47 as Stylistic Parody." *Papers on Language and Literature* 11: 227–41.
———. 1979. "Kenning and Riddle in Old English." *Papers on Language and Literature* 15: 115–36.
Storms, Godfrid. 1974. *Anglo-Saxon Magic.* New York: Gordon Press.
Swanton, Michael., ed. 1970. *The Dream of the Rood.* Manchester: Manchester University Press.
———. 1987. *English Literature Before Chaucer.* London: Longman.
Tacitus. 1970. *The Agricola and the Germania.* Trans. H. Mattingly, rev. S. A. Handford. Harmondsworth: Penguin.
Talbot, C. H., ed. and trans. 1954. *The Anglo-Saxon Missionaries in Germany.* New York: Sheed and Ward. Contains the "Lives" of Sts. Willbrord, Boniface, and others, with a selection from the correspondence of St. Boniface.
Tanke, John W. 1994. "*Wonfeax wale*: Ideology and Figuration in the Sexual Riddles of the Exeter Book." In Harwood and Overing, 21–42.
Thomas, Mark G., Michael P. H. Stumpf, and Heinrich Härke, 2006. "Evidence for an Apartheid-Like Social Structure in Early Anglo-Saxon England." *Proc. R. Soc. B* 273, 1601 (22 October): 2651–57. rspb.royalsocietypublishing.org, reference doi: 10.1098/rspb.2006.3627
Tiffany, Daniel. 2001. "Lyric Substance: On Riddles, Materialism, and Poetic Obscurity." *Critical Inquiry* 28, 1: 72–98.
Tolkien, Christopher, ed. and trans. 1960. *The Saga of King Heidrek the Wise.* Edinburgh: Nelson; reprint 2010, London: HarperCollins.
Tolkien, J. R. R. 1936. "*Beowulf*: The Monsters and the Critics." *Proceedings of the British Academy* 22: 245–95. See also Drout edition above.
———. 1953. "The Homecoming of Beorhtnoth Beorhthelm's Son." *Essays and Studies of the English Association* 6: 1–18.
Turner, Sharon. 1852. *The History of the Anglo-Saxons.* 7th ed. 3 vols. London: Longman.
Vendler, Helen. 1995. *The Breaking of Style: Hopkins, Heaney, Graham.* Cambridge, Mass.: Harvard University Press.

Walmsley, John, ed. 2006. *Inside Old English: Essays in Honour of Bruce Mitchell.* Oxford: Blackwell.

Webb, J. F., and D. H. Farmer. 1988. *The Age of Bede.* Rev. ed. Harmondsworth: Penguin. Contains Bede's *Life of Cuthbert,* Eddius Stephanus's *Life of Wilfrid,* and other works.

Weissbort, Daniel, and Astradur Eysteinsson, eds. 2006. *Translation—Theory and Practice: A Historical Reader.* Oxford: Oxford University Press.

Welsh, Andrew. 1978. *Roots of Lyric: Primitive Poetry and Modern Poetics.* Princeton, N.J.: Princeton University Press.

Whitelock, Dorothy., ed. and trans. 1955. *English Historical Documents c. 500–1042.* Vol. 1 of *English Historical Documents,* ed. David C. Douglas. London: Eyre & Spottiswoode.

———. 1968. "The Interpretation of *The Seafarer.*" In Bessinger and Kahrl, 442–57. Originally in *Chadwick Memorial Studies, Early Cultures of North West Europe,* ed. Sir Cyril Fox and Bruce Dickens. Cambridge: Cambridge University Press: 1950. 261–72.

Wilcox, Jonathan, ed. 2000. *Humour in Anglo-Saxon Literature.* Woodbridge: Brewer.

———. 2006. "Old English Translation." In Weissbort and Eysteinsson, 34–46.

Williams, Blanche. 1914. *Gnomic Poetry in Anglo-Saxon.* New York: Columbia University Press; reprint 1966, New York: AMS Press.

Williams, Edith Whitehurst. 1975. "What's So New About the Sexual Revolution? Some Comments on Anglo-Saxon Attitudes Toward Sexuality in Women Based on Four Exeter Book Riddles." *Texas Quarterly* 18, 2: 46–55.

Williamson, Craig, ed. 1977. *The Old English Riddles of the Exeter Book.* Chapel Hill: University of North Carolina Press.

———. 1982. *A Feast of Creatures: Anglo-Saxon Riddle-Songs.* Philadelphia: University of Pennsylvania Press; reprint 2011.

Wilson, D. M., ed. 1976. *The Archaeology of Anglo-Saxon England.* London: Methuen.

———. 1981. *The Anglo-Saxons.* 3rd ed. Harmondsworh: Penguin.

Withers, Benjamin C., and Jonathan Wilcox, eds. 2003. *Naked Before God: Uncovering the Body in Anglo-Saxon England.* Morgantown: West Virginia University Press.

Woolf, Rosemary. 1975. "*The Wanderer, The Seafarer,* and the Genre of *Planctus.*" In Nicholson and Frese, 192–207.

Wormald, Patrick. 1978. "Bede, Beowulf, and the Conversion of the Anglo-Saxon Aristocracy." In *Bede and Anglo-Saxon England,* ed. Robert T. Farrell. British Archaeological Reports 46. Oxford: BAR, 32–95.

Wrenn, C. L. 1967. *A Study of Old English Literature.* London: Harrah.

INDEX

This index contains author and subject entries from the Foreword and the various critical introductions, commentaries, and appendices. An index of the proper names in the poems can be found in the Glossary of Proper Names.

ACKNOWLEDGMENTS

I am indebted to many people for their support and advice in my years of working on this book. Swarthmore College has given me both financial support for my research and an intellectual home in which to teach. My students, with their love of these poems and their provocative questions, have kept me committed to the tasks of teaching and translating. Tom Shippey has been an inspiration and model for me over the years as I've much admired his scholarship on both medieval subjects and Middle-earth fiction. His reading of the manuscript, his offering of suggestions during the revision process, and his writing the foreword was a wonderful *giefu*, both gift and grace. My editor Jerome Singerman, like the Anglo-Saxon seafarer, held a steady hand in piloting this book through challenging waters. My wife Raima Evan read countless drafts, offering from her own *wordhord* numerous wise suggestions in my struggle to wrestle new words out of old. To my mentors who are noted in the Dedication, I owe the greatest debt. Their teaching and scholarship are part of the web of this work. Like the poets themselves, these mentors have passed on, but I hope my debt to them is partly paid in the offering of these poems. All these people helped me to shape a better book and bring these poems and proverbs, songs and stories, riddles and rich lore, to life again.